BLACK, WHITE AND GREY

BLACK, WHITE AND GREY

ETHICS IN SOUTH AFRICAN JOURNALISM

Franz Krüger

DOUBLE
STOREY
a juta company

First published 2004 by Double Storey Books,
a division of Juta & Co. Ltd, Mercury Crescent,
Wetton, Cape Town

© 2004 Franz Krüger

ISBN 1 919930 95 7

Editing by Priscilla Hall
Text design concept by Sarah-Anne Raynham
Page layout by Claudine Willatt-Bate
Cover design by Toby Newsome
Printing by ABC Press, Epping, Cape Town

CONTENTS

FOREWORD

By Henry Jeffreys

Bob Steele, the Poynter Institute's renowned journalism ethics thinker and writer, once said: 'If we are to value the work we do, we must better understand the values that guide us.'

The year 2003 was in many ways an *annus horribilis* for the journalistic media around the world as well as in South Africa. And things have not improved much since then.

The war in Iraq brought the long-simmering issue of 'embedded journalism' into the full, critical glare of the public spotlight as global media institutions scrambled to report on the war, literally from the lap of and on the terms of the US-led invasion forces. It raised serious doubts and concerns about the credibility, objectivity and partiality of the journalists and the media institutions involved in this dubious partnership.

Then there was the Jayson Blair affair, which brought shame to one of the world's leading media institutions, the *New York Times*. Blair's audacious fraud cost the two most senior editors of the *New York Times* their jobs and left the prestigious publication reeling as it reflected on how it allowed its most precious assets, credibility and public trust, to be so seriously compromised.

Back on the home front we had our own share of controversies that raised serious questions about the ethical state of our beloved craft.

Two high-profile journalists, one an editor and the other a celebrated columnist, were caught out in acts of blatant plagiarism. Of even greater concern was that some editors sat on the fence about whether the offending columnist's act warranted censure. We also experienced incidents of journalistic fabrication, perhaps not on the scale of a Jayson Blair, but still stunning in their audacity.

It was, however, the Bulelani Ngcuka spy allegations and the behaviour of editors and journalists involved in the matter that did the worst damage to the image and credibility of our journalism. As the whole sordid saga unfolded at the Hefer commission of inquiry into the allegations that the country's chief prosecutor had acted as a spy for the apartheid regime, one was left with the sinking feeling that something was seriously rotten in the state of South African journalism. We seemed to have lost the ethical plot.

This handbook comes at the right time, offering a practical contribution to assist with the much-needed process of rediscovering the ethical highway. It is designed to enable both budding and experienced journalists to deal effectively with the many and complex ethical challenges confronting them.

Its title is appropriate, since so many of the challenges confronting journalists in a transforming society such as ours are neither black, nor white, but grey.

The book will hopefully help journalists and editors to return to the basic values which allow them to claim their special and precious place in society: honesty, fairness, compassion, high standards and integrity. For without these, our craft is lost and our societal function dangerously compromised.

In the words of Bob Steele, these are the values that should guide us. We should, however, do more than simply understand them. We need to live by them. This book is a good place to embark on that quest.

Henry JJ Jeffreys
Chairperson of the South African National Editors' Forum (Sanef)
and deputy editor of Beeld
March 2004

PREFACE

Journalism matters. The modern world is quite simply unimaginable without the media, which provide a critical arena where societies meet, debate and skirmish. As a result, journalists are privileged in many ways.

Most profoundly, we work in greater freedom than any other profession. It's called freedom of speech, and it's probably the most important thing in any journalist's toolbox. But with it, as they say, comes responsibility. The trust people have in us can be quickly squandered. Ethics provide the guidelines for exercising our freedom. They set markers we can use to orientate ourselves.

For many, the idea of ethics evokes an image of the Ten Commandments, fixed and clear. Unfortunately, real life is often quite complicated. Although codes of conduct do quite a good job of setting out the do's and don'ts of the profession, applying them to real situations is often not at all straightforward. In many cases, our imperatives pull us in different directions – for instance, the public's right to know tugs against an individual's right to privacy. The title of this book is intended to reflect an approach which is prepared to see beyond simple black and white, and acknowledge shades of grey.

Good ethical decision-making requires thought, time and discussion. That may seem an unattainable luxury in South African newsrooms, too many of which are under constant pressure to produce more with less. But journalists have a responsibility to find the time for this work. It's possible to be a successful journalist without taking time to confront ethical issues, but you can't be a good one. I hope that this book will encourage journalists to take the time and trouble to explore ethical decision-making as a professional skill that is as important as any other.

Editors and owners, too, have responsibilities: they need to create the right conditions for careful, thoughtful and ethical journalism. In the long run, trustworthy journalism is also in the interests of the bottom line.

In South Africa the debate about journalism ethics has taken particular turns in recent years. Issues of transformation and race have sparked heated debates in the profession, and there have been calls for the codes themselves to be revisited, to bring them into line with the new South African reality. This book grew out of these discussions. Among other things, it attempts to measure the traditional standards of journalism against the demands of a changing society.

What you will find in this book

Besides the discussion of various areas of ethics, the chapters contain a set of *case studies* drawn from real events. They also include *talking points* – short contributions by some of the most prominent people in South African journalism. They provide additional voices on the various areas, offering a different perspective or sometimes discussing the way an issue plays itself out in particular circumstances.

The text is intended to be as practical as possible. I have, for instance, developed a tool to use when dealing with a particular dilemma. It's called the *ethics roadmap*. There is also a set of *discussions and exercises* that could be used in a classroom situation. Finally, a selection of *codes* has also been included – chiefly the industry codes used in print and broadcasting.

Acknowledgments

I owe a debt of gratitude to many people. They include the editors, who agreed to be interviewed so that their insights could inform book. Mandla Radebe and Rosemary Ramsay helped with the interviewing. My Wits students allowed me to test ideas. Barney Mthombothi and Latiefa Mobara offered advice and feedback. Ferial Haffajee, my almost co-author, helped with interviews and much useful feedback. Professor Anton Harber supported this project in many different ways.

I gratefully acknowledge the support of the South African National Editors' Forum and Rhodes University's journalism programme. The research for the book was carried out under a fellowship in the journalism programme of Wits University, and was funded by the European Foundation for Human Rights. I owe these two institutions a large debt of gratitude, since I would not have been able to complete the project without them.

Finally, thanks to my family – Lindy, Ruth and Thomas – who gave support far beyond the call of duty.

Franz Krüger

In memory of my father

The primary purpose of gathering and distributing news and opinion is to serve society by informing citizens and enabling them to make informed judgments on the issues of the time. The freedom of the press to bring an independent scrutiny is a freedom exercised on behalf of the public.
Press Code of Professional Practice, South Africa

Respect for truth and the public's right to information are fundamental principles of journalism. Journalists describe society to itself. They seek truth. They convey information, ideas and opinions, a privileged role. They search, disclose, record, question, entertain, suggest and remember. They inform citizens and animate democracy. They

give practical form to freedom of expression. Many journalists work in private enterprise, but all have these public responsibilities. They scrutinise power, but also exercise it, and should be accountable. Accountability engenders trust. Without trust, journalists do not fulfil their public responsibilities.
Australian Journalists' Association: Code of Ethics

1

FIRST QUESTIONS

Ethics is about right and wrong, and it's been around much longer than journalism, or media, or even the written word. Every human culture has systems of morality and standards according to which behaviour is judged. The Greeks regarded ethics as one of the great branches of knowledge, and the word itself comes from the Greek word *ethos*, which means character, or what a good person does.[1]

As a field of philosophical inquiry, it deals with morality, moral judgments and the meaning of concepts like right and wrong. At a more practical level, it considers what should be done in particular situations.

As such, it is clearly distinct from the law. Where ethics sets the highest standards of ideal behaviour, the law is concerned with minimums, with 'the bottom line below which we should not fall,' according to *Doing ethics in journalism*, a highly influential book by three American ethicists, Jay Black, Bob Steele and Ralph Barney.[2] The law, of course, carries sanctions of a more vigorous kind than any ethical code, whereas ethics appeals to the journalist's own responsibility and conscience. In these ways, the approach taken by the two disciplines is fundamentally different, even though many issues are addressed in both law and ethics: privacy is an example, as is the naming of children in certain circumstances.

A journalistic project may sometimes pass a legal test but not an ethical one, and vice versa. There have been instances when reporters have bought drugs on the street in order to expose the drug trade. Although that would have broken the law, most journalists would see it as justifiable in pursuit of an important story. At the same time, there is no law compelling a reporter to honour a promise of confidentiality made to a source, yet most journalists would see the need for honouring a promise of confidentiality as a cornerstone of ethical behaviour.

Media or journalism?

The ethics of media and of journalism are sometimes treated as if they were one and the same, but it is important to recognise the difference between the two. Journalism can hardly be conceived of outside its institutional context. One person alone could conceivably report and write on his or her own, but publication or broadcast requires technology, marketing departments, advertising and much more. They require an organisation, a media house. Media products contain much content that is not journalistic, from the weather report to small ads. And there is often tension between individual journalists and their company – sometimes about ethical issues. Professor Guy Berger, head of journalism and media studies at Rhodes University, writes: 'Journalism as a practice has a (fluid) degree of autonomy from, and even contradiction with, its institutional context. There is a critical distinction between the institutional whole and this one of its component parts.'[3]

This book will focus primarily on journalism ethics, in other words on the responsibilities of the individual journalist. This does not mean there are no issues for the organisations they work for. A Council of Europe resolution on journalism ethics pays some attention to the duties of owners and publishers. It says they should 'treat information not as a commodity but as a fundamental right of the citizen'.[4] It's a worthy ideal, not often taken seriously by companies. We will touch on issues of corporate ethics here and there, when they are relevant to our central concern.

WHY ETHICS?

We now turn to an important and fundamental question: why bother with ethics? For many people, morality is its own justification. We should behave properly because it's the right thing to do. The US ethicist Louis Day[5] highlights four reasons why societies develop systems of ethics:

- they serve society's need for stability, by giving us a framework which allows us to develop trust in each other;
- they serve a need for a moral hierarchy;
- they help resolve conflicts; and
- they help clarify values.

We will tackle the question from a slightly different angle, using as a starting point the self-image and role of journalism in society.

Journalists like to think of their profession in idealistic terms. Codes of ethics are a good place to find lofty and sometimes even elegant expressions of the view that journalism is basically about public service.

Metaethics considers the fundamental principles of ethics and seeks to describe different systems.

Normative ethics concerns itself with the particular principles that make for moral behaviour.

Teleological theories of ethics are guided by the consequences of actions. The rightness of an action is determined by its outcome.

Deontological theories of ethics call for certain things to be done because of their inherent rightness. Notions of duty and principle are central.

The fundamental idea is that when journalists rush around pushing their microphones into people's faces and asking embarrassing questions, they do it not for themselves but on behalf of the public. One of the oldest codes of ethics in the world is that adopted in 1926 by the US Society of Professional Journalists, which says: 'We believe that public enlightenment is the forerunner of justice.'[6] The meaning is clear, although the terminology is slightly archaic: the term justice is used here to mean a just social order. Today we would probably use the word democracy.

It is trite to point out the close connection between journalism and democracy. Citizens can exercise their democratic rights only if they are fully informed. The 2002 Declaration of Principles on Freedom of Expression in Africa says: 'Respect for freedom of expression, as well as the right of access to information held by public bodies and companies, will lead to greater public transparency and accountability, as well as to good governance and the strengthening of democracy.'[8]

A more sophisticated description of the relationship between journalism and democracy comes from Berger.[9] Making the useful distinction between media and journalism, Berger identifies 'four distinct species of democratic journalism':

- a 'liberal' view which sees journalists as 'the poor man's guardian', holding the powerful to account;
- a 'social democratic' view, where journalists see themselves as educators of the public;
- a 'neoliberal' view, which commits journalists to a pluralism of views, and highlights the importance of offering a platform for debates. This view owes much to the work of the German philosopher Jürgen Habermas, who developed the notion of media as public space; and
- a 'participative' approach, which takes the involvement of citizens in democracy even further than the neoliberal view, and sees democracy as incomplete if it relies only on periodic elections. This view would have journalism seek to further the involvement of citizens – particularly those outside the elites – in ongoing deliberation of public policy.

The four role conceptions are not necessarily contradictory, but offer different ways of thinking about the contribution of journalism to democracy.

It is a small step from here to the ideal of press freedom, also often invoked prominently in ethics codes. Because journalism is practised on behalf of the public, the media claim freedom not for themselves but for the citizenry in general. Japan's Canon of Journalism, adopted in 2000 by the Newspaper Publishers and Editors Association, the Nihon Shinbun Kyokai, says: 'The public's right to know ... cannot be ensured without the existence of media, operating with the guarantee of freedom of speech and expression.'[10]

> "Trust is our byword ...
> It is our heritage and
> our mission, and I would
> rather sweep the streets of
> London than compromise
> on that."[7]
> *Fergal Keane, BBC correspondent*

These are lofty ideals, which easily lay a basis for ethics. The bridge that takes us there is credibility. If journalists are to play a useful role in the way outlined, then audiences must trust their work. The editor of the *Sunday Independent*, Jovial Rantao, writes: 'Credibility is the lifeblood of our profession as journalists. Credibility is to us what oxygen is to the human body. Without it, we are nothing. Without it, not one person will believe a single word that we write. One of the basic tenets of our profession is to

4

ensure that the credibility of the information we gather on a daily basis is unquestionable.'[11]

So far, the equation is neat and simple: people have a right to know what's going on. Society 'contracts' journalists to provide information, on the understanding that they will work in an ethical and trustworthy way. QED.

The problem is that the reality of everyday journalism often seems very far from the ideal. It's hard to see the public served in covering yet another routine crime story. The idea of holding the powerful to account is vastly appealing, but stories that can claim that honour are few and far between. Watergate doesn't come along every day.

And the argument that the media provide a space for public debate is severely undermined by the fact that debating is an elite activity. With the significant exception of radio, the media do not penetrate very far into South African society. Illiteracy and poverty mean that millions of people have little access to the media. A government position paper that laid the basis for the establishment of the Media Development and Diversity Agency said: 'People in disadvantaged areas are left out of the information loop.'[12]

Professor Anton Harber, the head of the journalism and media studies programme at the University of the Witwatersrand, says ethics are important precisely because journalism is an imperfect profession.[13] In the 'global struggle between entertainment and serious information', ethics provides journalists with a defence against the pressure of market forces, he says.

The charge of the media studies academics

The idealised view of journalism has come under heavy attack from academic quarters. An entire industry of media studies has developed over the past half-century or so around attempts to analyse what journalists do ('academic hyperactivity', one scholar called it).[14] In this field, news is described as 'constructed' or 'manufactured', and seen as a 'cultural artifact'. In the following, we will try to develop an argument for ethics that takes these academic developments into account. Readers who regard this as unnecessary may want to skip the discussion.

The academic discipline of 'media studies' has become a large and complex field, and it is impossible to do it full justice here. But it would be use-

5

ful to outline the three broad perspectives that have developed, as identified by the academic, Michael Schudson.[15]

Money, media and power

The 'political economy' approach rejects any notion of free, independent or objective news media. Rather, it sees the media as serving an ideological function, legitimising the existing order on behalf of the ruling classes. Powerful elites dominate the media internationally and ensure that media products reinforce the dominant consensus. Where there is disagreement and debate, it remains within that consensus. In their 1988 book *Manufacturing consent*, Edward Herman and Noam Chomsky say the media 'inculcate and defend the economic, social and political agenda of privileged groups that dominate the domestic society and the state.'[16]

This rather extreme position was an attempt to debunk the classical liberal view, which sees the free market as a crucial element in the media and democracy equation. Only private media – which means those run for profit – can effectively function as a watchdog on the state, that argument goes. In the context of the campaign to extend private sector broadcasting, the media magnate Rupert Murdoch said: 'Public service broadcasters in this country [Britain] have paid a price for their state-sponsored privileges. That price has been their freedom.'[17]

In the mouth of a man like Murdoch, such a position is transparently self-serving. A view of the market as an entirely neutral force in the media world is completely unsustainable. One need look no further than South Africa's media landscape. Media products follow the money – and so poor people are left out in the cold, as noted above.

If money determines which audiences are served, it has also become a huge factor in deciding who can serve them. When liberal press theory was framed, the British media theorist James Curran points out, 'it really was the case that ordinary people could set up their trestle-table, so to speak, in the main market-place of ideas because it was cheap to publish. … Now at least £20 million is needed to launch a new national broadsheet, and over £15 million to establish a new popular cable TV channel in Britain.'[18]

Increasingly, journalism is market-driven. Editors are expected to construct 'products' that will be appealing in the marketplace. And journalists are aware of the influence advertisers sometimes have on coverage. At its most extreme, this can see companies withdraw advertising in response to unfavourable reports. More mild forms of influence come in the shape of free gifts, advertorial and the like. (We will discuss the ethical implications of these in Chapter 6.)

As journalists, we do not have to accept the view that we are simply propagandists for capitalism. But we cannot close our eyes to the influence of the economic system in which the media are organised. We are expected to report for particular audiences, and those audiences are defined in commercial terms.

> "News and news programmes could almost be called random reactions to random events. Again and again, the main reason why they turn out as they do is accident – accident which recurs so haphazardly as to defeat statistical examination."[19]
> *Unidentified British journalist*

Order out of chaos

Schudson groups a second set of analyses under the heading 'The social organisation of newswork'. Studies in this field have for instance classified reports on the basis of how they came to the attention of the news organisation, and whether they are accidents or routine. Others have investigated the relationships between journalists and official sources, and the way in which newsrooms are organised around beats, hierarchies and deadlines. A very interesting study by another academic, Peter Manning, shows how official sources have privileged access to reporters, and what it takes for other groups to get their views into the news.[20]

What these studies have in common is a focus on the 'constraints imposed by organisations despite the private intentions of the individual'.[21] News, in this view, is what newspeople make it.[22] The bureaucratic routines of the news operation completely overshadow the original event reported on – the 'real world' – as a determinant of news.

Again, journalists do not need to buy into the view in this form to accept that a large part of newsgathering is routine. Non-media people sometimes ask the question: 'How do you know that something is going to happen?' If we were to rely on chance and luck – being on the right street corner when an accident happens – newspapers would be very thin. Most stories come to us from scheduled court dates, press statements, media conferences. The easier it is to plan for an event, the easier it is to cover it.

And we should acknowledge that not all sources are created equal. Official sources – whether from the government or another major social group – get more space and airtime than others.

The culture of news

The final area focuses on the relationships between reporting and culture. Areas of investigation have included stereotypes in news reporting, such as the ways in which race and gender surface in the media. Studies of the coverage of gays in mainstream media also fall into this category. The concern has been to see how the media reproduce and reflect attitudes prevalent in the wider culture.

Other approaches have sought to explain aspects of journalism as a form of culture in themselves. News values have come under extensive scrutiny. The British theorist Stuart Hall says: '"News values" are one of the most opaque structures of meaning in modern society. All "true journalists" are supposed to possess it: few can or are willing to identify and define it.'[23]

Interesting work has also been done in showing the continuities and differences between journalism and other forms of story-telling.

At bottom, such approaches understand news reporting as an activity shaped by the culture around it, and see news as a cultural product. Do they undermine the claim to truthfulness so dear to journalists? Not necessarily: saying that journalism fits into a broader cultural picture is not to accuse it of being fictional, or distorted. It simply highlights that we do not operate without context.

So what's a hack to do?

This avalanche of academic criticism seems to have done a comprehensive demolition job on the shining self-image of journalists. We are told we are nothing but propagandists for the capitalist class, that we are functionaries of a production process that might as well be turning out toothpaste, and that we simply reproduce cultural values and preconceptions.

When confronted with this sort of thing, most journalists just shake their heads and walk away. Certainly, if we are functionaries of this kind, there's no room for any discussion of ethics.

And yet media studies do have important insights to offer. These have been touched on in the discussion of the three approaches taken. But there is a general point that needs to be made here: some of the academic approaches described remove the individual from the equation entirely. That is just crude and simplistic. But many others don't, seeking instead to understand constraints on the individual journalist. We cannot deny that such constraints exist.

Sociologists make use of the distinction between 'structure' and 'agency'. The former describes a recurring pattern of human behaviour – like an educational system, for instance. The latter is intention-al and undetermined human behaviour – like the way a particular student navigates his or her way through the system. Applying these concepts to the media, the aca-demics David Croteau and William Hoynes[24] discuss the interplay between the two at three levels: in the relation-ships between the media and other institutions, within the industry and between media and public. In all cases, there are external constraints – but there is also agency. Media organisations are constrained by a legal, political and economic context – but are able to act on their own and even influence others.

> "Within local [US] TV stations there is no question that tabloidisation is imposed from the top, while professionalism provides the language of resistance from below."[25]
> *Daniel C. Hallin*

The argument needs to be taken a significant step further, to get us back to the question of ethics. Rather than destroying the case for ethics, media studies cement it. If we recognise the constraints of 'structure', then ethics offer us a set of professional guidelines to follow as we exercise our 'agency'. They give us a reference point outside the immediate hurly-burly of the job, one that is inspired by the highest ideals.

In that sense, ethics and professionalism provide protection against some of the pressures journalists come under. When a marketing depart-ment leans on a newsdesk to cover a story just because it involves an advertiser, ethics give the desk an argument for refusing. They can prompt journalists to look beyond the routine set of predictable sources, to find fresh, original viewpoints. They can motivate journalists to match the fine sentiments of public service, despite whatever constraints there are. And here and there, a Watergate story does come along.

Ethics help media houses and individual journalists keep an eye on their own long-term interests in keeping faith with the public, when short-term considerations put them in jeopardy.

UNIVERSAL OR AFRICAN ETHICS

Before we proceed further, we need to consider the extent to which the values and principles encapsulated in media ethics need to be adapted for local circumstances. The Zambian academic Francis Kasoma has argued that the standards generally accepted are based in European morality, and that African journalists should look to their own moral heritage.

Kasoma says journalism based on African values would be kinder: 'There is too much of the cold Euro-American brand of news reporting in Africa ... Africa has the chance to restore the human touch to journalism,' he writes. [26]

In another essay, written together with a Nigerian colleague, Andrew Moemeka,[27] he argues that European journalism ethics are based on deontology – a school of ethics based on duty. Decisions are taken by asking the question: what is the duty of a moral person in this context? By contrast, African ethics are situational, taking more account of the possible consequences of an action for the community as a whole. They refer in this context to the pursuit of 'development journalism' – where the craft is practised in a way that furthers national development objectives. How-

Qagik **was a weekly news and current affairs show broadcast by the Inuit Broadcasting Corporation in the far north of Canada. Its style was based on the cultural values of the Inuit, its audience. This meant, among other things, that trauma was not covered since it was seen to be invasive, and reporters generally allowed the subjects of their reports more power to determine the shape of the story.** *Qagik* **means 'coming together' – underlining a consensus-seeking approach.[28]**

ever, the practice clearly fills the writers with some unease: although in favour of writing with an eye for social consequences, they warn that this should not mean simply following a government agenda. 'The basic problem ... is determining who decides whether news is, or is not, in the national interest. Such power should belong to journalists and not politicians,' they write.[29]

The first difficulty we have to contend with is that cultures offer something of a moving target. They are always changing under the influence of other cultures, economic circumstances, technological development and much else. Venerable African traditions like initiation have changed dramatically to adapt to urban environments, for instance. An appeal to African cultural values is an appeal to an idealised view of practices whose application in the real world can vary greatly. South Africa is profoundly but unevenly multicultural: in many spheres, Western culture is overwhelmingly dominant. This makes the identification of distinct values and practices even more difficult. Also, culture and politics are closely linked, and appeals to cultural values can be strongly political, as shown in the way in which the Inkatha Freedom Party has used Zulu culture for political purposes. In this context, any discussion of culture as if it was one clearly identifiable thing becomes very problematical.

Nevertheless, some specifically African cultural values can be clearly identified. One does not have to resort to an idealised abstraction of traditional culture to see the emphasis on community rather than individual that marks many practices. Another area of difference is to be found in attitudes to the dead. As Kasoma points out elsewhere, there is a close interrelationship between the living and the dead in African cultures.[30] Ancestors matter a great deal.

How exactly might these differences reflect in practical day-to-day journalism? Kasoma approvingly lists several ways: a journalist inspired by African values would serve everyone equally, but be 'a special spokesperson for poor and impotent people'.[31] He or she would show 'special love and care for the sick, aged and handicapped'.[32] In addition, there would be more democratic decision-making in the newsroom.

Many of these values resonate strongly with those espoused in Western journalism – at least at an aspirational level. The call for the weak to be given special consideration is not far from the Western notion that journalism's function is to 'comfort the afflicted and afflict the comfortable'. The appeal for journalists to build consensus and to work for the common good echoes the debate around civic journalism in the US. The call for less authoritarianism and more collective decision-making in newsrooms is similar to many modern approaches to management.

Perhaps the contrast being drawn is less between two sets of values than between African ethics and the *practice* in Western journalism. There are many voices who would agree with these criticisms of Western practice, without necessarily making reference to African values. Rather than seeking sharp differences between Western and African ethics, we should recognise the common ground. This approach would allow us to explore the valuable insights that African values can offer journalism on the continent and in the rest of the world.

Other writers have focused on the question of cultural common ground. The academics Clifford Christians and Michael Traber set out to find values applicable to communication shared by different cultures.[33] In a range of cultures from across the world – including African – they find what they call proto-norms, which include truth-telling; respect for the dignity of the individual; and the need to avoid harm to the innocent.

Another study compares codes of journalism ethics from many different countries. Drawing on three other comparative studies, the theorist Thomas Cooper identifies three contenders for the status of universal value: the search for truthfulness, responsibility (with subthemes of loyalty, professionalism and accountability) and freedom of expression.[34]

Tackling a slightly different but related question, the South African researcher Mandla Seleoane investigates whether there is a specifically African approach to freedom of expression.[35] He cites a range of African documents – from South Africa's Freedom Charter to the OAU Charter – which he says show no indication that Africans want their own, fundamentally different, approach to the ideal. Precolonial African societies allowed for free speech, he argues: 'If freedom of speech is in a sorry state in Africa, that has more to do with our governments than with the foreignness of the right to our ways of life.'[36]

Studies such as these show that different cultures have more in common than is sometimes thought. 'The world is not a composite of completely disjointed cultures and values; there also is cohesion,' writes the Norwegian media studies academic Helge Rønning.[37] However, the common ground remains at a very broad level. What are shared are proto-norms, as Christians and Traber call them, and they are applied differently in different cultures.

Perhaps the more interesting question is how the different norms are – or should be – applied in various societies and cultures. Western codes, for instance, accept the need to avoid unnecessary invasions of privacy. An argument might be made that African cultures are more respectful of other people than the European, and that this might translate into more respect for their privacy. The differences, then, would become ones of degree and of application, not of essence. Death is another area where the application of shared norms may differ, and we will discuss it later.

The intention here is to raise a possible direction for the discussion, not to settle the question. It is a discussion that has hardly begun in South African journalism.

FOUR PRINCIPLES

Doing ethics offers a set of guiding principles which have been very widely quoted[38] (see box on p. 14). They are grouped under three headings, but I would add a fourth.

1 **Truth-telling.** Seek truth and report it as fully as possible, in the formulation of Black et al. This speaks to the fundamental truth-telling function of journalism, and has two major subthemes: accuracy and fairness. The need for accuracy is obvious, and fairness fits in here

because its opposite, bias and unfairness, can badly undermine the truthfulness of a report. Fairness is so important that some writers subsume most ethical issues under this heading.

2 **Independence.** The second principle arises because our credibility is massively affected by any perceived or real conflicts of interest. We are unable to work if audiences discount our reporting because they see it as influenced by considerations outside of journalism, such as any personal, commercial or political motives. This principle also raises the need for journalists to be vociferous in their defence of media freedom.

3 **Minimising harm.** If truth-telling is the principle that drives us forward, this is the consideration that sometimes puts on the brakes. We have to recognise that people can get hurt by journalism: dealing with reporters can deepen a trauma suffered; reputations can suffer; people can be subjected to ridicule, recriminations and even physical danger; and public sensitivities can be offended. These things are not always avoidable – sometimes they are even necessary. But we should be aware of the potential harm, and try to minimise it.

4 **Accountability.** The fourth principle I add is accountability. Journalists should be prepared to explain and answer for their work, to their audiences and to the public at large. This is done in the handling of readers' letters, published corrections, and co-operation with the systems of self-regulation. These sorts of things build trust with audiences. They are very different from state regulation, which would undermine media freedom.

These four principles sometimes conflict. In fact, most ethical dilemmas arise when different ideals pull us in different directions. If things were always simple and straightforward, there would be little to say about ethics. We should not be afraid of these dilemmas and complexities, but should confront them honestly.

Public interest

In grappling with ethics, the notion of public interest plays a central role. We have already seen how important the concept is in journalism's understanding of its role in society. It will come up repeatedly in the chapters to come: in the context of the individual's rights to privacy, in relation to the demand for journalists to serve the national interest, and elsewhere. More often than not, it is also the key to settling particular dilemmas. Yes, a jour-

Guiding principles for the journalist

Seek truth and report it as fully as possible
- Inform yourself continuously so you can inform, engage, and educate the public in clear and compelling ways on significant issues.
- Be honest, fair, and courageous in gathering, reporting, and interpreting accurate information.
- Give voice to the voiceless.
- Hold the powerful accountable.

Act independently
- Guard vigorously the essential stewardship role that a free press plays in an open society.
- Seek out and disseminate competing perspectives without being unduly influenced by those who would use their power or position counter to the public interest.
- Remain free of associations and activities that may compromise your integrity or damage your credibility.
- Recognise that good ethical decisions require individual responsibility and collaborative efforts.

Minimise harm
- Be compassionate for those affected by your actions.
- Treat source, subjects and colleagues as human beings deserving of respect, not merely as means to your journalistic ends.
- Recognise that gathering and reporting information may cause harm or discomfort, but balance those negatives by choosing alternatives that maximise your goal of truth-telling.

Doing ethics[39]

nalist may reason, what I am proposing will harm a person's reputation. But I will go ahead because the public interest justifies it.

The courts recognise public interest, but it remains an imprecise tool. A distinction is often made between public interest and that which merely interests the public.[40] The Press Code of Professional Practice says:

The public interest is the only test that justifies departure from the highest standards of journalism and includes:

a) detecting or exposing crime or serious misdemeanour;
b) detecting or exposing serious anti-social conduct;
c) protecting public health or safety;
d) preventing the public from being misled by some statement or action of an individual or organisation;
e) detecting or exposing hypocrisy, falsehoods or double standards of behaviour on the part of public figures or institutions or in public institutions.[41]

These five points go some way to pinning the idea down, but there are still many areas of uncertainty. How serious is serious? Who is a public figure? What is hypocrisy? All of these elements of the definition can be stretched in various directions. Undoubtedly, journalists sometimes bend the concept to suit less than honourable purposes. Nevertheless, it remains an essential tool in considering many ethical problems.

. . . .

NOTES

1   Jay Black, Bob Steele and Ralph Barney, *Doing ethics in journalism: a handbook with case studies*. Needham Heights, MA: Allyn & Bacon, 1995. 5.

2   Ibid, 14.

3   Guy Berger, 'Grave new world: democratic journalism enters in the global 21st century', Grahamstown, 1999. Posted at http://journ.ru.ac.za/staff/guy/, accessed on 4 April 2003.

4   Council of Europe's Resolution 1003 (1993) on the ethics of journalism, par 15. Posted at http://assembly.coe.int/Documents/AdoptedText/ta93/ERES1003.HTM, accessed on 20 March 2004.

5   Louis Day, *Ethics in media communications: cases and controversies*. Belmont, CA: Wadsworth, 2000. 23.

6   Black, Steele and Barney, *Doing ethics in journalism*. 6.

7   Quoted in Stuart Allan, *News culture*. Buckingham: Open University Press, 2001. 48.

8   African Commission on Human and People's Rights, 'Declaration of principles on freedom of expression in Africa, adopted in 2002 in Banjul, The Gambia'. Posted at http://www1.umn.edu/humanrts/achpr/expressionfreedomdec.html, accessed on 1 April 2003.

9   Berger. 'Grave new world'.

10 Nihon Shinbun Kyokai (the Japan Newspaper Publishers and Editors Association), 'The Canon of Journalism, adopted June 21 2000'. Posted at http://www.ijnet.org/3a77356f18153.html, accessed on 31 March 2003.

11 *The Star*, 10 May 2002.

12 Media Development and Diversity Agency, 'A draft position paper'. Pretoria: Government Communication and Information System (GCIS), 2000. 24.

13 Personal communication.

14 Brent MacGregor, *Live, direct and biased: making television news in the satellite age.* London: Arnold, 1997. 44.

15 Michael Schudson, 'The sociology of news production revisited (again)' in James Curran and Michael Gurevitch (eds.), *Mass media and society.* London: Arnold, 2000.

16 Quoted in Stuart Allan, *News culture.* Buckingham: Open University Press, 2001. 57.

17 Quoted in James Curran, 'Rethinking media and democracy' in Curran and Gurevitch, *Mass media and society.* 121.

18 Ibid. 128.

19 Quoted in Michael Schudson, 'The sociology of news production revisited (again)' in James Curran and Michael Gurevitch (eds.), *Mass media and society.* London: Arnold, 2000. 176.

20 Paul Manning, *News and news sources: a critical introduction.* London: Sage, 2001.

21 Schudson, 'Sociology of news production'. 188.

22 MacGregor, 'Theories of news production'. 50.

23 Schudson, 'Sociology of news production'. 190.

24 David Croteau and William Hoynes, *Media/Society: industries, images and audiences.* London: Pine Forge, 1997. 20.

25 Daniel C Hallin, 'Commercialism and professionalism in the American news media' in Curran and Gurevitch, *Mass media and society.* 233.

26 Francis Kasoma, 'An introduction to journalism ethical reasoning in Africa' in Francis Kasoma (ed.), *Journalism ethics in Africa.* Nairobi: Acce, 1994. 34.

27 Andrew A Moemeka and Francis Kasoma, ' Journalism ethics in Africa: an aversion to deontology?' in Kasoma, *Journalism ethics in Africa.*

28 Described in Kate Madden, 'Video and cultural identity: the Inuit Broadcasting Corporation experience' in Felipe Korzenny and Stella Ting-Toomey (eds.), *Mass media effects across cultures.* Newbury Park: Sage, 1992.

29 Kasoma, *Journalism ethics in Africa.* 48

30 In François Nel, *Writing for the media in South Africa.* Cape Town: OUP, 1999. 267.

31 Kasoma, *Journalism ethics in Africa.* 31.

32 Ibid. 34.

33 Clifford Christians and Michael Traber (eds.), *Communication ethics and universal values.* Thousand Oaks: Sage, 1997.

34 Thomas Cooper, 'The ethics behind the effects: a comparison of national media codes of ethics' in Felipe Korzenny and Stella Ting-Toomey (eds.), *Mass media effects across cultures*. Newbury Park: Sage, 1992.

35 Mandla Seleoane, 'Towards an African theory of freedom of expression'. Paper delivered at the Freedom of Expression and Ethics in the Media conference, at Sandton, Johannesburg, 30–31 October 2001.

36 Ibid. 45.

37 Helge Rønning, *Media ethics: an introduction and overview*. Lansdowne, Cape Town: Juta, 2002. 46.

38 Jay Black, Bob Steele and Ralph Barney, *Doing ethics in journalism: a handbook with case studies*. Needham Heights, MA: Allyn & Bacon, 1995. 17.

39 Black, Steele and Barney, *Doing ethics in journalism*. 17.

40 Lord Wakeham, 'Can self regulation achieve more than law?' Wynne Baxter Godfree Law Lecture delivered at the University of Sussex, 15 May 1998.

41 Press Ombudsman of South Africa, 'Press Code of Professional Practice'. Johannesburg: Press Ombudsman of South Africa, 2001.

It is important that we acknowledge that, while South Africa enjoys a democratic government, its past still lies with us especially as far as race and racism are concerned.
Sunday Times: Charter

We will tell the story of South Africa in all its richness.
SABC: Radio News Mission Statement

We do not pander to personal or sectional interests but are solely concerned with the public interest.
Independent Newspapers: Code of Conduct

2

THE SOUTH AFRICAN MEDIA LANDSCAPE

History casts a long shadow over the South African present. Along with the broader society, journalists and the industry in which they work are products of that past. It shapes our newsrooms, products and audiences. And it gives us particular kinds of ethical dilemmas.

The ethical codes and principles we refer to when confronting these problems have been developed in very different circumstances. The influence of British and American journalism has been particularly strong. So dominant are these traditions that they sometimes like to appear universal, when they are in fact rooted in the histories of those societies.

This book is centrally concerned with testing these approaches against the South African reality, to see to what extent they apply and where they may need to be adapted or even jettisoned. Before looking in more detail at various ethical principles, we have to consider the context in which we operate. We need to investigate the shape of the South African media landscape, and how it came to be. We will also consider two major debates in South African journalism, around race and the role of journalists.

OWNERS, EDITORS, AUDIENCES

Historically[1] the South African media were dominated by white elites. Broadcasting was almost entirely controlled by the state through the SABC, while print was dominated by two English and two Afrikaans companies. The former were ultimately controlled by the mining conglomerate Anglo American, the latter were closely linked to various factions in the ruling National Party. Black-owned and opposition publications were a reasonably constant feature of the media landscape ever since the later decades of the nineteenth century, but always remained marginal to the mainstream. The 1980s saw a flowering of alternative media, ranging from independent news agencies and weekly newspapers to underground publications and organisational newsletters.[2]

When change came in the early 1990s, it affected the media profoundly. Even before the first democratic election of April 1994, a new board and new executives were appointed for the SABC in order to ensure that its power did not skew the crucial vote. Print saw a spate of ownership changes. International media companies entered the South African market. Most notably, the Irish tycoon Tony O'Reilly bought the Argus group and renamed it Independent Newspaper Holdings. At the same time, various deals were struck to spread ownership of media assets to black South Africans – both individual entrepreneurs and the investment vehicles of trade unions and other groups. Argus – as it still was – sold the *Sowetan* to New African Investments Limited, or Nail, and a consortium of black interests headed by Cyril Ramaphosa bought a substantial stake in Johnnic, which controlled Times Media Limited.[3]

In broadcasting, the SABC sold off seven stations, eight new stations were licensed by the Independent

Under apartheid, the SABC ran separate FM services for the various 'ethnic groups': Radio Zulu, Radio Venda and so on. Their mandate was to foster the 'national identity' of these different groups. The post-1994 SABC management retained the different language services, but renamed them and changed their mandate. Instead of being cultural prisons, discouraging their audiences from taking an interest in the wider South Africa, they used the various languages to open a window on the country and the world.

Broadcasting Authority, and together with a new free-to-air television station – e.tv – they took on the SABC channels. These developments benefited mainly black interests, with some investment from foreign groups. An entirely new class of broadcasting licence was created for community radio, and by September 1999 there were 86 such stations on air.[4] In these ways, the range of voices available in broadcasting increased substantially.

At the same time, the alternative press was in dire straits. Foreign funding – on which most had relied – was drying up, and one title after the other had to close. Only two groups were still alive when the new millennium rolled around: the *Weekly Mail*, renamed the *Mail&Guardian* after sizeable investment by the UK's *Guardian*, and East Cape News Agencies, renamed East Cape News.[5]

As ownership patterns shifted, the media came under pressure to make their staffs more representative. Media houses sought to appoint black, and to a much smaller extent women, editors. By June 2000, 12 out of 30 editors of major daily and weekly newspapers were black. In both SABC and private broadcasting, the majority of editors were black.[6] Through training and other initiatives, the demographics at lower levels of staff also changed, though precise figures are hard to come by. A significant number of these new appointees came from the dying alternative press and brought a fresh set of perspectives into the mainstream. The alternative press had a strong tradition of advocacy journalism, and this has to some extent fused with the more mainstream tradition.

In the broader scheme of things, the media have remained a minority sport. Newspapers and television are inaccessible to many, due to poverty and low literacy levels. Most newspaper distribution is focused on the urban areas, leaving out millions of people in the countryside. Language is another obstacle: hardly any titles are published in African languages. Radio has much broader reach, but gaps in signal distribution have left 18.6 per cent of the population – almost eight million people – without access to even this medium.[7]

The media market did not expand significantly when democracy came, even though the political and economic conditions might have given grounds for optimism. Figures from GCIS (the Government Communication and Information System) show that although literacy levels rose by 20 per cent between 1991 and 1995, this did not lead to a growth in newspaper sales.[8] Professor Guy Berger, head of the department of journalism and media studies at Rhodes University, writes: 'One of the problems facing southern Africa is this: there just [aren't] enough mass media. Things are better than they used to be, but as a region we remain media-thin rather than media-dense.'[9] Even within South Africa, he points out, there is a huge gulf in media density between urban centres like Johannesburg and other areas.

Economic logic would indicate that an expansion of the media market in South Africa depends on growth in the black middle class. Significantly, newspaper readerships at the upper end of the market have been struggling, but there are indications of some growth at the bottom end. The *Daily Sun*, launched in 2002 at the bargain price of R1, epitomises this development. Its dramatic growth – taking months to get within striking distance of 200 000 copies a day – has hurt the *Sowetan* badly. But perhaps more significantly, much of its growth seems to consist of new readers – indicating what may be the first real expansion of the market in many years.

> "Our readership is not very sophisticated. They are people thinking for the first time of extending their house, or buying a new car. And we are giving them the information they need to move along in this market."[10]
>
> *Daily Sun founder, Deon du Plessis*

A TALE OF TWO INQUIRIES

Undoubtedly, the media as an industry have seen some significant changes since 1994. But pressure for change has focused almost more sharply on content. Government and other critics of the media have dwelt on the kind of journalism being practised, the issues and stories tackled, and the ways they have been handled. The catchphrase used to cover both areas of change is transformation, a very elusive term.

Trying to pin the concept down, Lynette Steenveld, a journalism lecturer at Rhodes University, asks: From what, to what?[11] In response, Berger[12] offers three tests: race, democracy and development. The key thrust of transformation, he argues, is a move from racism, via a stage of positive discrimination, to a situation where race is no longer a factor. At the same time, transformation is about building democracy, and about moving from mass underdevelopment to development.

Changes in ownership, markets, titles and other aspects of the media as industry have been outlined above, and are relatively easy to quantify. But changes in journalism – or the lack of them – are hard to pin down. More often than not, they are in the eye of the beholder. Public debate generally swirls around the question of how   h transformation there has been in the media and in journalism, and whether it is enough. Rather than try-ing to settle such an elusive point, I will describe some of the ways in which the question has surfaced.

Two inquiries – the media hearings of the Truth and Reconciliation Commission (TRC) and the Human Rights Commission's inquiry into racism in the media – provided a focus for debate on the state of journal-ism. They were very different in tone; the media generally supported the first, while the second was greeted with suspicion and hostility. In differ-ing ways, they dealt with two central themes: the enduring issue of race, and the role of journalists, particularly in their relationship with the gov-ernment, whether old or new.

Looking back: the TRC media probe

For three days in September 1997, an SABC television studio in Auckland Park was turned over to the TRC. This time, journalists were not shining the spotlight, they were under it. The commission was hearing evidence on the role of the media under apartheid, as part of a series of inquiries into different sectors of society.

A range of journalists, black and white, mainstream and alternative, took the stand. Former senior SABC executives tried to explain the past: some saw little prob-lem in the role the broadcaster had played, while others were less sanguine. 'We didn't fire the guns, but we pol-ished them,' said a former newsreader, Pat Rogers.[14] The English press emphasised its opposition to the National Party govern-ment, but was attacked for not going far enough. Black journalists described racist practices in various newsrooms, from being forced to use segregated facilities to having their copy distrusted. A former senior jour-nalist at *Business Day*, NomaVenda Mathiane, highlighted the position of women. 'South African newspapers are the poorer for not having devel-oped black women,' she said.[15] Journalists from the alternative press described detention, assault and harassment at the hands of the authorities.

The Afrikaans press had an ambivalent attitude to the hearings. Naspers decided not to participate. The chief executive of Nasnews, the company's newspaper division, Hennie van Deventer, said: 'As far as the Truth Commission is concerned, I really cannot see that it will add anything,

> "Everyone spoke about the incompetence of black reporters and their advocacy. Even then, what was happening was the black guys would get the stories and feed in to some white journalists who would write the story."[13]
> *Joe Latakgomo, a former Sowetan editor*

except putting certain people in the dock.'[16] But 127 staff members defied the company and signed a declaration in which they confessed themselves 'morally co-responsible' on the grounds that they 'helped maintain a system within which [gross human rights abuses] could occur'.[17]

As a result of the hearings, the TRC found: 'With the notable exception of certain individuals, the mainstream newspapers and the SABC failed to report adequately on gross human rights violations. In so doing, they helped sustain and prolong the existence of apartheid.'[18]

Row on race: the HRC media inquiry

In 1998 the South African Human Rights Commission (HRC) received a complaint of racism against the *Sunday Times* and the *Mail&Guardian*. The complaint, which came from the Black Lawyers' Association and Association of Black Accountants of South Africa, initiated an inquiry that was to cause much more conflict with the media than the TRC probe had done.

The HRC decided to broaden the inquiry to cover all the media, and commissioned research from the Media Monitoring Project and a researcher, Claudia Braude. Their reports were published in an interim report in November 1999, and the HRC began to prepare for public hearings.

Much of the media had been opposed to the exercise from the word go. The *Mail&Guardian* called it a 'feebly disguised assault on the press',[19] and the editor of the *Daily Dispatch*, Gavin Stewart, placed it in the tradition of earlier inquiries into the press by the apartheid government. 'Investigations into the media have a depressing history in South Africa,' he said.[20] Other voices were strongly in favour. The CEO of Mafube Publishing, the former journalist Thami Mazwai, wrote: 'Must blacks not be taken seriously when they say the media are abusing their human rights?'[21]

The release of the interim report – and particularly Braude's research – raised the temperature significantly. Her findings were widely pilloried as unscientific and baseless. In one instance, she read a photograph of a stork and a crow on a rubbish container in Kampala, Uganda, as reflecting racism, and this argument drew particular ridicule. In a more careful but nonetheless devastating critique, Berger says: 'Braude went in search of racism in the media – and found it everywhere, much like the apartheid regime used to discover reds under every bed and behind every bush.'[22]

Opposition to the exercise grew further when the HRC indicated it would use its power of subpoena to compel unwilling editors to appear at hearings planned for early 2000 – a move reminiscent of the strong-arm tactics used by the apartheid government to compel journalists to reveal their sources. Confrontation between most of the media and the HRC seemed unavoidable. But an eleventh-hour decision to withdraw the sub-poenas in exchange for editors agreeing to participate saw the hearings begin on schedule in March 2000.

Drawing heavily from a submission by five black editors, the HRC iden-tified several categories of complaint: [23]

- The media are 'still controlled by white people and caters for white interests and reflects the world view of the white minority'.
- Racism can be found in the handling of corruption stories, in that 'news reports and opinion columns constantly create the impression that all blacks are corrupt and incompetent'.
- White experts predominate.
- It also quoted the black editors as saying they faced particular difficul-ties in asserting themselves 'in an environment where white cultural approaches prevailed'.

Mostly white editors defended themselves by saying that where particu-lar reports were highlighted as problematical, these amounted to poor journalism, not deliberate racism, and that this in turn was due to a lack of training and experience in newsrooms.

In August 2000 the HRC published its final report under the title *Faultlines*. While bitter about the way the media had handled the exercise, it offered only comparatively mild recommendations. Careful to avoid any impression that it wanted to undermine media freedom, it concentrated on issues like training in racism awareness. It urged that consideration be given to the amalgamation of the different monitoring bodies, and that codes of conduct be reviewed.[24]

SERVING THE NATIONAL INTEREST?

We have seen how the debate on the journalist's role in the new South Africa surfaced during the TRC and HRC inquiries. The issue is by no means settled, and has come to revolve around the question whether jour-nalism should serve the national or the public interest. Along with the question of race, it remains perhaps the most important controversy in

South African journalism today. It won't be possible to settle it here, but it is important at least to outline its parameters.

South African media traditions fall in a continuum between support for and resistance to the apartheid system. On the one end of the spectrum, the underground media of the ANC and related organisations saw themselves as instruments in the fight against apartheid. During the height of the repressive 1980s, one ANC-aligned journalist articulated a particularly extreme version of this view. If confronted with a policeman wounded in a shootout with ANC fighters, he said, it was the role and duty of a progressive journalist to finish the policeman off.[25] At the other end of the spectrum were the SABC and other media that built support for apartheid and demonised its opponents. In between, there were countless variations.

Ferial Haffajee, the editor of the *Mail&Guardian*, points out that the mainstream media, 'once harnessed into the service of the former state or bullied into submission … now protects its newfound freedom jealously'.[26] For them, freedom meant assuming a real Fourth Estate role in a way that had previously not been possible. The government's orientation was different, Haffajee points out. Rooted in the ANC's past view of the media as a tool of the struggle, it expected journalists to allow themselves to be harnessed to the greater good.

"Usually an impression is created that the national interest is to the media what a red rag is to a bull … My submission is that this is pretence par excellence because every day in editorials and in angles to a story openly and by implication the national interest is invoked, be it in encouraging or celebrating the national teams, be it around issues of corruption or HIV/Aids … and everywhere in the visions and mission statements of our media houses there is reference and appeal to the national interest."[27]
Joel Netshitenzhe, government spokesperson

The call for a patriotic media

These conflicting views have led to a fractious relationship between government and the media. Government and other critics have accused the media of failing to further – or even deliberately harming – the national interest. In the view of the then president, Nelson Mandela, the media were still controlled by whites who were opposed to change, and even those black journalists rising to senior positions were merely parroting what their white masters wanted to have said. In one meeting with South African National Editors' Forum (Sanef) members in June 1997, Mandela said: 'We do not have black journalists saying what they would like to say. They have to work on papers, they want to make a living. While there are a few exceptional journalists, many like to please their white editors.'[28]

At the Sun City indaba between Sanef and the government in June 2001, the then deputy minister in the presidency, Essop Pahad, spelt out in detail what the government's expectation was. He took as his point of departure the 'founding settlement' encapsulated in the Constitution and Bill of Rights. This settlement 'included a common commitment to striving for a non-racial, non-sexist and democratic society from which the legacy of racism and its manifestations of extreme poverty, disease and ignorance had been eradicated.'[29]

Pahad argued that a 'national agenda' of reconstruction and development arose from the founding settlement, and that the media had a patriotic contribution to make to further the agenda in areas such as HIV and Aids and others. As many others have done, Pahad also offered criticism of the media's 'culture of negativism'. 'Is there room for celebration of success in this notion of news?' he asked rhetorically.

The Constitution is used as a basic reference point in much government writing on the subject. A particularly sophisticated argument comes from the government spokesperson, Joel Netshitenzhe,[30] who recognises a 'hierarchy' which starts with the Constitution. It descends through lower levels 'which would be about how you implement those broad prescriptions of the Constitution'.

The notion of a hierarchy is a useful one. The Constitution is couched in terms broad enough to ensure support by most people. Democracy and human rights are very fine things, and fit neatly with the way journalists see themselves. In that sense, there is a national consensus on some very basic issues. These have changed over time: in the years of negotiation and violence that preceded the country's founding democratic election of 1994, most of the media threw their support behind the project to secure a negotiated settlement. Deon du Plessis, then editor of the *Pretoria News*, wrote at the time: 'Primarily, in our country, we must be passionately in favour of peace. Without peace we have nothing in our country; with it we have a chance. The public interest is served by peace and if it comes to a decision between peace [and] publication of certain material then peace must come first.'[32]

A prominent Aids dissident, Anita Allen, filed a complaint with the BCCSA (Broadcasting Complaints Commission of South Africa) against Tim Modise and other well-known SABC news anchors in 2002. The charge: sedition, for coverage given to critics of official policy on Aids. "Open rebellion against [government] policies amounts to a breakdown of law and order – exactly what is happening in HIV/Aids," she argued. Dismissing the complaint, the BCCSA chairperson, Kobus van Rooyen, said: "Even laws may be criticised."[31]

This kind of support for a national project is possible only when the issue is overwhelmingly clear and there is massive consensus on it, often when the very existence of the society is at stake, such as in times of war.

As it happened, fears of general collapse and violence were not realised, and South Africa settled into the order set out by the Constitution. While there may be agreement at this very broad level, differences of opinion begin to emerge very quickly as we descend down Netshitenzhe's hierarchy to more specific issues. For instance, most journalists would agree that fighting poverty and HIV/Aids are national priorities. But that's a very far way from supporting particular government policies on the issues.

The question is often asked: Who decides what is in the national interest? That right is sometimes claimed for the government, on the grounds that it has been democratically elected. But Netshitenzhe recognises that it can't be decided by decree. He says it is a 'sixth sense' of society as a whole, although he does slip in the significant rider that it is 'usually asserted by the formal authority within that nation'.

This kind of consensus develops in the general discussion going on across the whole society, everywhere from university lecture rooms and churches to dinner tables and taxi ranks. It often involves conflict. Litigation around HIV/Aids policy is an example of a contest to define the national interest, as the Steve Biko Foundation's Xolela Mangcu points out.[33] At the same time, it is not a fight of equals. Groups with money, or organisational and other muscle carry much more weight than those without.

> "Journalists are for democracy, but they would rather muckrake than muck in."[35]
>
> *Anthea Garman and Guy Berger, of Rhodes University's department of journalism and media studies*

The media provide the vehicle for much of this contest, which is why government officials are so anxious to get journalists 'on side'. Netshitenzhe says: 'Beyond the Constitution as such, we need to unite around a given consensus on some of these critical issues which are about the survival and thriving of our nation and our democratic system to forge ahead as one.'[34] The sentiment is understandable: as government spokesperson, his key function is to build as much social support as possible for government programmes and policies.

Journalists prefer the public interest

Journalists tend to see appeals to the national interest as politically loaded. And the more assiduously the government asserts its right to define the national interest, the more sceptical they become. Memories of the way the apartheid government used this kind of language are still quite fresh. Of course, comparing the two is unfair. The new government has a long liberation struggle, Nelson Mandela, and several clear victories in democratic elections to back its claim to legitimacy.

It doesn't make them angels. Any government makes mistakes, and journalists have always seen it as an important function to keep an eagle eye out for times when they falter. Haffajee writes: 'It is a muck-raking, shit-stirring, adrenalin rush of an occupation geared towards keeping society on its toes by doing what it does best: being a pain in the backside.'[36] And there is a strong suspicion that the temptation to dress up a sectional, short-term interest as 'national' may sometimes be too strong to resist.

Most editors are prepared to accept the Constitution as a reference point. The editor of *City Press*, Mathatha Tsedu, says the Constitution encapsulates 'the collective agreement that we've reached as a nation about how our interests are defined … as long as I'm not doing anything that is contrary to what the Constitution says, I am acting in the national interests'.[37]

The editor of the *Sunday Times*, Mondli Makhanya, says that considerations of national interest should apply only 'in very extreme circumstances', like war.[38] If the government was planning to intervene militarily in Zimbabwe, for instance, and premature publication of their plans might spark a war, then there might be an argument for holding back, he says, but nothing short of that.

The editor of *Business Day*, Peter Bruce, says short-term economic damage is not enough of a reason to suppress a story. 'Let's say I knew that the President was terminally ill – would I publish it? Yes, absolutely, without thinking about it if I was sure of my facts. And the rand would fall the next day, but I would look at the rand falling as not a big problem – it's a market thing out there and it would come back again.'[39]

Most editors distrust appeals to the national interest, and prefer to be guided by the concept of public interest. This uses the society as a whole and its citizens as its reference point, independent of the state. In that context, the government becomes one player among many – an important one, of course, but not the sole arbiter of what constitutes the society's interest. Makhanya says: 'I much prefer to use public interest because it is actually in the interest of the people who reside in this country.'

The editor of the *Sunday Tribune*, Barney Mthombothi, says: 'I am quite comfortable with "public interest" because you are talking about different media and they sell to different publics.'[40]

The issue has particular resonance for journalists at the SABC, which is trying to live down a legacy of blind obedience to the apartheid state. The head of SABC radio news, Pippa Green, says it would be undesirable to have the corporation's editorial code refer to the national interest: 'It would have opened the way to interference in certain types of stories.'[41]

The head of SABC TV news, Jimi Matthews, says: 'Hiding behind public and national is this thing called "the state", and I think it would be more honest for all of us if the state interest is included … I'm not sure that I could easily work for the state broadcaster.'[42] Matthews says the police have sometimes tried to suppress news stories with an appeal to the national interest. When he was still head of news at e.tv, for instance, the channel obtained builders' plans when the president's Cape Town residence was being renovated.

Matthews says police and security officials suggested it would be 'irresponsible' to run the story 'and thus not in the national interest', even though the intention was not to show the detail of the plans, simply to highlight a serious lapse of security. The story was run because 'it was in the public interest', Matthews says simply.

A debate about whether the SABC should be committed to serving the national or the public interest erupted in Parliament around the Broadcasting Amendment Bill during 2002. It ended inconclusively, with both terms included in the Bill as it was passed. But since both have been left undefined, it does not really resolve the issue one way or the other.

Once again, the difference between media and journalism

We have previously used the distinction between journalism and the media as an industry. In this context, too, it helps us find some additional clarity.

The media as industry have – and use – all sorts of options for serving social ends. News organisations have quite happily supported – and sometimes initiated – campaigns around community issues. The editor of the *Daily News*, Dennis Pather, says the news media have a role to play in 'promoting democracy'.[43] This has included promoting campaigns against poverty and encouraging entrepreneurship and projects in rural communities, he says. A number of newspapers regularly insert educational materials based on the school syllabus or issues of concern like HIV and Aids. Some newspapers make a point of printing the phone numbers of Aids helplines alongside reports on the pandemic, and advice columns are popular in both print and broadcasting. Logos like that of Proudly South African, or of various bids for South Africa to host international sporting events, have been woven into mastheads.

None of these things make journalists feel uncomfortable. Pather says they can be done 'without selling our souls as journalists'. But when it comes to reporting, national interest does not easily override journalists' passionate dedication to telling the story, and telling it fully.

TALKING POINT

Serving the public interest
Rehana Rossouw

As a journalist who spent her formative years trained by, and writing for, the alternative press in South Africa, I often look back at work I did 20 years ago and admit quite readily that I was a propagandist.

I am not embarrassed by this, though. I believe that the alternative press played a significant and vital role in mobilising resistance to apartheid.

Following the launch of *Grassroots* newspaper in Cape Town in 1980, community and anti-apartheid newspapers sprang up across the country, most of them supportive of community groups, left-wing trade unions and extra-parliamentary political organisations.

The articles we wrote and published ranged from 'How to draft a constitution for your organisation'; features on the miserable lives of black South Africans under apartheid; reports on the activities of the African National Congress, a banned organisation at the time; to exposés of government brutality and corruption.

Headlines often read: 'A victory for the people!' or 'State cracks down on peaceful protest'. Most of our articles were biased and one-sided. Bosses were not given space to defend their horrific working conditions and exploitative pay, and absolutely no attempt was made to give the police an opportunity to defend the fact that they opened fire on protesting school-children.

Articles on community struggles contained detail of how a protest committee was formed, what programme of action they devised, and the tactics they used to take on the authorities. This was no mere reportage, it was political education, organisation and mobilisation.

In the early 1990s the alternative press was in crisis. Largely dependent on foreign aid, they had no tools to build commercial enterprises, and the struggle they had fought for was won. The alternative press died, and many regarded this as a natural death.

But there is still a need today – in a democratic and free South Africa – for some of the journalism practised by the alternative press.

There is a particular need for education, and the media today fails miserably to meet this responsibility. With commercial imperatives ruling the roost, education initiatives are supported only when sponsors are prepared to fund the cost.

To combat the spread of Aids, the disease which has sprouted a new struggle in South Africa, requires education, mobilisation and organisation. So too, do initiatives encouraging civil obedience like paying municipal fees and registering to vote. The media report on 'municipal messes' and stay-aways from voting stations, but do not provide information required to access the services offered by government.

The arm's-length relationship between the organs of state and media today, touted as 'a free press in a free society', does disservice to the communities they serve. Many in the media fail to recognise the essential difference between supporting the political aims of the government and informing the public of the role of government and the tools they need to make government work for them.

Government, too, lambastes the media for failing in their duty to inform and educate, but does a pitiful job of disseminating information – both to the media and directly to the people they serve.

Government communicators regularly appeal to the media to serve the national interest, saying the media has a duty to fulfil this role. The media responds by arguing that the national interest is not necessarily the public interest. Both are right; and wrong. Both need to step back from their allegiances and examine what their duty is to society.

Whether it is done in the name of national interest or public interest, there is still a need for propaganda in South Africa, albeit at the simple level of publishing news and information people need to make them truly free.

(Rehana Rossouw is assistant news and features editor
at Business Day)

....

NOTES

1   The following must of necessity be a very brief overview of a large and complex field. For a fuller discussion, see Guy Berger, 'Deracialisation, democracy and development: transformation of the South African media 1994–2000', Grahamstown, 2000. Posted at http://journ.ru.ac.za/staff/guy/index.html, accessed on 23 April 2003.

2   For a fuller discussion of the later opposition press, see Les Switzer and Mohamed Adhikari (eds.), *South Africa's resistance press: alternative voices in the last generation under apartheid*. Athens, Ohio: Ohio University Center for International Studies, 2000.

3   Berger, 'Deracialisation'.

4   Ibid.

5   Switzer and Adhikari, *South Africa's resistance press*. xi.

6   Government Communication and Information System (GCIS), 'Media Development and Diversity Agency: a draft position paper'. Pretoria: GCIS, 2000. 20.

7   Ibid. 22.

8   Quoted in Guy Berger, 'More media for Southern Africa? The place of politics, economics and convergence in developing media density', Grahamstown, 2002. Posted at http://journ.ru.ac.za/staff/guy/, accessed on 23 April 2003.

9   Ibid.

10 Quoted in Anton Harber, 'The Sun also rises – daily', Business Day, 14 March 2003.

11 Lynette Steenveld, 'The transformation of the media: from what, to what?' *Rhodes Journalism Review* 16, July 1988. 4.

12 Berger, 'Deracialisation'.

13 Part of Independent Newspapers' submission to the TRC.

14 Quoted in *Rhodes Journalism Review* 15, November 1997. 30.

15 Quoted in *Rhodes Journalism Review* 15, November 1997. 31.

16 Quoted in *Rhodes Journalism Review* 14, May 1997. 26.

17 *Rhodes Journalism Review* 15, November 1997. 33.

18 Truth and Reconciliation Commission of South Africa (TRC), *Report* Vol 4. Cape Town: TRC, 1998. 189.

19 *Mail&Guardian*, 20–26 November 1998.

20 Quoted in the South African Human Rights Commission (SAHRC), *Interim report of the inquiry into racism in the media*. Johannesburg: SAHRC, 1999. 11.

21 Ibid. 12.

22 Guy Berger, 'Submission for HRC investigation into racism and the media', Grahamstown, 2000. Posted at http://journ.ru.ac.za/staff/guy/, accessed on 24 April 2003.

23 SAHRC, *Faultlines: Inquiry into racism in the media*. Johannesburg: SAHRC, 2000. 18–19.

24 Ibid. 80–4.

25 Personal communication.

26 Ferial Haffajee, 'Revisiting the ethical codes'. Paper prepared for conference on Freedom of Expression and Ethics in the Media: A South African Approach, at Sandton, Johannesburg, October 2001.

27 Speech delivered on Media Freedom Day, 25 October 2002, University of the Witwatersrand.

28 *Rhodes Journalism Review* 15, November 1997. 34.

29 Essop Pahad, 'Communication in a changing society: a news agenda for development'. Paper prepared for the Sanef/government indaba at Sun City, June 2001.

30 Joel Netshitenzhe, Speech delivered on Media Freedom Day, October 25, at the University of the Witwatersrand.

31 See BCCSA case 2002/12. Posted at http//www.bccsa.co.za.

32 Deon du Plessis, 'Confidentiality and public interest', *Ecquid Novi* 15,1, 1994. 95.

33 *Sunday Independent*, 4 August 2002.

34 Ibid.

35 'Editorial', *Rhodes Journalism Review* 14, May 1997.

36 *Mail&Guardian*, 20–26 November 1998.

37 Interview, 11 December 2002.

38 Interview, 9 December 2002.

39 Interview, 2 December 2002.

40 Interview, 2002.

41 Interview, 17 July 2002.

42 Interview, 27 November 2002.

43 Interview, 16 October 2002.

We will earn the respect of our listeners.
SABC: Radio News Mission Statement

As a public institution the BBC must account to the public for all its dealings.
BBC: Producers' Guidelines

Whenever there is an inaccurate or a misleading report, it shall be corrected promptly and given due prominence. An apology should be published whenever appropriate.
Ghana Journalists' Association: Code of Ethics

3

ACCOUNTABILITY AND PRACTICAL DECISION-MAKING

British newspapers have become thoroughly corrupt, according to the journalist Anthony Browne in the *New Statesman*: 'Print journalism is now the most corrupt realm of public life in Britain.'[1] Pointing to the widespread acceptance of freebies, he says every other sphere, from political parties to regulators and charities, 'has cleaned up its act, established rules of disclosure, and disciplined those who fall short'. Journalism's reluctance to follow suit makes its exposure of corruption elsewhere simply hypocritical. 'Journalists are the nation's anti-corruption squad, but there is no one to investigate our own corruption,' writes Browne.

Journalists prize their freedom, and the South African and many other constitutions guarantee it. But freedom does not mean licence. Journalists are not immune from the temptation to misuse their position for person-al benefit of one kind or another – even if Browne's description may not apply quite so starkly to South Africa. The president of the International Federation of Journalists, Jens Linde, says that journalists are often reluc-tant 'to become subject to a system of public scrutiny which actually works', just like politicians, lawyers, the military 'or any other group which exercises power'.[2] He adds: 'for journalists the obligation to accept scrutiny is special, for scrutiny is the sanction which journalists hold over others.'

Accountability does not mean allowing others to dictate what we do. It simply means:

- being prepared to take criticism and explain decisions;
- acknowledging and rectifying mistakes;
- being open about what we do and how we do it; and
- developing a set of standards for behaviour and methods of dealing with those who transgress.

Who should watch the watchdogs?

Other professions are regulated by law. Doctors and lawyers have to be registered, and can have their right to practise revoked if they fall foul of the rules of the profession. Journalism is different. Anybody can pick up a pen or a microphone and call themselves a journalist – there are no exter-nally determined standards that regulate the profession. The reason for this amazing privilege is that freedom of speech is such a precious thing, and any system to register journalists would compromise it. For that very reason, authoritarian governments are very fond of systems of licensing journalists. In 2002 the government of Zimbabwe introduced such a system.

In democracies, journalists are left to regulate themselves. Ed Linington, the press ombud, says anything else would 'eventually land up in the hands of the government'.[3] The former chairperson of the British Press Complaints Commission, Lord Wakeham, says: 'The case for self-regula-tion rests on the premise that in complex democratic societies self-imposed rules are likely to carry a greater moral authority, and consequently, to work with greater effectiveness than externally imposed rules.'[4] In Britain there has been sustained pressure for increased legal restrictions on media freedom. Wakeham says self-regulation has a num-ber of practical benefits too: it is cheap, quick and flexible, and is therefore easily accessible to ordinary people.[5] In addition, most people have a particular sensitivity to being judged by their peers.

In South Africa, as in Britain, the media fall under the authority of bodies set up by the industry and dominated by journalists. The Media Institute of Southern Africa (Misa) also supports the establishment of voluntary media councils in those countries that don't have them, even though some journalists in the region fear that a lack of experience may lead to such bodies taking bad decisions, creating undesirable precedents.[6]

The danger of self-regulation is of course that journalists will 'look after their own' in a way that undermines public confidence in the system. If it is to have any value at all, press councils must on occasion be prepared to take a sharply critical look at what is being done in the media.

> "I don't want to belittle [the Broadcasting Complaints Commission of South Africa], but 99% of those complaints are by privileged white people who've got nothing better to do than to complain about something. I'm not saying they shouldn't have rights because they're privileged whites. But we are talking about being accountable to the people."[7]
>
> *Guy Berger, Rhodes University*

While the emphasis here has been on self-regulation, it should not be forgotten that even in democracies there remain many legal constraints on journalists. People who feel they have been libelled can sue for damages; there are provisions governing hate speech, rules around the coverage of courts, protection of minors and other things.[8]

In addition, some people point to the market as a mechanism of accountability. The argument is that readers, listeners and viewers can vote with their feet if they do not like what they are given. Media that are in tune with their audiences will prosper; those that are not will wither and die. The argument is based on an idealised view of consumer choices and the market. In any event, popularity is not the same as ethics: yellow journalism often does rather well. While not without some validity, the argument should be treated with considerable caution.

The architecture of self-regulation

Newspaper journalists are subject to the jurisdiction of the Press Ombudsman of South Africa, which replaced the South African Press Council in 1997. The ombud's office falls under a Founding Bodies Committee, among whose members are representatives of journalist unions, editors' forums, the Newspaper Association of Southern Africa, and magazine and community press owners. Funding comes from print media companies to ensure that no potential conflicts of interest may arise. Anybody can complain to the ombud, on condition that they waive their right to legal action. But this does not mean that newspapers can be harassed by frivolous, fraudulent, malicious or vexatious complaints, or those that do not reveal prima facie a contravention of the code. An offending newspaper can be ordered to publish a finding – no fines or other punishments can be meted out. The ombud deals with the editor on behalf of his or her newspaper, not individual journalists.

According to Linington, his ombud office dealt with 144 complaints in 2003.[9] Linington says he first tries to settle complaints by mediation. This may just take a telephone call or a letter to the affected editor.

If this fails, a matter may be decided on the basis of written submissions, or a hearing may be held. It is an informal affair: no minutes are taken, and lawyers are not allowed to speak. (Some complainants do bring lawyers, says Linington, who then spend their time advising their clients through scribbled notes or whispers.) There is an appeal panel, headed by a judge, to whom either party can appeal if they are unhappy with the ombud's ruling.

All over the world, broadcasting is subject to more regulation than print. The frequency spectrum used for radio and TV is a limited resource, and so governments have set up systems to license broadcasters. In South Africa, this power is wielded by the Independent Communications Authority of South Africa (Icasa). Licences are issued with a range of conditions, including signal strength, coverage area, ownership, proportion of advertising and local content. Icasa ensures compliance through the Broadcasting Monitoring and Complaints Committee (BMCC).

Icasa requires licensees to adhere to its code of conduct, which covers the full range of media ethical issues, not just those affecting journalists (see Appendix 3). To make things a bit more complicated, though, members of the National Association of Broadcasters (NAB) are excluded from this requirement, on the basis that they have accepted their own code, and subject themselves to the discipline of another body, the Broadcasting Complaints Commission of South Africa (BCCSA).

The overwhelming majority of radio and television stations are members of the NAB, leaving Icasa's BMCC to deal only with community broadcasters on content issues (of course, it ensures that NAB members adhere to their other licence conditions). For our purposes, though, the BCCSA is the more important body.

Set up in 1993, the body shares many similarities with the press ombud. It is funded by broadcasters, through the NAB, and consists of seven representatives of the public and seven from the industry. Members serve for five years, and a chairperson for five too. Complainants may be required to waive their right to legal action, but this is not a requirement as with the press ombud. An adjudicator first attempts to settle the matter, and can rule on the complaint. Appeals are heard by a tribunal. Lawyers may appear before the BCCSA, and it is empowered not only to require corrections to be broadcast, but can also impose a fine of up to R40 000.

Around 700 to 800 complaints are received per year, says the BCCSA chairperson, Kobus van Rooyen.[10] Informal mediation is not as common as with the press ombud, he says. Complaints about language, sex and violence play a much more prominent role in broadcasting than in print.

The rules we live by

The press ombud operates on the basis of the Press Code of Professional Practice. The BCCSA used to have a code that was virtually identical because it was based on the press code. But during 2003, Icasa's code came into effect, and the BCCSA now uses this code. In addition, many organisations have developed their own documents.

The usefulness of codifying the ethics of the profession is not universally accepted. From the perspective of some governments, codes of ethics (together with the system of self-regulation) are not sufficient to keep journalists honest, and the more vigorous powers of law are required.[11] At the other end of the spectrum, some see even a voluntary code as an infringement of media freedom. And in the litigious US, there are sometimes fears that codes can undermine journalists in the courtroom. Some lawyers fear that in a defamation suit, for instance, a plaintiff can use a written code against the news organisation being sued.[12] In South Africa, the debate has no particular strength. Codes are generally seen as a useful

"Carefully written codes highlight and anticipate ethical dilemmas so we don't have to reinvent a decision-making process each time we face a new dilemma; they inspire us about our unique roles and responsibilities; they make each of us custodians of our profession's values and behaviours, and inspire us to emulate the best of our profession; they promote front end, proactive decision-making, before our decisions 'go public'."[13]
Bob Steele and Jay Black,
US ethicists

tool – so much so that some organisations seem to go through regular cycles of reworking their codes.

What makes a good code? There is a natural inclination to view a code as a list of 'thou shalt nots'. No code can do without what Bob Steele and Jay Black call this 'red light tone', but they say it should be balanced by a 'green light tone emphasising duties and responsibilities'.[14] With a little thought, it's not hard to work out ways of describing the ideal of ethical behaviour rather than focusing only on the problem areas.

There is some debate about how detailed a code should be. South Africa's press code explicitly points out that it cannot cover every contingency, and that the press should be judged by its spirit rather than its narrow letter. Black et al. say codes can't 'delineate all the territory likely to be encountered, and they aren't much help when negotiating the vast foggy terrain through which journalists travel daily'.[15]

On the other hand, *Die Burger* prefers more detail. Its code runs to 12 pages, with detailed guidelines augmenting the basic principles. The deputy editor, George Claassen, developed the code, and says the breadth of previous codes made them too vague. He says the detail will make the code easier to use by younger journalists.[16]

For a code to be useful, it must be accepted by those expected to stick to it. Joe Thloloe, e.tv's head of news, said although the station had a code, it became necessary to draft a new one. 'Essentially nobody seems to know how it was written, when it was written and it hasn't been in use as a document. That is why we need something that people will be committed to,' he said when the service began developing its new code. Thloloe felt that the process of drafting a code can help ensure the 'buy-in' of staff.

During 2003 the SABC undertook a highly public process to redraft its editorial policies. The amended Broadcasting Act of 2002 required the corporation to develop policies and then lodge them with Icasa. One of the issues that arose particularly sharply for the SABC was the question of whose code it should be. The previous code said prominently: 'Authority for editorial decisions … vests in the editorial staff'[17] – explicitly excluding non-news management and the board. But the draft editorial policies distributed for public comment declared the SABC's chief executive to be the editor-in-chief, and instituted a system of upward referral for contentious issues. The proposal was heavily criticised by opposition parties and media commentators as well as the SABC's own editorial staff. The final version, released early in 2004, softened the provision and shifted responsibility closer to the editorial staff again.[18]

The advertising industry has its own separate code, policed by the Advertising Standards Authority.

Time for change?

Codes need to be reviewed regularly. Even though it's clearly undesirable to write in provisions around every new controversy, they need to be kept in tune with changing circumstances and thinking. With this flurry of redrafting in various media houses, the question is whether the overarching codes used by the regulators have kept up with the times.

The Press Code of Professional Practice – which is followed closely by the news provisions of the Icasa code – came into force in 1997, when the Press Council was replaced by the Press Ombudsman. The new code replaced a Press Code of Conduct that dated back to 1962 but had seen several revisions over the years. The new code saw substantial changes to the preamble and the section on discrimination and dropped some things seen as 'left-overs from the apartheid era', according to Linington.[19]

Nevertheless, gaps remain. There is a startling silence on issues of independence and conflict of interest. Internationally, this has become a major area of concern. The *New York Times* has several policies dealing with various aspects of ethics. But in January 2003, the paper added a new 53-page code of conduct that is entirely focused on questions of conflict of interest.[20] And as we have seen, some sharply critical voices have raised concerns in Britain. In South Africa some industry practices have begun to confront the issue. *The Star* has a well-developed policy on freebies, as well as travel and motoring journalism. And the *Sunday Times* collects all free gifts given to staff, auctions them off and donates the proceeds to charity. But the absence of any reference to the issue in the industry codes themselves is a significant gap.

Journalists might also discuss whether gender and race issues are dealt with adequately. Given the importance of these issues in our history, one would expect more guidance in the industry codes. We will discuss what is there, and what is missing, in later chapters.

The question of changing the codes and the monitoring bodies came up sharply during the Human Rights Commission (HRC) inquiry into racism in the media. Its report was particularly critical of the press ombud, saying the office was 'laid back, not very well publicised, takes no proactive action and could be more effective than it is'.[21] The HRC suggested that print should also fall under Icasa's code, or alternatively that a new regulatory framework for the whole media – print and broadcasting – should be considered. This should be under the control of and funded by the media. 'In other words, what already exists should be strengthened and established by legislation.'[22]

Turning to the codes of conduct, it recommended that they be reviewed 'to ensure that they are consistent and in line with the current constitutional requirements and that they properly reflect the role of the media in a democratic society'.[23]

Debates about the shape of regulation are not unique to South Africa. Wakeham identifies five issues that have arisen internationally:

- Should third-party complaints be accepted (in other words by parties not directly affected by a report)?
- Should a press council be proactive, initiating its own investigations?
- Should councils take up press freedom issues?
- How closely can codes define values like 'taste' and 'decency'?
- Should powers to fine and suspend, familiar in broadcasting, be introduced to the press?[24]

The South African regulators are clearly against being given the power to initiate an investigation without their having received a complaint. Linington says: 'Basically what you're doing is becoming policeman, prosecutor and judge and there is inherent unfairness in that.'[25] The other questions have so far not arisen very sharply in South Africa.

Most editors interviewed were willing to consider a review of the codes, but could not immediately think of any gaps that needed to be filled. Linington bridles against the HRC's recommendation that the system 'should be strengthened and established by legislation' since this would amount to state take-over, but concedes that issues like gender might need some more attention in the press code.

The HRC's suggestions did not lead to any change in the system of regulation. Just over a year after the release of the *Faultlines* report, a conference jointly hosted by the HRC and the South African National Editors' Forum (Sanef) considered issues arising out of the report, but ended inconclusively. The codes and the structures checking on South Africa's journalists were left unchanged.

Accountability begins at home

It's far better to avoid having to deal with complaints lodged with the press ombud or BCCSA. There are various ways in which individual news media themselves can engage with their audiences. Most editors say that they correct errors promptly and with due prominence – despite a natural reluctance to admit mistakes. Most codes also spell out this requirement, although it's easier to follow in print than in broadcasting. There is sometimes criticism of the prominence given to corrections: an error in a front-page lead is rectified in a tiny block on page 17. The editor of *Business Day*, Peter Bruce, decided to place the paper's Getting It Right boxes as close as possible to the position of the report being corrected. Burying them elsewhere is unethical, he says: 'People miss them.'[26]

Complaints are a fact of life in the media. Sometimes they are reasonable, and sometimes not. Linington writes: 'Some South African editors simply send all complaints to their attorneys; are extremely defensive in response to complaints; frequently ignore letters of complaint or reply abruptly and dismissively; publish a letter of complaint with an arrogant footnote; refuse to publish a letter rebutting some damaging report but fail to tell the writer or explain the reason.'[27]

Some news organisations have appointed an internal ombud to deal with public complaints. In the US, these are sometimes called public editors. Whether it is a formal office of this kind or simply a willingness to listen, the principle remains the same. News organisations do well to set up a system to deal quickly and sympathetically with complaints. It's good for business, Linington points out, since complaints are a form of feedback and the way they are handled can build – or damage – credibility.

PRACTICAL DECISION-MAKING

Let's now take a step backwards from institutions and codes into the newsroom, where journalists – reporters, producers, sub-editors, photographers, graphic artists or others – confront issues of practical ethics every day. In the title of their much-quoted book, the US ethicists Jay Black, Bob Steele and Ralph Barney call it 'doing ethics'.[28] Making good ethical decisions is a skill that can be developed. And it is every bit as important as all the other skills that a good journalist needs to develop.

> "We try to apply our minds prior to the event and not dream up the ethics subsequently, which is what tends to happen quite often on newspapers."[29]
> *Johan de Villiers, executive editor of The Star*

In developing this skill, we should begin by understanding that ethics involves a clear set of principles that can be described with reasonable accuracy. Too often, ethics are seen as an undefined, fuzzy area best tackled by gut feel. In fact, we will make better decisions if we adopt a more deliberate, analytical approach. This section will attempt to point out some ways in which we can improve our decision-making.

Ethical principles often compete. Dilemmas usually arise when different values pull us in different directions. Very often, real life situations are not painted in simple black and white. We need to be willing to explore the shades of grey too. That means balancing competing values.

• •

There are two different approaches to take in tackling ethical issues. One asks about the likely consequences of various courses of action; the other relies on notions of duty.

The first, based on the philosophical approach known as **teleology**, allows journalists to weigh the impact of a story or technique. Dealing with the possible use of hidden cameras to get footage of a paedophile ring, for instance, the reporter would ask the question: what will that technique do to the audience and those involved? It's a popular approach to ethical dilemmas, but it is not without its drawbacks. For one thing, it lends itself to an 'ends justify the means' argument, and it can lead to the interests of majorities trumping the legitimate interests of minorities. Sometimes the damage that could be caused to one person – a crime victim, for instance – should weigh more heavily than the benefit to the mass of the audience. Finally, of course, predicting consequences is an uncertain task.

The second, based on **deontological** approaches in philosophy, is guided by duty. It asks the question: what are my obligations in this situation? This requires a specific set of rules that can be referred to. In the above example of the hidden cameras, the journalist would look for rules about deception and act accordingly. This approach avoids some of the pitfalls of the other, but can be rigid. In real life, most decision-making takes both approaches into account.[30]

• •

But it does entail taking decisions. Academics may enjoy the luxury of simply describing a dilemma and leaving it unresolved, but working journalists don't. Deadlines are unforgiving and decisions have to be taken, often under considerable time pressure. A problem story will have to be run, amended or pulled.

Always, the quality of ethical decision-making will be improved through discussion. This may mean a quick chat with a colleague, or it may involve a formal discussion with a group of senior editors. The editor of *The Star*, Moegsien Williams, says: 'Newspapers must never take impulsive decisions.'[31] There should always be 'a process where there is a discussion, there is a bit of consideration, there's weighing up the pros and the cons,' he says. Of course, this is not always easy on deadline.

Decision-making is also improved by involving people of varied backgrounds and viewpoints. This is particularly important in the South African context, where racial and other divisions run so deep.

An ethics roadmap: Three steps to resolving a dilemma

Several excellent models have been developed to guide journalists through a decision-making process if they are faced with an ethical question. The US ethicist Louis Day has developed what he calls the situation definition, analysis and decision (Sad) formula.[32] The American Society of Newspaper Editors and the Poynter Institute have developed an interactive Ethics Tool which allows journalists to involve others in an online discussion as they work through ten steps.[33] The following draws from these and other sources in order to create a simple, practical roadmap that journalists can follow to find their way through an ethical dilemma. Appendix 1 offers this roadmap as a form that you can work through.

Step 1: Define the issue

Firstly, you should make sure you have all the necessary facts at your disposal. This means being able to **summarise the situation** as if you were explaining it to an editor. It is important to pay attention to any areas of factual uncertainty.

Secondly, you should **formulate the question**. What exactly needs to be resolved? It is surprisingly useful to force yourself to formulate the question precisely. Ethical questions often feel fuzzy, and forcing yourself to commit to a form of words that define the issue is a good technique to ensure you think exactly.

Step 2: Think through the issue

There are a number of things that you must consider as you grapple with your problem. Firstly, work out the **public interest**. Why are you doing this story? Why does your audience have an interest in it?

Secondly, you need to identify the people or groups who stand to be affected – the **stakeholders**. The most obvious of these are sources, the subject of a story, their family and your news organisation. How will they be affected? What are their motivations? Are these legitimate?

Thirdly, identify the **principles** involved. Most often, a dilemma arises because different ethical imperatives collide. For instance, the right of the public to information may clash with an individual's right to privacy. In order to resolve an issue properly, we need to be able to define the principles at stake. These could be any of the issues that form the chapters of this book.

Fourthly, look at **guidelines and precedents** These could include ethical codes, rulings by the industry watchdogs, examples from other fields, personal experiences, and so on.

Fifthly, **identify the options**. It is important to think laterally in formulating different possible courses of action. Publishing a story or killing it are not the only options. Imaginative solutions are often the way out of a dilemma.

Step 3: Decide

Finally, you have to commit yourself to a particular course of action. And you should be willing to defend that decision to all stakeholders, including colleagues, the audience and the subject of the story. In a situation of controversy, challenges from various quarters must be expected and will have to be dealt with. Dennis Pather, the editor of the *Daily News*, says the best test of having taken a good decision is 'to stand up in public and defend your decision'.[34]

The case studies below will apply this model to concrete examples. In the interests of readability, the various steps will not be specifically signposted, but they should nevertheless be clearly discernible.

Readers should be more than consumers
Cyril Madlala

After ten years of liberation, it is worth considering whether South Africa's democracy would not have been enhanced by a vigorous but loyal alternative media.

It would be vigorous in the pursuit of the truth about the conduct and performance of the new ruling elite, yet remaining, and being seen to be, loyal to this democratic dispensation. Armed with impeccable struggle credentials, it would be taken seriously by a substantial lot of South Africans who can influence the behaviour of those who wield power. In turn, it would respect its audience as more than just consumers, treating it instead as citizenry.

What liberated Afrikaner perspective of the new South Africa would we be reading in the *Vrye Weekblad*? Would we be dismissive of the former editor Max du Preez's observations just because he is white and therefore not entitled to be critical of a black president in South Africa?

What impact on this democracy would the *Weekly Mail* be making if financial constraints had not forced it to seek new business partnerships? What would *South* be making of the muddled politics of the Western Cape?

The answers are of academic interest now – except in KwaZulu-Natal, where *Umafrika* is trying to serve a new South Africa, or more specifically, a province where the present remains marked by the scars of past conflicts. The media are also affected by these divisions. Unsurprisingly, Inkatha remains ill at ease with *Umafrika*, a newspaper that was such a pain when the organisation ran the erstwhile KwaZulu government. Equally, the ANC more readily embraces the paper as one of its own, since it identified with the cause the organisation championed.

Ten years after liberation, much has changed. The ANC and the IFP have found themselves in a provincial coalition government, an arrangement born of a necessity to co-exist merely because it would have been impossible for one to govern without the other.

The media landscape has also changed. Ten years ago, unshaven comrades in t-shirts, hiding from the police, would sneak into the newsrooms of these alternative newspapers for interviews. These days they are immaculate in their expensive suits as they appear on SABC television.

Come to think of it, three minutes on the SABC 1 is worth a thousand times more than the three hours a comrade would have spent with a sympathetic comrade journalist not so many years ago. The comrades are in control of the state broadcaster now, and who needs an *Umafrika* or a Du Preez who thinks he can lecture to this government about the morality of its ways as he did to PW Botha's government?

What has been lost, however, is a media tradition that had a different relationship with its audience. Stories of detention, torture and murder at the hands of the Security Branch were not aimed at boosting newspaper sales. They were a mirror to the defiance, the pain and the unwavering commitment of those who sacrificed their lives for a democratic South Africa.

Those newspapers saw themselves as accountable to the South African people, then engaged in a desperate struggle for dignity and freedom. These days, what matters to newspapers is the bottom line and political correctness. Readers are no longer seen as citizens, they are just consumers.

I suggest there is a vacuum to be filled by a vigilant media whose commitment to this democracy is beyond doubt and who would have the ear of the constituency that is important to the ruling class. Otherwise, who will make the rulers listen?

(Cyril Madlala is publisher and editor of Umafrika)

Case study 1
Leaks, agendas and RS452

The year 2003 delivered a story full to the brim with ethical issues, which catapulted journalism into the spotlight as almost never before. Suddenly journalists had become actors – some said they were tools – in a large and dimly understood power play, and their methods and ethics were scrutinised by a judicial commission of inquiry, as well as by public opinion.

The complex tale is an obvious choice as this book's first case study. Although no story of best practice, it illustrates a wide range of ethical issues. The discussion here will also provide a concrete illustration of how such challenges should be thought through.

Timeline

24 July 2003:	The national director of public prosecutions, Bulelani Ngcuka, holds a confidential briefing with editors to refute a smear e-mail against him doing the rounds, and gives details of his investigations into the deputy president, Jacob Zuma.
7 September:	*City Press* reports claims Ngcuka may have been an apartheid spy.
19 September:	Ranjeni Munusamy, who initiated the *City Press* report, resigns from her job at the *Sunday Times* after having been suspended for passing the story to the rival paper.
19 September:	The retired judge Joos Hefer is appointed to investigate the spy accusation against Ngcuka.
22 September:	First detailed account of Ngcuka's confidential briefing of editors appears in *Business Day*.
22 October:	Hefer refuses an application by Munusamy to have her subpoena withdrawn.
26–28 November:	Vusi Mona, by now the former *City Press* editor, testifies at the Hefer Commission.
30 November:	*City Press* retracts the spy story and apologises to Ngcuka.
20 January 2004:	Hefer finds Ngcuka was 'probably never' a spy.

We should begin on 7 September, when *City Press* published a sensational report under the headline 'Was Ngcuka a spy?' The story said that the national director of public prosecutions, Bulelani Ngcuka, had been investigated by the ANC in the late 1980s to establish whether he was an apartheid spy. The evidence largely consisted of an ANC intelligence report, which said he had been identified as 'possibly, but not conclusively' a spy with the code-name RS452. Ngcuka himself was quoted, through his spokesperson, as declining to comment.

The report was accompanied by a front-page editorial, justifying the decision to run the story. This placed the claims firmly in the context of an investigation Ngcuka's office was conducting into the financial affairs of the deputy president, Jacob Zuma, who had been ANC intelligence chief at the time of the ANC probe. The *City Press* editorial commented: 'if indeed Zuma once investigated Ngcuka, the public should have been told. … It would help provide a political perspective of what is really going on in the Zuma–Ngcuka saga.'

It emerged in the next few days that a senior political reporter of the rival *Sunday Times*, Ranjeni Munusamy, had passed the story on to *City Press* after her own paper declined to publish it. She was suspended by the *Sunday Times*, and then resigned.

In a front-page editorial on 21 September, Mathatha Tsedu, at the time *Sunday Times* editor, said the paper had decided not to run Munusamy's story for three reasons: firstly, it had too many holes; secondly, its publication 'would have served interests other than those of the public'; and thirdly that it might have exposed the paper to legal action.[35]

In a statement justifying herself, Munusamy said her story had never been that Ngcuka was a spy, but just that there had been an investigation that had suspected him. She argued that the publication was in the public interest, since it could help explain the 'vicious public exchange between Zuma and Ngcuka', and accused the *Sunday Times* of suppressing an important report.[36]

It soon emerged that agent RS452 had in fact been a former civil rights lawyer in the Eastern Cape, Vanessa Brereton. Meanwhile, President Thabo Mbeki had appointed a retired judge, Joos Hefer, to investigate whether Ngcuka had been a spy and whether he had abused his position as a result. Hefer subpoenaed Munusamy and several editors to give evidence to his inquiry, to the general disquiet of the profession.

Supported by several media organisations, Munusamy asked Hefer to withdraw the subpoena, saying she needed to protect her sources and had been threatened. Hefer turned down the request, but said Munusamy would be allowed to object to particular questions. Munusamy appealed against the decision, and lost in the Bloemfontein Appeal Court.

One editor who did not object to being called to the stand was *City Press*'s Vusi Mona, who in the meantime had left *City Press* under a cloud (see Case Study 9 on p. 109: The public relations editor). He testified about an off-the-record briefing Ngcuka held in July, which he said had been a 'vitriolic character assassination session'. He also testified Ngcuka had said Zuma was in trouble because he had 'surrounded himself with Indians'.

He said his decision to break the confidentiality of the briefing was justi-fied by the fact that it violated the constitutional rights of those Ngcuka attacked.[37] Mona was sharply criticised by other editors for his decision. Under blistering cross-examination, he later conceded that the spy report had been inaccurate, that the decision to publish it had been reckless, and he apologised to Ngcuka.[38]

In the wake of his ignominious exit from the commission, his former paper published a front-page editorial retracting the initial spy story, apologising to Ngcuka, and distancing itself from Mona.[39]

So much for the events. I have concentrated on the main aspects that are relevant to our purposes. But what are the ethical issues that arise? In terms of the approach outlined in the roadmap above, we need to move on to formulating the various questions that arose in the course of these events, and analyse and then judge them.

Question 1: Was it in the public interest to know that Ngcuka was suspected of being a spy 20 years ago?

The argument is sometimes made that it is completely uninteresting whether Ngcuka was a spy or not. Mbeki himself made oblique references to the matter in his weekly column on the ANC website, pointing out that the ANC had chosen a path of reconciliation and had served with people who had occupied high positions in the previous government.[40] Many saw his intervention as a subtle warning to those making the claims against Ngcuka.

The argument doesn't hold water. For one thing, the past is still too recent to be buried quite so easily. South African society still cares deeply about which side people were on during the apartheid years. And people have a particular distaste for traitors.

Also, it was in the public interest to know of any old enmity that would explain the hostility between Zuma and Ngcuka. The suggestion was made that Ngcuka was misusing his important and powerful office. Information to sustain such a claim would also have been strongly in the public interest. Significantly, Hefer was initially tasked with establishing not only whether Ngcuka was a spy but also whether he misused his power.

Decision: For the moment, we can say that claims that the country's prosecutions chief might have been a spy were of substantial public interest.

Question 2: Was there enough evidence for publication?

But the previous conclusion holds true only if there are substantial grounds for believing the suspicion to be well founded. The fundamental difficulty with the *City Press* report is that it failed to make enough of a distinction between the fact that there was an investigation, and its conclusion. As we have seen, Munusamy later sought to make this distinction. 'My story was never that Ngcuka was a spy, because it is impossible to prove that beyond reasonable doubt now,' she wrote.[41] Significantly, it was not an argument Mona used in his testimony before the Hefer Commission.

Although *City Press* did not explicitly suggest that Ngcuka was a spy, tone and handling suggested the claim should be taken seriously. No attempt was made to interrogate the reasoning of ANC intelligence in reaching their tentative conclusion. Certainly in the public mind the suggestion was presented as one to be taken seriously. Over the weeks that followed, more and more evidence emerged to disprove the claim.

Decision: There was not enough evidence for the report to pass the accuracy test.

Question 3: How much weight should be attached to the evidence of the report's sources?

The strength of the *City Press* report should also be considered in the light of the people who provided the evidence. The main sources for the report were the former ANC intelligence operatives Mo Shaik and Mac Maharaj. Shaik's brother, Schabir, was Zuma's financial adviser, and had been charged with fraud, corruption and tax evasion by the Scorpions. These charges also implicated Zuma. Mo Shaik had drawn up the original intelligence report, and had then reconstructed it in response to the case against his brother. Maharaj was also under investigation by Ngcuka's office.

Their disclosures were designed to show that Ngcuka had improper motives for acting against them and Zuma. But the question of motive was later turned on the accusers: in the light of their lack of evidence, it became clear that they were motivated by a desire to get back at him and deflect his investigations.

The *Sunday Times* decided not to run the story partly because it felt the claims were designed to further the agendas of a couple of powerful sources. *City Press*, too, alluded to the problem: 'The question has to be asked why these allegations are surfacing now while Ngcuka is investigating matters involving the deputy president,' it wrote in its front-page editorial. But asking the question is not enough under the circumstances. The paper should have handled the story quite differently.

The fact that information is leaked by somebody who stands to gain from its publication is not reason enough to rule out publication. People rarely pass on damaging information without a motive of some sort. But it means journalists have a duty to treat it with a great deal of caution, and seek independent corroboration.

In this case there was no independent corroboration. At most, it could be accepted that an investigation had been done.

The story might have been easier to accept if the spotlight had remained clearly on the accusers. If the claim had been firmly linked to them, their motives highlighted and their reasoning thoroughly interrogated, *City Press* might not have been judged so harshly.

As it was, the paper was seen as allowing itself to be misused by its sources for their own ends. Of course, Munusamy accused the *Sunday Times* of having allowed itself to be misused in a campaign by Ngcuka against Zuma. It is true that the Scorpions had developed a substantial appetite for media coverage, and made extensive use of selective leaks to build their public image. Ngcuka's off-the-record briefing with editors was an obvious example.

Perhaps the most disquieting aspect of the whole story was that journalists became players in a political game that nobody really understood. Where sources have motives, journalists should be careful. When those sources are powerful and are playing for high stakes, we should be doubly careful. We should try to understand those motives as clearly as possible, and be honest with our audiences about what is at stake.

Decision: The motives of the principal sources were so suspect as to further weaken the case for publication.

Question 4: Was Munusamy disloyal in passing on her story to a rival newspaper?

Munusamy was suspended by the *Sunday Times* for disloyalty, in passing on the story to a rival paper. She justified her decision by saying her paper's refusal to publish the story was ethically questionable. At a debate some time later, the veteran journalist Allister Sparks said that this behaviour was intolerable. It was like a soldier refusing to carry out orders, he thundered. Munusamy retorted that even soldiers have the right to refuse orders that conflict with their consciences.

All employers expect loyalty. Sparks argued that the honourable course of action would have been to resign and then take the story elsewhere. There is something underhand about passing on a major story to a direct rival. But the issue is not nearly as weighty as some of the other ethical issues at stake. A journalist's relationship with an employer can impact on his or her credibility among audiences, but it does so in a more indirect way.

Decision: If she felt so strongly about her story, Munusamy would have done better to leave the *Sunday Times* and then pass it on.

Question 5: Was Mona justified in breaking confidentiality about Ngcuka's off-the-record briefing?

City Press published details of the meeting, and Mona testified to the Hefer Commission about its content. He claimed to have thought it would be acceptable to disclose what was said as long as it was not attributed to Ngcuka. This argument is quickly dealt with: an off-the-record briefing is not the same thing as a statement 'not for attribution'; it is meant for background only.

He also said the agreement of confidentiality fell away as the spirit and letter of the Constitution was violated. But even if Ngcuka had over-stepped the mark in some of his statements, it seems to be stretching things to call them unconstitutional. In any event, Mona should have left if he was uncomfortable with the tone of the briefing, according to Sanef: 'Mr Mona may have had reasons for disquiet at what he says took place at the briefing, but the professional rules of journalistic conduct provide for an ethical standard of conduct to deal with such situations.'[42]

Decision: Mona had insufficient grounds for breaking confidentiality.

Question 6: Did journalists have the right to object to giving evidence at the Hefer inquiry?

An impressive array of media organisations backed Munusamy in her decision to fight the subpoena against her. They included Sanef, the Freedom of Expression Institute, the Media Institute of Southern Africa, the Media Workers' Association of South Africa, and the International Press Institute.

According to the veteran journalist Raymond Louw, the objection was based on the constitutional right to media freedom, and the possibility of physical harm befalling journalists. Both, he wrote, revolved around the possibility that the commission would try to identify her sources.[43]

But there were also some dissenting views. The Caxton professor of journalism and media studies at the University of the Witwatersrand, Anton Harber, wrote that journalists could not claim an absolute immunity from testifying. Sometimes they had a good reason to refuse, but not always. In Munusamy's case, testimony would not endanger anybody's life or inhibit future reporting, he wrote.[44]

Another veteran journalist, Max du Preez, wrote: 'Journalists are not special citizens with special rights.' He also made the distinction between testifying (which was acceptable) and identifying confidential sources (which was not).[45]

Hefer, and later the Bloemfontein Appeal Court, made use of just this distinction. Both ruled that Munusamy should testify, but would be allowed to challenge questions about who her sources were.

The difficulty of Munusamy and Sanef's argument was that it relied too heavily on the protection of sources. Once that had been removed by Hefer's concession, there was no substantial argument left. Later it was argued that she should testify only 'as a last resort' – but since her report began the whole exercise, it evoked little sympathy.

Sanef underplayed a much more substantial argument around independence. Public trust relies on journalists being able to remain independent of outside agendas. They should be visible in the public domain only in their professional capacities. The public should hear from them through their reporting. When they go about their newsgathering work, they interact with people as journalists – they collect information for publication or broadcast. If they then later use the information for other purposes, people can rightly cry foul.

In general, journalists should maintain a measure of independence even of the state. Of course, that cannot be limitless. But only exceptional circumstances justify their stepping outside their role. For instance, journalists may come across information of an imminent and serious threat to an individual or a group. In those cases, it seems to me, independence must take a back seat – ethics demand that such a threat be averted or stopped.

Other situations are not as clear-cut. For instance, should journalists assist in the administration of justice by giving evidence to secure a conviction? Most journalists would be uncomfortable with doing so, as a general rule. For some, the seriousness of the crime would make a difference. The line where independence ends and civic duty begins is a hard one to draw.

Even though it is starkly absent from our codes, as we have seen, the question of independence is crucial to journalism ethics. In the Munusamy case, Sanef made the point that the principle of not testifying should be fought for regardless of the particular report at stake, reflecting the general disquiet in the profession about whether *City Press*'s spy report was really worth defending. But the argument of independence would have been undermined by the very powerful perception that the *City Press* report failed the independence test so thoroughly. As we have seen, the paper allowed itself to become the plaything of the agendas of some powerful and aggrieved men.

Decision: Journalists cannot claim absolute immunity from involvement in judicial processes, but there should be strong reasons before they give up their independence in this way. For the other journalists subpoenaed, there were not sufficient grounds to compel them to testify. Because of the flaws in the original report, Munusamy's argument resisting the subpoena was weaker.

. . . .

NOTES

1   'You can't trust those dirty, lying hacks', *New Statesman*, 10 June 2002.

2   Jens Linde, 'Independence and ethics in journalism: An international perspective' in John Mukela (ed.), *Essays and conversations on media and democracy*. Maputo: NSJ Trust, 2001. 98.

3   Interview, 27 January 2003.

4   Quoted in Ferial Haffajee, 'Revisiting the ethical codes'. Paper prepared for the conference on Freedom of Expression and Ethics in the Media: A South African Approach, at Sandton, Johannesburg, October 2001. 57.

5   Lord Wakeham, 'Can self regulation achieve more than law?' Wynne Baxter Godfree Law Lecture delivered at the University of Sussex on 15 May 1998.

6   Jeanette Minnie, 'Independence and ethics: a southern view' in John Mukela (ed.), *Essays and conversations on media and democracy*. Maputo: NSJ Trust, 2001. 123.

7   John Mukela (ed.), *Essays and conversations on media and democracy*. Maputo: NSJ Trust, 2001. 136.

8   For a brief overview of the law, see Gwen Ansell, *Basic journalism*. Johannesburg: M&G Books, 2002. 173–96; or Johan Retief, *Media ethics: an introduction to responsible journalism*. Cape Town: OUP, 2002. 25–34.

9   Personal communication.

10 Interview, 30 January 2003.

11 See Francis Kasoma, 'Media ethics or media law: the enforcement of responsible journalism in Africa', *Ecquid Novi* 15, 1994. 1.

12 Bob Steele, 'Ethics codes: the lawyers' take'. Posted at http://poynteronline.org/column.asp?id=36&aid=18920, accessed on 1 May 1 2003.

13 Bob Steele and Jay Black, 'Codes of ethics and beyond'. Posted at http://www.poynter.org/content/content_view.asp?id=5522, accessed on 18 March 2004.

14 Bob Steele and Jay Black, 'Media ethics codes and beyond', *Global Issues* 6, 1 April 2001.

15 Jay Black, Bob Steele and Ralph Barney, *Doing ethics in journalism: a handbook with case studies*. Needham Heights, MA: Allyn & Bacon, 1995. 14.

16 Interview, 8 November 2002.

17 SABC, 'Ethical code for editorial staff'. Johannesburg: SABC, undated.

18 SABC, 'Editorial policies'. Johannesburg: SABC, 2004.

19 Telephonic interview, 28 November 2003.

20 *The New York Times*, 'Ethical journalism: code of conduct for the news and editorial departments'. New York: *The New York Times*, 2003.

21 South African Human Rights Commission (SAHRC), *Faultlines: inquiry into racism in the media*. Johannesburg: SAHRC, 2000. 36.

22 Ibid. 81–2.

23 Ibid. 83.

24 Quoted in Haffajee, 'Revisiting the ethical codes'. 57.

25 Interview, 27 January 2003.

26 Internal memo, 8 April 2002.

27 Press Ombudsman of South Africa, 'First quarterly complaints review'. Circulated November 2002.

28 Black, Steele and Barney, *Doing ethics*.

29 Johan de Villiers: Interview.

30 Based on Black, Steele and Barney, *Doing ethics*. 40–3.

31 Interview, 13 September 2002.

32 Louis A Day, *Ethics and media communications: cases and controversies*. Belmont, California: Wadsworth, 2000.

33 Available to registered users of the site, the Ethics Tool is at https://www.poynter.org/ethics/Default.asp.

34 Interview, 16 October 2002.

35 *Sunday Times*, 21 September 2003.

36 Statement by the *Sunday Times* senior political correspondent Ranjeni Munusamy on the *Sunday Times* announcement of her suspension, 15 September 2003.

37 *ThisDay*, 28 November 2003.

38 *Business Day*, 28 November 2003.

39   *City Press*, 30 November 2003.

40   '*Letter from the President*', 17–23 October 2003.

41   Munusamy statement, 15 September 2003.

42   *The Star*, 17 October 2003.

43   *ThisDay*, 16 October 2003.

44   *Business Day*, 24 October 2003.

45   *The Star*, 27 November 2003.

News reporters must/ should at all times tell the truth when reporting their stories.
Icora FM, community radio station in Eshowe, KwaZulu-Natal: Ethics Charter

Every journalist has a duty to tell, adhere to, adore and faithfully defend the truth. A journalist shall make adequate inquiries, do cross-checking of facts, in order to provide the public with unbiased, accurate, balanced comprehensive information/ news.
Journalists' Code of Ethics, Tanzania

Newspapers must take care not to publish inaccurate, misleading or distorted material including pictures.
UK Press Complaints Commission: Code of Practice

4

GETTING IT RIGHT: ACCURACY

Soon after taking over the editorship of the *Mail&Guardian* in 2002, Mondli Makhanya nailed his colours to the mast: 'I will build on our reputation to make the *M&G* the absolute authority on everything of significance in South Africa. Every word, sentence and paragraph we publish will be absolutely true.'[1] Brave words, which clearly highlighted the importance of accuracy.

Getting it right is, quite simply, the starting point for journalism ethics. If our business is truthtelling, then accuracy must always be our first concern. It's also an area that audiences take very seriously. Even apparently unimportant things, like spelling errors, have a profound effect on the credibility of individual journalists and media, as well as the profession as a whole.

Unfortunately, mistakes are far too common. The press ombudsman, Ed Linington, says accuracy is 'nearly always a factor' in complaints he sees.[2] People lay complaints on many grounds, but it is rare that they do not also claim that the newspaper got it wrong in some respect. And Johan de Villiers, executive editor of *The Star*, says: 'I have come to the sad conclusion that every time we write about something I know about we get it wrong … we get dates, names and locations wrong.'[3] He points out that mistakes can get a life of their own. Journalists often check things in newspaper archives – and then repeat errors that have found their way into print.

The South African National Editors' Forum (Sanef) has identified accuracy as one of eleven areas of concern in South African journalism. The issue is taken so seriously that the Stellenbosch Commitment – drawn up at the Skills Indaba held in the town in September 2002 – suggests 'industry and educators [should] put internal, punitive measures in place to combat inaccuracy'.[4]

What's to be done?

Reporters have a responsibility to get it right. Moegsien Williams, editor of *The Star*, says news organisations place a great deal of trust in their staff. It sometimes keeps him awake at night, he says, that 'we actually get our youngest reporters to go and cover some very, very serious court cases for instance, on the implicit understanding that they will not come back with wrong information.'[5]

The basic rule, of course, is simply: make sure. For many years, a yellowing poster in the stairwell of the *Daily Dispatch* reminded staff arriving for duty: 'Don't chance it, check it.' And Trisha Greene, an editor at the *Charlotte Observer*, told reporters: 'Don't trust anyone. If your mother tells you she loves you, check it out.'[6]

Despite this rather radical view, there is a difference between a story quoting the vicar as saying the church fête was spoiled by rain, and one claiming high-level corruption in government. The more controversial and weighty the issue is, the greater the need to find corroborating evidence.

At the same time, absolute proof is often elusive. Even the courts some-

"Those two streets don't even intersect. How could two cars collide there?"

"He's lived here for 40 years, and they can't even spell his name right?"

"That's not even the correct name for that hospital: I know because my sister works there."

"I knew that was wrong the minute I read it … and if they got that wrong, it makes me wonder what else they get wrong."[7]

Comments from US members of the public on accuracy

59

times have to decide on the balance of probabilities, despite having far more time and the greater investigative resources of the police at their disposal. Journalists have to seek as much verification as possible, and then make a judgment call on whether the story stands up or not. We should take as much care as possible, particularly with important stories, but there is always an element of risk. Recent judgments in South African courts have established the principle that journalists can defend themselves against a libel suit even if the story turned out later to be untrue – as long as they can show they investigated thoroughly.

Journalists look in a number of directions to find evidence. There's instinct and gut feel: not enough, certainly, but a useful starting point. Does the story ring true? Does the source appear to know what he or she is talking about? These are some of the questions that can be asked. (For further discussion on evaluating sources, see Chapter 10.) Very often, the next step is to find another source who can bear out the claim. Some organisations have rules about multiple sourcing. The BBC, for instance, says it is 'good practice' not to run reports from one news agency 'unless it can be substantiated by a BBC correspondent or another agency'.[8]

Many South African organisations aspire to these sorts of standards, particularly where the original sources are anonymous. But in practice, many stories appear on the basis of the flimsiest of evidence.

Sometimes, news organisations will ask a source to sign an affidavit. Where the accusation is serious, a sworn document gives the editor some comfort in case it comes to a court case. The source can be held to his or her word.

Perhaps the strongest form of proof comes in the form of documents: minutes, letters, reports or the like. Documentary evidence is taken very seriously, but it is often very hard to come by. And it is as well to remember that documents can be forged. In 1983, media around the world ran extracts from newly discovered diaries by Adolf Hitler. The best German historians had examined the documents and pronounced them authentic. It was an international sensation – but the diaries turned out to be counterfeit, an elaborate and skilfully executed hoax.

Additional measures

In line with the Sanef view on accuracy, a number of South African media organisations have taken further steps to reduce mistakes. The *Sunday*

Times expects its reporters to do an accuracy check, filling in a detailed questionnaire with a colleague. The form contains questions on everything from spelling to fairness, and has to be signed off by both (see full questionnaire in Appendix 5). It's an onerous system, and may be impractical in organisations with daily deadlines.

E.tv instituted a points system, where each mistake counts a minus point. Each bulletin's points are counted up and circulated, encouraging staff to keep the error count low.

The *Cape Argus* tried a 'name and shame' policy, where those responsible for errors were publicly pilloried. The paper also found that many errors arose from poor note-taking, and the editor, Ivan Fynn, says he has had to take steps to encourage reporters to return to using the humble notebook.[9]

Since the advent of computers, some journalists – not just at the *Cape Argus* – have begun typing notes directly into their terminal while conducting a telephonic interview. Sometimes, they then write the story directly on top, erasing the original notes in the process. This is a very bad habit, says Fynn. It is essential to be able to check back on notes, to deal with queries. Computer notes, even if they are saved separately, are open to manipulation and can't be used in court, he pointed out in a circular to staff.

> "Verifiable 'facts' are different from allegations, hypotheses, hunches offered up by sources. Information that you cannot confirm – from personal observation or 'provable' data – should be subject to a higher standard of scrutiny."[10]
> *Alan Stavitsky, National Public Radio*

Some larger organisations have used fact-checkers – staffers, often students or interns, whose job it is to go over reporters' stories and double-check the facts.

An example of a very extensive system comes from the *Chicago Tribune*.[11] Among other measures, the paper uses an outside proofreading agency to read the paper line by line, looking for errors. These include typos, missing or extra words, and even missing or extra spaces. For every mistake, a form is filled in to establish why it was made. Howard Tyner, the editor, says the system has demonstrated that between one-half and two-thirds of mistakes are avoidable. And it reduced errors from 4.5 per page in 1992 to 2.5 in 1997.

It is difficult to see how South African media organisations could afford such an onerous system. But it certainly demonstrates an impressive seriousness in tackling the issue.

The whole picture

Accuracy is about more than spelling people's names right – as important as this is. The Stellenbosch University ethicist Johan Retief says it 'starts with the ability to gather *all* the *relevant* facts'.[12] He points out that leaving out even one important detail can distort a story, but that including irrelevancies can also undermine it.

One hears people complain that they have been quoted out of context. Very often, it simply means they are embarrassed but can't really claim to have been misquoted. Nevertheless, context is important. In July 1999 the *Sowetan* published a front-page picture of a burly white man driving his bakkie with his dog beside him, while a black worker sat in the back. The headline was 'It's a dog's life!' and the accompanying report commented on racism and conservatism in towns like Brits, where the picture was taken and 'where animals were often treated better than blacks'.[13] The people in the picture were not identified, but the number plate was clearly visible. As a result, a Brits businessman received hate mail and death threats. He told *The Citizen* the picture was a distortion, and his employee had been on the back to stop gas bottles from rolling around.[14]

The ethical obligation to be smart[15]

It is staggering how often reporters rush out on an assignment with only the vaguest idea of the area they are about to cover, be it fiscal policy, Aids science or military technology. The Poynter Institute's Bob Steele quotes a reporter as saying: 'I don't have to understand it. I just have to write about it.' He comments: 'We too often fail our journalistic mission and flunk our ethical obligations because we just aren't smart enough about the subject matter we cover.'[16]

Journalists are mostly generalists: for many, the attraction of the profession is precisely the opportunity to dabble in many different fields. There are a few recognised specialisms: sport, politics, entertainment, more recently health and a few others. But these are very broad areas, and many others are completely left out.

It stands to reason that the better you know a subject, the more intelligently you can cover it. And as journalists are called upon to cover issues of increasing complexity, this places more pressure on the reporter who wants to do a good job. We can't be experts on everything we have to cover. But we can prepare properly, taking some time to read up on the subject at hand.

For media organisations, it comes down to a question of resources. A huge American newspaper with a reporting staff running into many hundreds can afford to keep a range of specialists on staff, and can afford to give them the time to keep abreast of their field. They are not going to find themselves suddenly sent out on a breaking crime story. But few – if any – South African organisations have that kind of capacity. Nevertheless, even with limited resources, news organisations should value expertise, and try to develop it among their staff.

Plagiarism

Plagiarism occurs when a writer uses an idea, a distinctive formulation or set of words from another without acknowledging the source. This kind of intellectual theft has become a major problem at universities, particularly since the Internet has made it very easy to cut and paste material. Journalism is not immune, and some prominent columnists have been disgraced after being found to have stolen other people's work. The great *New York Times* was shaken when it emerged that a reporter, Jayson Blair, had copied pieces of his reports from elsewhere, among other forms of dishonesty. Ultimately even senior editors had to leave because of the scandal.

People caught out have all sorts of excuses. They may say it was accidental – a turn of phrase stuck in their mind and they forgot where it came from. This can happen, but it becomes more difficult to accept the borrowing of large chunks.

Even in small doses, plagiarism is taken seriously because it is simply theft. James Fallows, the Washington editor of the *Atlantic Monthly*, says: 'This is something you never, never do. Every line of work needs clear rules. If you're a soldier, you don't desert. If you're a writer, you don't steal anyone's prose. It should be the one automatic firing.'[17]

Although plagiarism is serious, there are complexities that sometimes make it difficult to define. Trudy Lieberman, a contributing editor to the *Columbia Journalism Review*, writes that the dictionary definition 'stretches around a mountain of sins. Is plagiarism the theft of an idea, one word, two words, three words, four sentences, five paragraphs, long passages, or simply the research of others boiled down to yours? Is it a rearrangement of another's words and thoughts, or a near verbatim match with a different word substituted here and there?'[18]

Perhaps the simplest advice to give is this: if in doubt, credit.

Changing quotes

Quotes are enormously valuable in written journalism. They add colour and authority to a report, by signifying that these are the actual words real participants in the event have used. (Of course, some are flat and boring, and add little of value. But good quotes lift a story.) When we put something in quote marks, we're indicating that these are the exact words used by the source – and that's what they should be.

But at the same time, speech is a very different thing to the written word. Even the most articulate person does not speak as they would write. There are ums and ahs, hesitations, sentences that fizzle out and are begun again, and much else. Transcribing these faithfully into cold type would make the person look like an idiot. So we strip out the things that are characteristic of the spoken word – even while we are taking notes.

People make mistakes when they speak. Those situations need some thought. If the American president refers to Mozambique as the capital of Maputo, it may reflect an ignorance of the region that is quite telling. And we may want to report the error. Somebody else may make a grammatical mistake through being unfamiliar with English – in South Africa, many of us are working in languages that are not our mother tongue. In that situation, it would be malicious to report it as is.

But sometimes, deviations from standard English are a matter of dialect – and making those changes would remove some of their colour and authenticity. (There is only one dialect which should be eradicated root and branch, and that is bureaucratese. When journalists are confronted with this dialect, they have a duty to turn it into plain English. Here's an example: 'The establishment of a task team to liaise with a task team working on [prison] overcrowding within the security cluster at implementation level.'[20] But that's another matter.)

Sometimes newspapers use the bracketed word (*sic*) to draw attention to the fact that an error in a quote is the speaker's and not the paper's. And, more rarely, one sees the use of brackets inside quotes to indicate where changes have been made, or of dots to show ellipsis. These methods are valid, but sometimes look a bit fussy.

In general, the most elegant and honest solution to the problem is to

> "My own opinion is that all quotes are cleaned up. It works in stages. You clean up as you listen. You filter out the 'well, you knows'. The second stage is taking the notes. You clean it up again. Then when you decode it, you clean it up again. Then when you publish it certain words are carved away. There are levels and levels and levels. And we do it all with perfectly good motives."[19]
>
> *Donald Fry, Poynter Institute*

take the words out of quote marks entirely, or to leave only the most telling phrases in quotes. It goes without saying that the meaning of quotes should never be changed – whether in direct or indirect speech.

Rumour, myth and urban legend

Ask most journalists whether they will report on rumours, and they will draw themselves up slightly and say, no, never. And as a first response, that's undoubtedly valid. After all, we deal in facts that can be substantiated and corroborated. But are there circumstances that justify an exception?

Take for instance the belief that sex with a virgin can cure Aids. It's hard to say how prevalent it is, but it has gained some currency. Some health workers and other observers believe it may be a factor contributing to the horrifying phenomenon of baby rape. If that is so, then an entirely false belief is having a real impact on society, and t becomes a perfectly valid subject for journalistic attention. In a way, the myth has become reality – not in its content, but in its effect. When dealing with such things, we must make it clear that we are dealing with a dangerous myth. Anything else would be inaccurate.

Checking back

Sources often ask for an opportunity to look at reports before they are published or broadcast, and journalists differ greatly in how they respond. Some are categorical in refusing. The argument is that it opens the door to manipulation of the report. People may have second thoughts about what they said, or want to influence the shape of your report. Mathatha Tsedu, the editor of *City Press*, says: 'I would only countenance that in a situation where the story is of a technical nature, … just saying "is this accurate?"'[21]

Others are more prepared to accommodate sources. Fynn says quotes should be read back to sources if asked, as a matter of courtesy. 'Remember that this is not the same as seeking their permission to publish the story or giving them licence to edit t,' he adds in a circular to staff.[22]

Both agree on that important proviso: you should never agree to give the source any say over the shape of your report. Changes can (in fact, should) be made to correct errors of fact – but nothing else.

Productions and reconstructions

Television and, to some extent, radio journalism rely on production. The Norwegian academic Helge Rønning calls it 'one of the most trivial practices on television news': somebody is introduced 'over footage of the interviewee walking, or on the telephone, or reading a document – all activities staged for the camera'.[23] Even when a photographer just asks a subject to face into the light, he or she is intervening in the situation to shape the image. Is that acceptable?

Most journalists would accept some degree of production. There is not much harm in getting the minister to pick up a document at his desk and 'read it' for the camera, or in asking a question again in the hopes of getting a clearer soundbite. What is off limits, though, is where an intervention of this kind tries to reshape the situation (see box alongside). Finding the line between the two is not easy, but a very conservative approach is probably advised. Production should be kept to a minimum.

Some television documentaries make use of reconstructions where footage of the actual event is unavailable. This need not be a problem, as long as it's clearly identified as such. The Canadian Broadcasting Corporation says: 'Journalistic programmes must not as a general principle mix actuality (visual and audio of actual events and of real people) with a dramatised portrayal of people or events. The audience must be able to judge the nature of the information received. The mixture of forms renders such a judgment difficult because it may lend the appearance of reality to hypothesis. Should a situation arise in which such a mixture of forms is the only adequate method to convey the necessary information, the dramatised portion must be well identified.'[25]

The satirist Pieter-Dirk Uys describes being interviewed by the BBC while he was touring the country doing voter education before the 1994 election. "The producer is not shy to suggest retakes on the interview to get the answers he wants," says Uys. "One doesn't want to go as far as to suggest any slanted material, but it is a new experience for me. 'Why do you want to do it again? Wasn't I clear?' I'd say. 'Yes, but we thought it was a little vague on the violence and crime aspect.' 'But there is no violence and crime aspect,' I'd smile. 'We don't have guns. We don't need guns.' 'No, we feel your optimism about the election is out of step with the reality.' 'We are optimistic,' I'd purr. The election was going to be a disaster, they'd decided, and my bushy-tailed hope wasn't helping the story."[24]

The lying camera

Digital technology has revolutionised photojournalism. Photographers have always used techniques like cropping, burning and dodging to enhance images in the darkroom. But digital technologies make it possible to change a photograph completely after it has been taken. *National Geographic* took advantage of these opportunities to move Egyptian pyramids closer together, and *Die Burger* altered a photograph of Nelson Mandela releasing a white dove during his first public appearance after being elected president in 1994. They lowered the dove to bring it closer to his hands. The editor, Ebbe Dommisse, said afterwards it had not been a good decision, and put out a memo saying that readers should be told if a photograph had been manipulated.[26]

If the result is clearly identified as digitally altered, the audience will 'read' it like a graphic and no harm is done. But readers expect photographs to reflect reality of some kind. The late photographer Monty Cooper wrote: 'With more and more illustrative pix appearing daily, no image can be taken for granted. No image is immediately recognised as the truth.'[27]

Of course, no photograph reflects reality in an uncomplicated way; they are all products of human creativity. But digital manipulation crosses a line simply because it exploits readers' expectation that what they see in the photograph existed 'out there' at some point. Robin Comley, pictures editor of *The Star*, says she will allow photographers to digitally change density and colour intensity. But when it comes to moving objects around, the answer is 'Absolutely not. A thousand million percent absolutely not.'[28]

· ·

Accuracy:
a test of five questions

Journalists should ask these questions to check their reporting:
1. Have spellings, names, numbers and dates been checked?
2. Are the key facts backed up by independent sources?
3. Are the sources reliable?
4. Is there enough context to tell the story fully?
5. Do headlines, straps, captions, etc., accurately reflect the story?

· ·

Getting it right on air
Pippa Green

Early in 2003 Judge Pius Langa of the Constitutional Court called me to enquire about a report on one of our afternoon news bulletins that quoted the leader of the opposition, Tony Leon, commenting on a recent judgment of the Constitutional Court about floor-crossing.

We'd reported that Leon had accused the Constitutional Court of making a 'political judgment' – a rather serious accusation for a politician to be making in a country that prides itself on the independence of the judiciary.

I checked the tape. In fact, Leon had used the phrase 'politically astute', quite a different meaning. A slight change in diction had created an impression that the leader of the opposition was accusing the Constitutional Court of making judgments that suited the ruling party.

Radio's strength is often its weakness. It is swift, sometimes too swift to catch mistakes like these. And it is fleeting. Listeners may hear just one sentence of a newscast – hearing the 'political judgment' sentence without an attribution might make it sound like a statement of fact.

Perhaps what is remarkable is not that the error was made but that more are not. The sheer breadth of the platform of the public broadcaster poses more challenges to accuracy than in most media. The Radio News division of the public broadcaster produces a total of 242 bulletins and about 35 hours of current affairs a day. Thirteen languages are in use – the 11 official languages plus the two San languages of the Northern Cape, !Xû and Khwedam. Although it is a unified division, it is highly decentralised.

Constant monitoring is impossible. To manage such a platform requires two key tools: one is gatekeepers scattered judiciously throughout the division at bulletin desks, as assignment editors, and as executive producers of our current affairs shows. The other – far more challenging – is to establish common editorial values and professionalism throughout the news division.

In some ways, this is done through daily editorial line conferences that link up editors around the country. But often that is not sufficient. Much of my job is about building up relationships of trust so that the decisions made on the ground are editorially defensible.

Our research shows that most of our listeners (between 15 and 18 million to our bulletins and current affairs shows) believe what they hear on radio. It is a medium that has a much higher credibility rating than newspapers, even if this reputation may sometimes be undeserved.

In the light of its reach and credibility, it is small wonder that the political stakes around the public broadcaster in general and radio in particular are high. Political parties wait like hawks to pounce on mistakes.

In early 2004 a reporter filing copy for the hourly bulletins from an election rally in KwaZulu-Natal reported that 'about 1000 people had already arrived'. A local politician at the rally berated her because the story, filed before the rally began, implied that the party in question could attract only 1000 supporters. Actually, she was quite correct in her assessment of numbers at the time, and this made the attack easy to defend. The point, though, is that the burden of credibility on the public broadcaster is extremely heavy.

If radio news, as marginalised as it often is, sets a standard of expectation for accuracy, it becomes crucial to protect the platform from political and commercial influence and to focus on editorial standards.

Another example of bad inaccuracy involved (to my shame) the Constitutional Court. Six suspects escaped from a Roodepoort court after being handed guns from the gallery. The magistrate and the state advocate told an SABC reporter the suspects weren't handcuffed in court because the Constitutional Court had ruled that this was a violation of their rights – an easy narrative to believe in the wake of a spate of decisions that have lent weight to the prejudice that the court is 'too liberal'.

In fact, the magistrate and the state advocate were wrong. The Constitutional Court had made no such ruling, nor had they even considered a case about handcuffs in court. There are plenty of reasons why this story fell through our gatekeeping cracks, but it's no use explaining that to anyone.

We were quick to correct the facts, yet we had misinformed the public and our credibility took a knock. At the end of the day, these are the only things that are remembered.

(Pippa Green is head of Radio News and
Current Affairs at the SABC)

Case study 2
Lies on the pavement

On 23 July 2002 the ANC's former chief whip, Tony Yengeni, was in the Pretoria High Court to hear his legal team argue that fraud and corruption charges against him should be dropped. The charges arose from his acceptance of a massive discount on a luxury 4x4 vehicle from a company wanting to sell arms to the government. In a black suit and dark sunglasses, Yengeni stopped outside court to buy a newspaper, and an enterprising photographer caught him in the act of handing over money to the newspaper vendor. Clearly visible under the vendor's feet were two blue *Pretoria News* posters.

It was a great opportunity for a bit of self-promotion, and the next morning's paper ran the picture prominently on its front page with the headline 'News-maker'.[29] That morning's *Sowetan*, meanwhile, ran an almost identical picture on page three.[30] The major difference was that the vendor was now standing on *Sowetan* posters. According to the caption, Yengeni was buying a copy of that paper. Clearly, one of the two images had been altered.

The former editor of the *Sowetan*, John Dludlu, says he soon began getting calls for comment. He immediately launched an investigation and suspended two staff members.

Two days later, the paper gave an account of the incident under the headline 'When a picture does not tell the full story'.[31] In a signed article alongside both versions of the picture, Dludlu said it was true that Yengeni had bought a copy of *Sowetan*, but that 'other elements of the picture might have been digitally manipulated to replace a poster of *Pretoria News* with a *Sowetan* one'.

Dludlu commented: 'This is unacceptable and I view such dishonesty in a serious light … I am deeply embarrassed by this. I would like to apologise unreservedly to all readers and Mr Thabo Leshilo, the editor of *Pretoria News*, for this. I will ensure that this does not occur again.'

The photographer was able to show that he had sent through the image in an untouched form, but another staff member was disciplined.

Dludlu says the manipulation seemed to have been undertaken after he saw the promotional opportunities of the picture.[32] He says he was presented with the picture, in which the newspaper being bought could not be identified. If it was *Sowetan*, Dludlu says, he wanted 'to put him on the posters and tell the readers to read the newspaper and find out which newspaper Tony is buying'. The posters were hardly noticeable in the small image that he saw.

He was assured it was *Sowetan*, and then the image was altered without his knowledge – presumably to extend the promotional opportunity.

The episode highlights how easily technology can be used to falsify a situation. Dludlu points out that the technical opportunities to make the changes existed at many different points in the production process. The photographer, the photographic desk, the design team and the sub-editors all have the capacity to change images.

Dludlu deserves credit for acting swiftly and decisively to deal with the situation. He explained, apologised and took action against those responsible. Hopefully, it has demonstrated that this kind of manipulation is unacceptable.

Case study 3
Paper tricked into losing its head

The *Daily News*, then Zimbabwe's only independent daily newspaper, in April 2002 published a report about a particularly brutal killing of an opposition supporter by young thugs aligned to the ruling Zanu (PF) party.[33] The report described how the 53-year-old woman, Tandina Tadyanemhandu, was beheaded while two daughters were forced to watch.

Her husband, Enos, was quoted as saying that his 17-year-old daughter had met him as he was approaching his village home in Magunje district, about 150 kilometres north of Harare. She was crying, and told him what had happened. 'When I saw my wife's remains, the head and the body were clearly separated,' he was quoted as saying. 'I had to push them back together.' He also told the paper he had reported the matter to the police and been told to bring the suspects in himself. The opposition Movement for Democratic Change issued a statement confirming the story, and it went around the world as a particularly appalling example of Zimbabwean brutality.

The only problem was, the story was untrue. Aside from the husband's graphic account, there was no other evidence. Police and local officials denied the incident had taken place, and reporters were unable to find a grave. The *Daily News*'s editor, Geoff Nyarota, retracted the story and apologised to Zanu (PF), saying the paper had been misled. 'It is difficult to believe Mr Tadyanemhandu could have made up such a detailed story. But if his wife's so-called grave cannot be found, then that must be exactly what he did – create the elaborate story,' said Nyarota.

The story did not end there. Nyarota and several other reporters were arrested under the country's Access to Information and Protection of Privacy Act, which makes it an offence to publish false information without verifying the facts. Among them was the UK *Guardian*'s Zimbabwe correspondent, Andrew Meldrum, whose trial was the first to go ahead.[34] He was acquitted in July but immediately deported.

It was not clear why Enos Tadyanemhandu made up such an appalling story. There was some talk that the paper might have been deliberately led into a trap in order to embarrass it, but there was never any real evidence.

One has to have sympathy for the journalist confronted with such dramatic information from a first-hand source who was prepared to go on the record. But the lesson is clear: information must be cross-checked. This may be fraught with particular difficulties in Zimbabwe, where official sources are less than helpful to independent journalists, but it has to be done nevertheless.

The slip had major consequences. The authorities were quick to exploit the opportunity offered by this lapse to discredit, and take legal action against, the independent and foreign media.

The editor of South Africa's *Sunday Independent*, Jovial Rantao, wrote in a column that the case had undermined the standing of an otherwise respected newspaper. 'It is sad that all the hard work that this newspaper had done … is [over]shadowed by the dark cloud of the false report.'[35]

Case study 4
The harder they fall

Darrel Bristow-Bovey was at the top of his game. In a few short years he had shot to prominence as one of South Africa's foremost columnists. His dry, satirical observations appeared in an astonishing range of newspapers and magazines; his books sold well; and he had been both a winner and a judge in the Mondi awards for journalistic writing. He was very popular because he was very good.

And then a Rhodes University student on an internship at the *Saturday*

Star spotted a curious coincidence. A passage in Bristow-Bovey's book *The naked bachelor* was remarkably similar to one in *Notes from a big country*, by Bill Bryson. The passage dealt with statistics about serious injuries Americans have suffered involving unlikely household items, like beds, pens or ceilings.

The student, Rob Boffard, wrote a report that was headlined 'Darrel puts the "copy" in copycat', in which he accused the famous columnist of plagiarism.[36] The report contained Bristow-Bovey's response: 'One reads, one adapts things. I have the kind of memory that remembers things like this. I may have done the same thing with other pieces of information from all over the place. I'm sure if you really examine the book, you will find hundreds of these.' He added there was no 'legal or sensible' basis for the accusation of plagiarism, and accused Boffard of simply being out to tarnish his name.

The incident sparked an extensive public discussion, and many readers sprang to Bristow-Bovey's defence. He was amusing and clever, they said, and borrowing a little from somebody else was not a serious crime.

His reputation dented, Bristow-Bovey continued to write. A few months later, when the matter had faded from public view, he offered an apology of sorts in *Business Day*.[37] He had 'thoughtlessly imported' a joke together with some statistics from Bryson's book. 'I was foolishly careless, and I regret it deeply,' he wrote. But at the same time, he pointed out that the disputed material represented a tiny proportion of his work. He insisted he was not a plagiarist, and said he was surprised by calls that the incident should cause newspapers and magazines to stop using his columns.

But just days later, that's exactly what happened. A reader pointed out that his column in the *Cape Times* showed uncredited similarities with a section of *The English*, a book by the British TV personality Jeremy Paxman. The paper dropped his column, and *Business Day* in turn cancelled a column he wrote for them. Bristow-Bovey told *The Star* that circumstances had made it impossible for him to continue writing columns in South Africa.[38]

Was it really just a lot of fuss about nothing, as many of Bristow-Bovey's fans argued? He was churning out a lot of material every week, after all. It's hard to be original and funny all the time, and mistakes do happen. Simon Ndungu, of the Freedom of Expression Institute, conceded early in the controversy that it was possible to slip by forgetting a reference, 'but he should make sure it doesn't happen again. It's a moral issue.'[39]

It is quite likely that the pressure to produce had something to do with Bristow-Bovey's slip. But it remains hard to believe that he could have inadvertently copied large chunks of material without realising what he was doing.

Plagiarism remains a serious matter. Columnists are chosen for the individual voice they offer their readers and they can't serve up somebody else's material without breaking trust with their readers. It's intellectual theft, it's dishonest.

....

NOTES

1   Quoted in 'The big investigative piece', *The Media*, November 2002.

2   Interview, 27 January 2003.

3   Interview, 2002.

4   South African National Editors' Forum (Sanef), 'Back to basics: the Stellenbosch Commitment'. Johannesburg: Sanef, 2002.

5   Interview, 13 September 2002.

6   Quoted in François Nel, *Writing for the media in South Africa*. Cape Town: OUP, 1999. 80.

7   Quoted in Robert J Haiman, 'Best practices for newspaper journalists', Freedom Forum, Washington, undated. Posted at http://www.freedomforum.org/publications/diversity/bestpractices/bestpractices.pdf, accessed on 19 March 2004.

8   BBC, *Producers' guidelines*. London: BBC, 1996. 23.

9   Interview, 8 November 2002.

10 Alan G Stavitsky, *Independence and integrity: a guidebook for public radio journalism*. Washington: National Public Radio, 1995. 19.

11 The following description comes from Robert J Haiman, 'Best practices for newspaper journalists', Freedom Forum, Washington, undated. Posted at http://www.freedomforum.org/publications/diversity/bestpractices/bestpractices.pdf, accessed on 19 March 2004. 9–12.

12 Johan Retief, *Media ethics: an introduction to responsible journalism*. Cape Town: OUP, 2002. 51.

13 *Sowetan*, 22 July 1999.

14 *The Citizen*, 23 July 1999

15 Borrowed from the title of a 'Talk about Ethics' column by Bob Steele, 9 July 2002. Posted at http://www.poynter.org/column.asp?id=36&aid=785, accessed on 19 March 2004.

16 Ibid.

17 Quoted in Trudy Lieberman, 'Plagiarize, plagiarize, plagiarize … only be sure to call it research', *Columbia Journalism Review*, July/August 1995.

18 Ibid.

19 Quoted in Doreen Carvajal, 'The great quote question', *FineLine: The Newsletter on Journalism Ethics* 3,1, January 1991.

20 Letter to *The Star*, 3 April 2003, by Tsoeu Ntsane, spokesperson for the minister of correctional services.

21 Interview, 11 December 2002.

22 'Publish in haste, repent at leisure', 1 November 2002.

23 Helge Rønning, *Media ethics: an introduction and overview*. Lansdowne, Cape Town: Juta, 2002.

24 Pieter-Dirk Uys, *Elections and erections: a memoir of fear and fun*. Cape Town: Zebra, 2002. 93.

25 Canadian Broadcasting Corporation, 'Journalistic standards and practices (2001), section IV B 3.1'. Posted at http://cbc.radio-canada.ca/htmen/policies/journalistic/index.htm, accessed on 19 March 2004.

26 Montgomery Cooper, 'Ethics and the digital revolution in Southern Africa' in Chudi Ukpabi (ed.), *Handbook on journalism ethics: African case studies*. Windhoek: The Media Institute of Southern Africa (Misa), 2001. 163.

27 *Rhodes Journalism Review* 10, July 1995. 26.

28 Interview, 2002.

29 *Pretoria News*, 24 July 2002.

30 *Sowetan*, 24 July 2002.

31 *Sowetan*, 2 July 2002.

32 Interview, 18 October 2002.

33 Sapa report, 23 April 2002.

34 *The Guardian*, 13 June 2002.

35 *The Star*, 10 May 2002.

36 *Saturday Star*, 12 July 2003.

37 *Business Day*, 11 September 2003.

38 *The Star*, 18 September 2003.

39 *Saturday Star*, 12 July 2003.

There are generally more than two sides to any issue, and balance cannot necessarily be achieved by simply offering two opposing views.
e.tv: Ethical Code

All sides of the core issue or subject should be reported.
Press Council of India: Norms of Journalistic Conduct

Journalists will have opinions of their own, but they must not yield to bias or prejudice. For journalists to be professional is not to be without opinions, but to be aware of those opinions and make allowances for them, so that their reporting is, and appears to be, judicious and fair.
Canadian Broadcasting Corporation: Journalistic Standards and Practices

5

GETTING ALL SIDES: FAIRNESS

The idea of objectivity has not always been with us. According to Stuart Allan,[1] it developed in the years after World War Two as a result of technological and other changes in the newspaper industry. Journalists began wanting to be professionals, and developed a view of themselves as impartial observers of events, faithfully reporting the facts. Professionalism, in this view, demanded an ability to put aside any personal beliefs and preconceptions – any subjectivity. Objectivity became a central tenet of journalism. The most commonly used image is that of the mirror: journalists liked to think of themselves as simply reflecting an image of society.

The metaphor suggests its own limitations, for mirrors can only offer a partial view, and can be pointed in different directions. Even though the image is still often used, the notion of objectivity has fallen from favour. The editor of the *Sunday Tribune*, Barney Mthombothi, says: 'There is no newspaper that does not have its own point of view, we speak from different angles and we see things differently.'[2] Two people can see the same car accident and give vastly differing accounts of what they saw. And the editor of the *Sunday Times*, Mondli Makhanya, points to the gulf that exists between black and white journalists in their perceptions of the situation in Zimbabwe and other things.[3] Journalists simply cannot become people without history, perceptions or beliefs.

Sometimes people say that even if objectivity is unattainable, it remains an ideal to strive for. And certainly it reflects values and attitudes one would not want to jettison: evenhandedness and honesty, to name just two. But increasingly, journalists are finding that there are other concepts they can use which capture those values without getting weighed down with the baggage that the idea of objectivity carries.

In a guidebook for American public radio journalists, Alan G Stavitsky expresses discomfort at the idea of objectivity, adding: 'Reporting that is fair, accurate and balanced is true to the ideals of journalism. Such reporting filters out bias in the traditional spirit of objectivity, while allowing reporters to apply their personal insights and engagement with the issues they cover.'[4]

> An SABC board member, Thami Mazwai, caused an outcry when he told the parliamentary portfolio committee in August 2002: "You can't afford to be driven by old clichés, such as objectivity [and] the right of the editor."[6]

A similar attitude is taken by South Africa's press code, which does not talk about objectivity at all. It refers instead to 'accuracy, balance, fairness and decency'.[5] I prefer to follow the same approach. Fairness is easier to work with than objectivity: it's less of an impossible dream.

Fairness and balance

The concept of fairness can become very broad. Based on a detailed survey of American readers' attitudes, Robert J Haiman of the Poynter Institute has written a guide to best practice for journalists that puts almost everything under this heading, from diversity to admitting that there's no story. 'The public has a much broader, deeper and richer definition of a fair press' than journalists, he writes.[7]

The Stellenbosch University ethicist Johan Retief adopts a more specific approach, outlining three elements of a definition:

- No party should be misrepresented by 'choice of words or by the lack of proper context';
- All parties should get their say; and
- Coverage should be given to different groups in relation to their importance.[8]

'The other side'

In months of painstaking work, the *Sunday Times* had assembled evidence that the ANC leader Tony Yengeni was given a luxury 4x4 vehicle at a massive discount from a firm involved in bidding for a part of the government's arms procurement package. Before the story could run, he had to be given a chance to put his side of the story, and so the paper flew a reporter to Cape Town to give him the opportunity. When the story appeared in February 2001, it contained all the evidence the paper had – and also Yengeni's response.

It was a classic illustration of the principle of fairness in action. No matter how sure journalists are of their facts, how much evidence they have compiled, there's an absolute requirement to allow the subject of the allegation to give his or her side of the story. It's the cornerstone of journalistic fairness, and it's rightly drummed into reporters from the first day they step into a newsroom.

Fairness demands that real efforts are made to get the other side's comment, and the more serious the claims are, the more trouble must be taken: in the Yengeni case, a reporter was flown to Cape Town. It's not good enough to make one half-hearted phone call and then take refuge behind the formula 'X was unavailable for comment'. It is also important to allow a reasonable amount of time for the person to formulate a response. It is unfair for reporters to phone somebody half an hour before deadline and expect a response to six months of investigations. But equally, a story cannot be held hostage by somebody's inability or unwillingness to respond in reasonable time.

The response should also be given due weight and prominence in the story. It is unfair to tack a single line of response onto the end of an intricate story. The subject of an accusation deserves to be allowed to respond to the various aspects of the story, and for his or her voice to be heard reasonably prominently.

Of course there are occasions when despite our best efforts, that comment remains elusive. Then the person should be given an opportunity to respond as soon as possible after the initial story appears.

Broadcasters sometimes have to deal with an accusation being made unexpectedly by a guest or caller live on air. In such a situation, it's only fair to get the accused person's response as soon as possible.

More than two sides

Fairness in the Yengeni situation is easy and obvious. 'He said she was a crook, but she denied it': it's a simple formula we apply every day. But when situations are a little more complicated, it can become more difficult to satisfy the requirement of fairness.

For one thing, there are often more than two sides to a story. If residents of an upmarket suburb want to set up access booms for security reasons, then the residents and the local authority are in the front of the queue to be quoted. But several other groups will also be affected, and should be considered: police, domestic workers in the area, shopkeepers, the security company who will run the access points, members of the public whose access will be affected, and others. To reflect the complexity of such a situation requires a bit of lateral thinking, initiative, and time – which admittedly is often in short supply.

Falling off the edge

It's not always obvious who 'the other side' is. Let's take an example: the minister of safety and security releases crime statistics in Parliament. It's been a long time since figures were released, and the story runs prominently in many media. In most cases, it is accompanied by critical comment from opposition parties. Why them? Crime victims and independent crime analysts could just as easily have been chosen as 'the other side'.

The example illustrates one of the major factors that influence who ends up getting quoted: simple practicality. The statistics were released in Parliament, and the parties were immediately and easily accessible, and were dead keen to have their say – as always.

There are other factors, too, that influence who gets their view into the news. The academic Daniel C Hallin[9] says journalists divide the world into three regions:

- the sphere of consensus, where journalists 'do not feel compelled to present opposing views or to remain disinterested observers';

- the sphere of legitimate controversy, where opposing views are sought; and
- the sphere of deviance, where groups unworthy of being heard are found.

Criminals fall into the sphere of deviance: nobody thinks that in a hijacking story, fairness requires you to get comment from the criminal. It gets interesting on the borders between these spheres. For instance, where does the dispute between orthodox science and the dissident view on HIV/Aids fall? Increasingly, South African media are regarding the dissidents as belonging to the sphere of deviance – which means their views don't need to be sought out.

The debate about privatisation and other aspects of economic policy provides another good example. The voice of left-wing critics in most media is strongly overshadowed by centrist and conservative views. And yet they arguably represent a significant and widely held view. Sometimes, these opinions are called 'ultra-left' – effectively labelling them as deviant, in terms of Hallin's categories.

Other academics have spoken about a 'hierarchy of credibility':[10] some sources carry more weight than others. In fact, this hierarchy often coincides with the division of power in broader society: the minister is more authoritative than a middle manager in his or her department; the hospital superintendent's comment is worth more than a nurse's. The working journalist can benefit from looking beyond these easy assumptions: often people further down the hierarchy can give much better information than the person at the top.

"Do you want to speak to the man in charge or the woman who knows what's going on?"
Sign on an office wall

All of this points to some of the complexities of the requirement to be fair and balanced. As journalists, we have the power to choose who to speak to. 'It's a question of journalistic judgment,' says the editor of *Rapport*, Tim du Plessis, 'some groups are just fringe.'[11] We are obliged to take decisions about the relative significance of different viewpoints: it would be manifestly unfair to do otherwise.

But we should take those decisions with great care. In South Africa, more than most other countries, we should be aware of the fact that yesterday's fringe group can become tomorrow's mainstream. After all, it's not that long ago that the ANC was shunned by most mainstream South African news media as 'terrorist'.

In fact I would argue that fairness requires journalists actively to seek out groups that may be marginal and yet have something interesting and important to say. It's unfair to accept simply that powerful groups have better access to us by virtue of the paraphernalia of their PR departments. We should seek out the quieter voices. Too many groups fall off the edge of news coverage, and our journalism is the poorer for it.

Beware of the middle ground

One often hears the justification: 'Both sides were unhappy with our report, so we must have done something right.' This must rank as one of the most idiotic, facile clichés around.

Being in the middle is no guarantee of virtue. In fact the truth is sometimes on one side. It would be a brave – and foolish – person who would now claim that the truth about apartheid was somewhere in the middle between those who fought it and those who defended it. In the US, Senator Joe McCarthy's claims about supposed communist infiltration of American institutions in the early 1950s highlighted the problem with an uncritical "he said, she said" approach to fairness. The academic Matthew Kieran says: 'It is not that the facts [the media] reported were inaccurate, nor would anyone think that such charges should be left unreported … Rather the reports failed to question whether the charges being made were themselves plausible, had any basis in fact, and thus were fair or not.'[12]

Where rubbish is being propagated, it's bad journalism to treat it with the same seriousness as more credible claims.

Campaigning and fairness

In South Africa – and elsewhere – there is a long and honourable tradition of campaigning journalism. Under apartheid, many journalists in both the alternative and mainstream media saw their duty as being to fight against a great evil. More recently, *The Star* has taken a very strong view on the HIV/Aids pandemic. Significantly, the Press Code of Professional Practice (although not the Code of Conduct for Broadcasters) explicitly allows such advocacy. 'A newspaper is justified in strongly advocating its own views on controversial topics,' it says.

One of the founding editors of the *Weekly Mail*, Anton Harber, says advocacy can be an essential ingredient of success for a newspaper. As long as the paper doesn't play with facts and is careful not to divide its readership, strongly held views can be very popular. He says a paper should fight in a way that maintains credibility, which means engaging with the other side and remaining intellectually honest.[13]

When it came to apartheid, journalists took different routes. Some became activists, campaigning for a wide range of issues. Others felt that simply applying the tools of the trade would make the truth clear enough. Mthombothi says: 'I think most of the people that I know that took positions against apartheid actually let their own work speak for itself without themselves going out and campaigning. You actually write about [apartheid], you expose the inequities, you expose the oppression.'[14]

The press code has its own answer: advocacy is fine, it says, as long as fact and opinion are clearly distinguishable and there is no misrepresentation, suppression or distortion of relevant facts.

Separating fact from opinion

It is useful to remind ourselves of the three basic formats of journalism: reportage ('this has happened'), analysis ('this is what it means'), and opinion ('this is what I think about it'). The borders between these types of writing are often blurred. Haiman found this blurring was the cause of some claims of bias and hence accusations of unfairness. He writes: 'When these columns of opinion appear in news sections or on section fronts, readers can be confused, as one reader put it, about "what is supposed to be factual news and what is their editorial opinion."'[15]

The Kaiser-Wiggins rule, developed at the *Washington Post*, says that the public deserves at least "one clean shot at the facts of what happened before all the motive-seekers and opiners descend on the story".[16]

In South Africa there are similar trends. Headlines are often strongly opinionated, and a reporter will be expected to report the story on one day and then write a leader about it the next.

Financial pressures make it unlikely that South African newspapers will be able to hire teams of full-time leader writers and columnists, and as a result it is likely that reporters will continue having to move from one format to another. Nevertheless, the distinction between fact and comment is worth maintaining as much as possible. There is evidence that audiences respond badly to reporting that is overly opinionated.

Fairness: It's a tough challenge

So far, we've discussed different implications of the requirement to give all sides of a story. It should be noted, though, that you can give all sides and still be unfair. The tone of the story can indicate bias, for instance: the simple choice of the word 'claims' can indicate disbelief. Retief also highlights the importance of putting things in the right context.[17] Headlines, the juxtaposition of words and pictures, omissions and many other things can undermine the fairness of a report.

It's important, too, to bear in mind that fairness is achieved over time. Even if an individual report lacks some perspectives, that can be redressed later. *Cape Talk*'s news editor, Andrew Bolton, points out that this is particularly important for radio journalists, who deal with such a brief, fast medium.[18] If one bulletin brings an Israeli view of the latest incident in the Middle East, the next can use a Palestinian view.

Journalists need to rise to the challenge of fairness, as difficult as it sometimes is. We may have difficulties with the notion of objectivity, but no journalist can do without a commitment to fairness.

> "Its primary office is the gathering of news. At the peril of its soul it must see that the supply is not tainted. Neither in what it gives, nor in what it does not give, nor in the mode of presentation, must the unclouded face of truth suffer wrong. Comment is free but facts are sacred."[19]
> *CP Scott, editor and proprietor, Manchester Guardian, 1922*

. . . .

Fairness:
a test of five questions

Journalists should ask these questions to check their reporting:
1. Have all affected parties been spoken to?
2. Have they all been given the appropriate weight and consideration?
3. Has the report gone beyond the obvious sources?
4. Does the reporting reveal any bias?
5. Is the story as a whole being given the right weight?

. . . .

In defence of passion
Anton Harber

Good journalism, we are taught in the text-books, is dispassionate, factual and objective, written by reporters who have learnt to give all sides of the story and not allow their own views and feelings to interfere.

But hold on. In South Africa we have a fine and proud tradition of journalists who fought against apartheid, who railed against it in all their writing and who spent their time exposing its evils and promoting its enemies.

So which is it? Do we honour those who stand aloof and present us with a range of cold, hard facts which allow us to make up our own mind in a well-informed and considered way; or do we favour those who stick their neck out for what they believe in and use their journalism to further these ends?

We have to be careful in praising campaigning journalism, because we know that it also gave us the worst of apartheid-supporting newspapers and broadcasters. Advocacy gave us the best journalism of our history, and the worst, both the courageous journalism we want to remember and honour, and the myopic reporting that we want to bury and forget.

Some would say that advocacy was necessary in a time of conflict and repression, and particularly important in assisting the downfall of the apartheid government. Now, however, we have stability, democracy and free speech – and in this atmosphere it is no longer appropriate and we should adopt the professional ethic of objectivity and neutrality.

But I still think that some of the best writing on subjects like HIV/Aids and South Africa's role in helping Zimbabwe solve its current problems comes from those who write with self-declared partisanship.

The crucial difference for me is not whether writers use an impersonal, dispassionate voice or an opinionated one, the question is whether the writers are honest, critical and independent in their thought.

What do I mean by this? If campaigning journalism means ignoring some of the facts and not dealing with the other side of a story, then it is myopic, dangerous and dishonest – as was much of the pro-apartheid reporting in the Afrikaans press and at least some of the anti-apartheid reporting in the alternative press.

But if advocacy is done intelligently and honestly – in that it does not hide different views or uncomfortable facts – then it is engaging and effective. Advocacy can be fair – and it is at its best when it is so.

If neutral journalism is just a pretence that serves to disguise the fact that the author has a point of view and is not giving balanced treatment – as is so often the case – then it too is dishonest and ineffectual. When it succeeds in achieving genuine balance and fairness, then it can produce fine and worthwhile reading.

The key factor is honesty. Journalism which doesn't acknowledge that there are many points of view is a journalism that pulls the wool over people's eyes. But journalism that acknowledges and engages with different views, and does not hide facts which contradict one's own view, offers rich and stimulating material.

You can produce either of these options by using the techniques of dispassionate neutrality, or the techniques of passionate opinion – both are valid. But both fail if they do not treat their subject honestly and their audience with respect. And by this I mean trying to help the audience understand the issue or event, and all its implications, and not trying to distort it by commission or omission.

Most great news media will use both neutral voices and advocacy voices – depending on which one is appropriate to the story being reported.

Both can be enjoyable. But, one must admit, there are few things more stimulating to read than well-written and provocative advocacy.

Like this piece.

(Anton Harber is Caxton professor of journalism and media studies at the University of the Witwatersrand)

Case study 5
Minister Motormouth

In April 2001 the minister of safety and security, Steve Tshwete, went on national television to name three prominent ANC leaders as being involved in a plot to oust or harm President Thabo Mbeki. Rumours of the plot had been circulating for some time and had been prominently reported in the *Sunday Times* a few days before the broadcast. But this was the first time the three had been named. They were no lightweights: the former ANC secretary-general Cyril Ramaphosa, the former Gauteng premier Tokyo Sexwale, and the former Mpumalanga premier Mathews Phosa. All three had left active politics for careers in business but remained important figures in the ANC. Some months later, Tshwete was forced to admit there was no truth in the claims, and to apologise to the three. It was an astonishing episode. But even more astonishing are some of the details of what led up to the broadcast.

Stories about the plot had been doing the rounds for some time. A key source was James Nkambule, a former leader of the ANC Youth League in Mpumalanga, who had made various attempts to get the media to report his allegations against Phosa, an old political rival, and others. Nkambule had been expelled from the party, and was at the time facing charges of embezzlement of state funds.

Barney Mthombothi, at the time chief executive of news at the SABC, says several interviews had been done with Nkambule in which he made his claims.[20] In the first of these, he'd insisted on appearing anonymously. But the stories did not make it to broadcast. There was no independent evidence to corroborate Nkambule's claims; he clearly had an axe to grind and his own credibility was not beyond question. Mthombothi says he came under pressure from people within the SABC to broadcast the claims despite these concerns, but resisted.

The story entered the public domain only when Tshwete told the *Sunday Times* that the police were investigating the plot since there were fears Mbeki could be harmed. Tshwete referred darkly to high-profile leaders of the party, but gave no names. The paper ran the story prominently, under the headline 'ANC cracks down on Mbeki rivals'.[21]

Tshwete had also been speaking separately to the SABC, making similar statements – but still refusing to name anybody. A careful report was compiled, and Tshwete was invited to the studio for a live discussion during the television bulletins of 24 April 2001. During the Xhosa bulletin at 7.30 p.m., the newsreader Noxolo Grootboom innocently asked Tshwete: '*Ngobani bona lababantu?*' (Who are these people?) And he named Phosa, Ramaphosa and Sexwale.

Tshwete appears to have immediately regretted his indiscretion. He emerged from the studio saying: '*Ndibhanxile ngoku!*' (I've messed up!) and refused to answer when asked the same question during the 8 p.m. English bulletin.

The story of course ran prominently in the next day's newspapers. Still, there was no substantive response from the three men accused. Tshwete came under heavy fire, even from within the ANC, for his handling of the affair. The 'plot story' rumbled on for months, until Tshwete finally in December stood up in Parliament to say there had been no substance to the story, and to apologise to the three men.

This is not the place to discuss the political implications of the incident. But it does raise some interesting ethical issues for journalists.

How do you deal with claims of this kind? For one thing, you look for corroborating evidence, particularly if the source has such an obvious motive. But given the nature of the allegations, this was hard to get.

Nkambule named the three, and throughout the time that these rumours were circulating it was remarkable that their names were widely known in media and political circles. Numerous attempts were made to get their response, but they would not comment. Is it acceptable to run a story if you've given the 'accused' a chance to respond, even if they don't take it? It's a common practice, but Mthombothi says: 'We could have actually taken the view that we bounced the thing off them and therefore we have every right to run it. [But] I think in the first instance you need to convince yourself that there is a grain of truth in what is being said before you can run it.' In this case, it would have been unfair to run the story on the basis of the word of one individual, and journalists rightly stayed away from it.

But the situation changed dramatically when Tshwete decided to get involved. Once a minister of state – and a senior one at that – put his weight behind the claim, it had to be taken more seriously. He not only said there was believed to be a plot, but disclosed that the authorities were taking concrete measures to deal with it: a high-level investigation had been launched, and security around the president stepped up.

A form of corroboration often used is that the police – or another official body – is investigating. This is not strong proof because it's easy to lay a complaint with the police, who almost invariably launch at least a cursory probe. But in this case, since it came from the minister, it had more weight. The *Sunday Times* placed its report firmly in the context of political infighting in the ANC, putting some distance between itself and the claims.

Tshwete's inadvertent naming of the three was clearly libellous, and highlights the dangers of live broadcasting. He could have been sued, and so could the media carrying the claim.

Was the reporting of the affair fair to the three? Clearly not. But it's hard to see how journalists could have handled the situation differently. Tshwete misused his status to conduct what seems to have been an internal political battle. Even though it was widely seen as nonsense at the time – and turned out to be exactly that – a minister is hard to ignore. But the affair certainly undermined his own credibility.

Case study 6
Flat-earthers, round-earthers

In September 2000 the *Mail&Guardian* published an article under the headline 'All the president's scientists: diary of a round-earther'.[22] It was a diary written by a participant in the Presidential Aids Advisory Panel at the height of President Thabo Mbeki's public flirtation with the views of people who dispute that HIV causes Aids. The panel brought together roughly equal numbers of orthodox and dissident Aids scientists in an ultimately futile attempt to get them to find common ground.

Run across two pages, the diary gave a fascinating inside view of personalities and arguments as the two sides grappled with each other over several days. The anonymous writer, whose sympathies were firmly on the orthodox side, used the terms 'flat-earthers' and 'round-earthers' to describe the two sides.

The press ombud received a complaint from the Forum for Debating Aids in South Africa, a dissident group who said the item contravened almost every clause of the press code. 'It was inaccurate, unfair, unbalanced, out of context, omitted material information, contained exaggeration and misrepresentation, was malicious, did not distinguish between fact and opinion, and there had been no attempt to verify the facts or to seek comment in advance of publication from those on whom it reported critically.'[23]

During the hearing of the complaint, the central issue was whether the item was a news report or not. The group's president, Elliot Small, argued that the item should be judged like a factual report, while the *Mail&Guardian* said that it was comment and that the provisions of the code did not apply to a diary of this kind. All the newspaper had to do was to establish that it was authentic and kept by a credible member of the panel.

The complaint was rejected, on the grounds that the item was comment. But the judgment asked the question: 'Does a newspaper escape all responsibility for an article simply by saying it was written by a credible person in a particular position to know, as this diary was?' At least, the paper should allow space for a contrary view. This the editor, Phillip van Niekerk, had done.

But the responsibility did not mean it had to double-check every fact, 'interview every person mentioned critically, find out whether there was any relevant material that had been omitted and insert it'. The most serious comment seemed to be describing the dissidents as flat-earthers, but this did not go beyond the bounds of fair comment.

The forum took the matter on appeal, where it found more sympathy. One of the members of the appeal panel, Robin McGregor, came out strongly in favour of the forum. He said the article was 'seriously biased against dissident views'.[24] It was also 'snide, sarcastic and offensive' and was incomplete because it did not cover the media conference at the end and the agreements made. Another member of the panel, Dennis Pather, backed the paper's position completely.

The judgment delivered found a middle path: it upheld the ombud's ruling, except that it said the diary had omitted some material facts – that there had been an agreement to collaborate on certain tests, and so on. The paper was ordered to allow the forum to state its case in 400 words. It was a very mild slap on the wrist, however, since Van Niekerk had made exactly this offer to the forum before it came to the ombud.

I would support the view expressed by Pather and the ombud. Firstly, balance does not need to be achieved in a single item. The *Mail&Guardian* had given space to a dissident view on other occasions, and offered to publish a response from the forum. That adequately answered the need for balance.

Secondly, everyone – except the forum – accepted that the item was comment, not reportage. In covering a public controversy of this kind, the media need to allow the different views reasonably free rein. Trying to temper strongly held views would distort the nature of the debate. As the ombud's ruling said, it would amount to censorship. These were the views of a member of the panel, after all, not those of the newspaper itself. It is true, of course, that the newspaper was not absolved completely from responsibility for what was written, but columnists and commentators are usually given very wide latitude, particularly if they are from outside the newspaper.

Case study 7
Reporting yourself

The SABC makes news more than most South African media organisations. As the public broadcaster, everything from licence fees to internal politics attracts a lot of attention. Covering controversies in one's own backyard poses particular challenges.

In April 1999 one of South Africa's best-known journalists, Max du Preez, was effectively dismissed by the SABC. The 8 p.m. bulletin of SABC3 reported management's decision not to renew his contract.[25] The news item said the editor-in-chief, Phil Molefe, refused to comment, but then said it was 'believed' the decision was due to 'several incidents of gross insubordination towards management'. In one incident, Du Preez was said to have sworn at a senior editor in the newsroom.

The Freedom of Expression Institute (FXI) laid a complaint with the BCCSA on the grounds that the item was unbalanced, not having given Du Preez a chance to respond. 'It is a violation of the public-owned airwaves by its appointed managers, who used it to service their conflicts. The presentation of the item was done in a cavalier and arrogant fashion which did the public a disservice,' the complaint said. In a fairly rambling submission, the FXI also said: 'The incident begs an investigation into the state of editorial independence at the SABC because of the real danger of self-censorship setting in.'

In his judgment, the chairperson of the BCCSA, Kobus van Rooyen, found:

- that the accuracy of the item could not be judged since the dispute was being adjudicated elsewhere;
- that the item should have stopped with Molefe's 'no comment'. The claims after this point made against Du Preez needed to be balanced with his comment, and in that sense the item broke the broadcasting code's provisions on balance; and
- that there was no basis for the claims of a lack of independence.

The judgment also made the comment that 'not in one of the more or less 100 SABC cases which have come before the BCCSA in the last six years was there any evidence that the SABC had compromised its independence'. The finding should be broadcast, Van Rooyen ordered.

The unwillingness to find on the item's accuracy is probably understandable, and the conclusion of a lack of balance can't be argued. It is a fundamental requirement of fairness to allow the subject of an un-favourable report a chance to respond. Of course that is awkward if the person has just been fired by the organisation, but it does not change the duty. As Van Rooyen suggests, the SABC might have been able to get away with it if it had simply reported the fact that Du Preez's contract had not been renewed. But as soon as allegations of misconduct were spelt out, he had a right to be heard.

The issue of independence requires a little more thought. There are several difficulties here. For one thing, the FXI used this particular case to draw inferences of broader trends and dangers. But the BCCSA tribunal really had only these particular facts to consider, and should have stuck with them. It is not clear why the BCCSA felt it necessary to mount a broad defence of the SABC in the way that it did.

The second difficulty is that independence is not something covered in the BCCSA code. As we have seen, this is a major gap. It means that the tribunal had no guidelines for judging the FXI's complaint. Fortunately, we have the luxury of being able to look elsewhere for guidance.

Black, Steele and Barney set out several elements of the principle of independence, including: 'Seek out and disseminate competing perspectives without being unduly influenced by those who would use their power or position counter to the public interest.'[26] In this case, it is hard to avoid the conclusion that the handling of the report was driven by the self-interest of the SABC's management rather than by strictly editorial considerations.

Independence in the first sense refers to an ability to make news judgments without being influenced by outside agendas. In a later judgment (to which we will return below), Van Rooyen said: 'Editorial independence can only be placed at risk when an external force is active in demanding changes to a news item. The present matter deals with an internal dispute and there is no evidence that an external source was active in influencing the news editor.'[27]

As I see it, that is too limited a view. Independence should be taken to include all agendas that are not part of normal news values. That must include agendas from elsewhere in the same organisation.

One should not be too starry-eyed about this. Most organisations have great difficulty in reporting themselves fairly. But in this case, the attempt to besmirch the name of a respected journalist was particularly crass. The tribunal would have been hard-pressed to make a general finding about the SABC's independence, but the circumstances do justify a conclusion that the SABC failed the independence test in this case.

The story did not end there. On the day after the judgment was handed down, 4 June 1999, the SABC reported its findings as directed. But it angled the report on the comment that there had been no evidence of compromised independence in over a hundred cases against the SABC, only mentioning the adverse finding right at the end.

This item drew another complaint, in which it was argued that the BCCSA finding had not been broadcast correctly, and that the original error of not including Du Preez's viewpoint had not been rectified.

The tribunal dismissed the complaint on the grounds that it had not ordered the report corrected, only that its finding should be broadcast; and that this had been done. 'The essence of the summary of the judgment was conveyed to the public,' the tribunal found.

Again, the BCCSA was kinder to the SABC than was warranted. Although it was correct in saying that no aspect of the judgment had been left out, the emphasis of the report was deliberately chosen to play up the positive comment on the SABC's independence, and to play down the negative finding. Of course, the SABC merely played the ball the BCCSA had bowled. But accountability demands that media organisations give due prominence to the rectification of mistakes, and this principle was not observed.

. . . .

NOTES

1   Stuart Allan, *News culture*. Buckingham: Open University Press, 2001. 12–26.

2   Interview, 17 July 2002.

3   Interview, 9 December 2002.

4   Alan Stavitsky, *Independence and integrity: a guidebook for public radio journalism*. Washington: National Public Radio, 1995. 16.

5   Press Ombudsman of South Africa, 'Press Code of Professional Practice'. Johannesburg: Press Ombudsman of South Africa, 2001.

6   *Business Day*, 21 August 2002.

7   Robert J Haiman, 'Best practices for newspaper journalists', Freedom Forum, undated. Posted at http://www.freedomforum.org/publications/diversity/bestpractices/bestpractices.pdf, accessed on 19 March 2004. 4.

8   Johan Retief, *Media ethics: an introduction to responsible journalism*. Cape Town: OUP, 2002. 86.

9   Quoted in Allan, *News culture*. 69.

10 Paul Manning, *News and news sources: a critical introduction*. London: Sage, 2001. 15.

11 Interview, 15 October 2002.

12 Matthew Kieran, *Media ethics: a philosophical approach*. Westport, Connecticut: Praeger, 1999. 48.

13 Personal communication.

14 Interview, 17 July 2002.

15 Haiman, 'Best practices'. 50.

16 Quoted in Robert J Haiman, 'Best practices for newspaper journalists', Freedom Forum, Washington, undated. Posted at http://www.freedomforum.org/publications/diversity/bestpractices/bestpractices.pdf, accessed on 19 March 2004. 54.

17 Retief, *Media ethics*. 86.

18 Interview, 8 November 2002.

19 Quoted in Stuart Allan, *News culture*. Buckingham: Open University Press, 2001. 7.

20 Interview, 17 July 2002.

21 *Sunday Times*, 22 April 2001.

22 *Mail&Guardian*, 8–14 September 2000.

23 Quoted in the ombud's adjudication.

24 Appeal panel ruling.

25 The following details are drawn from the ruling of the BCCSA tribunal, case no 1999/11.

26 Jay Black, Bob Steele and Ralph Barney, *Doing ethics in journalism: A handbook with case studies*. Needham Heights, MA: Allyn & Bacon, 1995. 17.

27 In the ruling of the BCCSA tribunal in the second case involving the dismissal of Du Preez, brought by H Lorgat, case no 1999/21.

We do not allow advertising, commercial, political or personal considerations to influence our editorial decisions.
SABC: Editorial Code

Die Burger is independent of the authorities at all levels, as well as all pressure and/or interest groups.
Die Burger: Code of Ethics

Journalists and their employers shall conduct themselves in a manner that protects them from real or apparent conflicts of interest.
Code of Conduct for Journalists and the Mass Media, Kenya

6

KEEPING YOUR DISTANCE: INDEPENDENCE

A politician steers a major government contract towards a company of which she is a director. A doctor accepts payments from a pathologist's laboratory for each test referred there. In return for a fee, a staff member in an emergency call centre routinely tips a tow truck company off about car accidents before alerting an ambulance.

These are all instances in which we have no difficulty identifying the conflict of interest that undermines the independence and integrity of the person involved. Concern about these issues has grown in all areas of public life. Wherever public trust is at stake, standards of expected behaviour are becoming higher. Journalism is no exception.

That is as it should be. We have already discussed the importance of trust in journalism, and it's clear that a journalist's credibility sinks like a stone as soon as audiences can say: 'Ah, she's only reporting this because she belongs to party X, or because she's married to Y, or because she's in the pay of company Z.' People are quick to spot bias and ulterior motives, and will then simply discount the reliability of the story, or of the journalist's work in general, or even of the media organisation involved.

Independence is one of the fundamental principles of journalism ethics because it sets up a defence against conflicts of interest and competing loyalties. It says publicly that our work is guided by no allegiance except that to professional standards and the audiences. In *Doing ethics in journalism*, Jay Black, Bob Steele and Ralph Barney write: 'Journalists must remain free of associations and activities that may compromise their integrity or damage their own or their organisation's credibility.'[1]

It is critically important to recognise the difference between the reality and the perception of conflicts of interest. If we own a house whose value is likely to drop dramatically because it is near the planned route for a new railway line, and we set out to find as much dirt on the project as possible, we can rightly be accused of misusing our position as a journalist to further a personal agenda – defending the value of our property. The ethical problem is very similar to those affecting other professions sketched earlier.

When an actual conflict of interest is discussed, one often hears people say, Yes, there is a potential conflict here, but we'll just be scrupulously fair. Of course it is possible to report fairly on a story in which we have a stake. But that doesn't deal with the problem of perceptions. Credibility may be affected if people know about a conflict of interest – even if no fault can be found with the actual reporting. Black, Steele and Barney describe the difference like this: 'Credibility is what others think of us; ethics is what kind of people we actually are. One is image, the other substance.'[2] It may be tempting to say substance matters but image does not, but this would be dangerous and foolish. In fact, trust is built on what people think of us, and it is just as important to avoid the perception of conflict of interest as it is to avoid the reality.

Die Burger's code of ethics captures the distinction by posing two questions: 'Can you say in all honesty that the relevant favour or offer – whether it's a cup of coffee, a cigar, a week in Mauritius or a visit to the Middle East on the invitation of the Arab League or to Israel on the invitation of the Jewish Board of Deputies – won't have an influence on your impartiality? Will your readers be sure of your credibility, even if you don't have any doubts?'

So what should a journalist do to avoid these problems? Some associations are best avoided, like close friendships with people one reports about. There are others one can do little about, like family relationships. If stories arise that fall into this category, it is best to pass them on to a colleague.

In South Africa the discussion about conflicts of interest remains relatively undeveloped. In 1992 a survey of editors by the *Rhodes Journalism Review* on their policy towards freebies revealed little more than generalities. There's no free lunch, they agreed, but seemed to feel that virtually anything was acceptable as long as the editor was informed. A typical comment came from Jim Jones, then editor of *Business Day*: 'I generally assume staff members cannot be "bought". That's backed up by a requirement that any "large" freebie be disclosed to the editor.'[4] The most detailed thought seems to have gone into the question of shareholdings by financial journalists.

> "The answer is to raise the qualifications, salaries, status and self-respect of journalists."[3]
> *Ken Owen, former editor of the Sunday Times*

Since then, some media organisations have developed far more precise guidelines. (See below for some examples of South African best practice.) But many others maintain a *laissez-faire* approach that is at odds with the standards they apply to politicians and others. The editorial code of the SABC contains a strong and unambiguous statement on the issue (see p. 94), but the recently developed editorial policy fails to flesh out these principles. The document merely says the news division will develop its own internal guidelines on political involvement, family or financial interest, gifts, free travel, and so on.[5] As for the industry codes, we have already seen that they are completely silent on these important issues (see Chapter 3).

We need, now, to consider the different kinds of conflict that may arise.

Blood is thicker than ink

The editor of *Rapport*, Tim du Plessis, tells the story of how his newspaper covered the story of a prominent Pretoria businessman who fathered a child with a domestic worker. The man denied paternity, and refused to pay maintenance even after DNA tests showed he was the father of the child. The paper was about to publish a report naming the man when Du Plessis received a phone call from the man's wife. He says: 'She was in tears and said, "You are going to destroy my life. I run a business in conservative Pretoria. If people know who my husband is, my business is going to be ruined."' To make matters worse, she turned out to be a close friend of Du Plessis's parents. 'It was terrible – that's the worst thing that can happen to an editor,' he says. 'My father died when I was very young, and her family was very good to my family then.' After consulting colleagues and considering the matter, he called her back an hour later and said the story would be published. 'I have a certain professional responsibility,' Du Plessis says he told her.[6]

The incident is a perfect example of how family ties can create a conflict of interest. One may argue about Du Plessis's decision on the basis of the harm the story may have caused to an innocent person. But his determination not to be swayed by family ties is impressive. Normally, a reporter can avoid a story involving family or other personal connections by passing it on to a colleague, but that was not an option in this case. It must have been a very tough call.

> The 2003 Iraqi war introduced a new term: 'the embedded journalist'. The US military made provision for journalists to be attached to, or embedded in, particular military units. Supporters of the practice argued it allowed journalists to report first-hand from the front. Opponents said it would be impossible to maintain independence, and that journalists would simply become propagandists. There were no journalists embedded with the Iraqi military, although some reported from Baghdad.

Financial interests

Business reporters face a particular temptation in that their work can move markets. A journalist could make a lot of money on the side by buying shares and then reporting in a way that pushes their value up – and some have done so. Alternatively, reporters sometimes get information which is not yet in the public domain, and which could help them make a mint in a form of insider trading. Clearly, that kind of profiteering is completely unacceptable. The editor of *Business Day*, Peter Bruce, says: 'Journalists aren't allowed to trade actively in the shares that they write about. In other words, if you're the banking writer and we see you writing a story about Investec, and I find out that you bought Investec shares quite heavily last week and your story moves the share price up, I would see to it that you are fired.'[7]

Rules of this kind are well established in most news organisations. Bruce says he has not had a case of the rules being broken on his paper. In any event, journalists are no longer as often in a position to access privileged information since corporate government rules have restricted journalists' access. Bruce says: 'People in companies aren't allowed to say anything to a journalist that they wouldn't say to their shareholders first. If they do, they get into trouble.'

As with so many conflict of interest issues, a key element in handling potential financial temptations is disclosure. Journalists are required to disclose any holdings they have. Some editors have put their share portfolio into a 'blind trust' – in which somebody else manages them without their active involvement.

A citizen's rights

Like any other citizens, journalists have political rights. They include the right to vote, belong to political parties, campaign for them, and stand for election. However, it is not advisable for a journalist to exercise much more than the vote. What a journalist does in the privacy of the polling booth remains secret and can't affect his or her credibility. But any public activity is best avoided: being seen as politically partisan can be very damaging to one's reputation.

If journalists decide to stand for election, it is best to step away from journalism for the time being. If they are elected, they obviously move into a new role. If not, should they simply step back into their old role? The BBC allows this: 'They are not to be excluded from topical editorial work just because they used to be politically active.'[8] However, this seems to take the issue a little lightly. After a hard-fought election campaign, how likely is it that our journalist/ politician will be able to put those political passions aside? The Stellenbosch University ethicist Johan Retief comments: 'He or she will always be associated with that party. He or she will have no credibility, whether writing against the opposition or about his or her own party.'[9]

During the lengthy and complex process whereby the ANC draws up its lists of candidates, a party branch put forward the name of an SABC journalist. But she had not been asked, and could not be held responsible for being associated with the party. The SABC gave her clear alternatives: she should either take the political route, with all its uncertainties, or publicly make it clear she was not available for nomination. She chose the latter.

The same considerations apply to non-political situations: a motoring editor, for instance, might decide to accept a job as spokesperson for a major motor manufacturer. But if he tires of it, should he be allowed straight back into his old job? In the case of a high-profile position like this, there may be an argument for enforcing a 'cooling off' period, as is now required of senior government officials moving into the private sector.

A citizen's duties

Our discussion of the demands for a patriotic media (see Chapter 2) has shown that journalists claim a measure of independence even from the state and its organs of justice. It is a claim many outside the profession find difficult to accept. South Africa has a worrying crime problem: how can anybody duck the responsibility to do their bit to fight it? Journalists get access to information that can help put criminals behind bars – why would they not use it to do so? Sometimes one also hears the accusation that this claim is simply a hangover from the past. There may have been justification for journalists wanting to distance themselves from the previous regime and its police, it is said, but the new government surely deserves better.

The journalist's real social responsibility is met by doing his or her job, providing trustworthy and independent accounts of what is going on. Being seen as proxies of the police and justice system would undermine our ability to do our job. The head of news at e.tv, Joe Thloloe, says: 'It is up to the police to go and do their investigations rather than try and use me as a journalist. The problem here is we have to maintain our integrity to the point where people can continue to trust us rather than looking at us as police informants or the agents of the police.'[10]

Co-operation with the police can endanger journalists. *Cape Talk*'s news editor, Andrew Bolton, describes how intelligence agencies wanted to use a reporter 'to assist in investigations' into urban terrorism in Cape Town. The staffer was getting death threats, says Bolton, and the request was turned down.[11]

> **"To be seen as colluding with authority – any authority – damages hard-won reputations and may even put correspondents' lives in danger."**
> *Former BBC correspondents in a letter to The Times on the decision by the corporation to allow staff to testify in the war crimes trial of the former Yugoslav strongman, Slobodan Milošević*

The debate around this issue is usually understood as being about the protection of sources. But co-operation with the police and courts can take many different forms. Some journalists have been asked to spy; others have testified in court; while yet others have faced police requests for their notes, videotape or other material.

> **"I don't accept that journalists are exempt from moral obligations or international justice."[12]**
> *Jacky Rowland, BBC correspondent, on her decision to testify*

There is little unanimity among journalists about such situations. Most would accept the basic need to maintain their independence from the authorities, but some apply the principle more absolutely than others. Johan de Villiers, executive editor of *The Star*, feels that changed circumstances require a more cooperative attitude: 'In the old days, when the police wanted your photographs of demonstrations, it was a fair bet that they wanted to see who was there so they could round up people – which was clearly for political purposes. We are currently in the situation where, for instance, there are crime scenes that our photographers witness. I have a problem in withholding the information.'[13]

For others, the severity of the crime involved makes a difference, and most would agree that a journalist has a duty to prevent present and serious danger to the lives of people. Most would freely make material available that has been published or broadcast, since it is in the public domain in any event. But before such material can be used as evidence, police need an affidavit to confirm its accuracy – and at this point, differences again emerge. Some journalists see no problem in supplying such a statement, others do.

The justice system does not recognise that journalists have any special privileges, and Section 205 of the Criminal Procedures Act can be used to force anybody – including reporters – to give evidence. Andries Cornelissen, a reporter from *Beeld*, was in 1993 sentenced to a year in jail for refusing to answer questions in court. He had reported on a speech by Peter Mokaba, leader of the ANC Youth League, in which the firebrand used the slogan 'Kill the boer, kill the farmer'. Police were investigating a case of incitement against Mokaba, and claimed they could only pursue the case with Cornelissen's help.[14] The sentence was later overturned on appeal, with the judge recognising the special role of the media.[15] He accepted that testifying in the case would have damaged Cornelissen's professional standing, and that the police had not seriously tried to find other witnesses. However, the provision remains a potential problem for journalists, despite discussions between the media and the authorities.

Moonlighting

Journalism is not the best-paid profession, and many people in the field look for ways of augmenting their pay packets. Companies have various policies: some rule moonlighting out completely, others positively encourage it as long as it does not impact on them in any way. A radio reporter who occasionally writes for a newspaper, for instance, can help build the profile of his or her station.

In many cases the organisation expects to be asked, so that an editor can check for any problem areas. A news organisation would legitimately disapprove of a staff member working for a rival group, for instance, or frown on the use of their resources for these purposes. These situations involve considerations of corporate self-interest rather than professional ethics.

But there are opportunities for moonlighting that set broader ethical alarm bells ringing. Radio journalists, for instance, are sometimes offered opportunities to voice commercials. If their voice is known in a news context, it would undermine their credibility to be heard selling a car or government policy.

It's also very problematical for a journalist to do public relations work on the side. The pay may be good, but the costs to credibility are substantial, whether you're acting for a company, government department or any other body.

The honeyed onslaught of the marketers

A never-ending stream of gifts flows into newsrooms, everything from shirts to cellphones, pens to crates of beer. Towards the end of every year, the stream grows into a torrent as marketers exploit the season of goodwill to curry favour with journalists. The *Sunday Times* probably has the best system to deal with these freebies: they are all handed in, no matter how small. Once in a while they are auctioned off to staff, and the proceeds go to charity. Other organisations will allow staff to accept small gifts, but insist that anything larger be politely returned.

The industry has a particular weakness for free trips, which are dressed up with varying degrees of success as being intended to help the journalist cover a particular story. An airline, for instance, might take a planeload of journalists on a flight across the country to show off a new aircraft. The Canadian Broadcasting Corporation (CBC) has a very strict prohibition against this practice: 'Travel and accommodation costs are a form of programme expense and are not to be absorbed by outside agencies.' Exceptions will be considered 'only for journalistic purposes and only when no commercial transport is available,' the CBC says.[16]

In South Africa most organisations argue – with some justification – that budgets simply do not allow for such a purist position. Some use free trips as a perk to supplement salaries, or as rewards. Ivan Fynn, the editor of the *Cape Argus*, says: 'We have some young reporters who have never flown out of Cape Town. If there's a trip to Jo'burg or Durban, it's better to send someone like that because it gives them a broader view of what's going on.'[17]

Travel and motoring journalism in South Africa is completely unthinkable without freebies. When launching a new model, motor manufacturers take motoring journalists to exotic locations, where they spend a few days in the lap of luxury while trying out the car in question. No South African media organisation will pay for that kind of exercise. Travel writers write about destinations where they have been invited.

Under the circumstances, it is best to manage the offers of free trips in a transparent and fair way. *The Star* has a detailed Trips Charter, which sets out – among other things – that invitations must go to the editor, explains a process to be followed in deciding whether to accept, and says that articles written as a result must acknowledge the sponsorship.

The marketers' efforts are enthusiastically supported by those of the media companies themselves. Thloloe, says: 'Every company in the country wants to be covered and they want to be covered in a particular way. So those pressures are enormous. People sit around working out strategies of getting onto our screens and our responsibility is to try and keep them at bay. It is a constant battle, obviously the marketing people within the media will always be coming in saying, "Can you try this, can you do that?" because they want to sell airtime and they think they might strike a deal if we manage to get their clients onto the news bulletin. It is a very difficult area, we are constantly having to push commercial interest out of the news.'[18]

In a tight media market, the temptation to blur the lines between editorial and commercial consideration is great. There are many variations:

- A newspaper launches a fund to collect money for a child who needs an operation – hoping to boost circulation;
- The company's own promotional events are covered in great detail – the classic picture of the smiling editor handing over the prize in a promotional competition;
- Free copies of the paper are handed out to a major conference, and the marketing department asks for coverage of the event;
- Radio news bulletins are sponsored;
- A deal is made for ongoing coverage of a particular soapie in return for advertising;
- Newspapers publish 'surveys' on companies or industries, sometimes with the bylines of the paper's writers;

- Salespeople offer 'value-adds' – editorial space equivalent to the value of advertising space booked;
- Newspapers print a 'wrap-around' that looks like the front page but is devoted to advertising;
- Editors come under pressure to kill a story because it's embarrassing to an advertiser – or a company withdraws advertising because of a report it does not like;
- Radio stations allow sponsored slots, where the sponsor's product shapes the nature of the slot – like a coffee company paying for a regular interview with somebody who has to be 'wide awake';
- There is also the practice of content being shaped by business strategy – known as market-driven journalism;
- Online publications may provide direct links from inside a news story to an advertiser's site.

And the list goes on and on. Some of these practices are objectionable, others are innocent. The reality is that journalism has always had an economic context, and it would be naïve to expect media products not to be shaped by the need to attract a particular target audience, for instance.

Where commercial and editorial considerations meet, the waters are always murky. It is almost impossible to draw clear lines about what's right and what's wrong; our best guide is common sense and a willingness to discuss particular situations. But it is essential to develop a keen sense of the issue, and to be vigilant for those occasions when commercial agendas, rather than professional ones, determine decisions on coverage. It happens easily.

Home affairs

Some of the ugliest brawls in the media have pitted editors against their bosses. A particularly entertaining scrap is described in Case Study 10 below: when Donald Trelford, editor of Britain's *Observer*, exposed repression in Zimbabwe's Matabeleland province, the newspaper's proprietor, Tiny Rowland, was outraged. He felt his business interests in Zimbabwe would be compromised, and he demanded that Trelford go back to Zimbabwe to have another look. The two men had a furious public row, but ultimately made up.[19]

The principle of editorial autonomy is a treasured cornerstone of journalism ethics, particularly in the British

"We report matters regarding ourselves and colleagues with the same vigour and candour as we would other institutions or individuals."
The Independent Newspapers Code of Conduct

tradition. It holds that media owners should appoint editors on the basis of a general agreement about policy, and then leave them alone. Proprietors should look after the business, pay the bills and bank the profits, while editors are the kings or queens of content. They can be fired if the company is not happy with their direction, but they should be able to run their papers without interference.

In reality, the clash between Rowland and Trelford is just one instance where owners have been unable to keep their fingers out of the editorial pie. There have been many others. In South Africa, too, editors have been pressured by their companies over political, editorial and other issues.

Less dramatic but very powerful pressure has come through fundamental changes in the role of the editor. These days, no editor would be allowed to ignore the commercial interests of the paper and its owners. In fact, editors are expected to integrate editorial and commercial considerations on a day-to-day basis. Trevor Ncube, the *Mail&Guardian* owner, expressed this expectation bluntly at a Sanef seminar in August 2004. 'Being in business is about defending the bottom line. Journalists incorrectly assume we are not a business, that papers are somehow different to sweets and Coca-Cola,' he said. As he put it, the 'Chinese wall' between business and editorial needed to come down.[20]

Statements like these show that threats to independent journalism can easily come from within. We have discussed some of the forms that pressures from the marketing departments can take. The notion of editors being without any interest in or regard for mere money may be a little antiquated, but it is critically important for editors and journalists to keep an eye on pressures from their own companies.

This is not to say that proprietors are the enemy. It is perfectly possible to maintain a constructive relationship. In fact, far-sighted owners and companies will understand that respect for editorial independence and ethics is in their long-term commercial interest.

Sometimes, the company itself makes news – and it's very difficult to cover stories of this kind fairly and independently. Most news organisations will say they report themselves just as they would anybody else. It's a noble sentiment that is rarely observed. Circulation figures are a good example: no matter how badly the newspaper's sales figures have plummeted, newspapers always report them in the most rosy tones. The SABC often makes news, and has struggled on occasion to deal properly with its own controversies.

Business media sometimes have to report on the activities of their own companies, or associated firms. Mostly, they will acknowledge the link in the copy or at the bottom of the report.

Worthy causes

There are many NGOs and other groups that fight Aids, poverty, illiteracy or any one of hundreds of other causes. Journalists are sometimes too quick to relax their guard when dealing with these groups, trusting them and their information more easily than other groups.

The Norwegian academic Helge Rønning describes the relationship of Western aid NGOs with journalists as an 'unholy alliance'.[21] He says they shape the images of Africa portrayed in the media according to their own agendas. 'Often the only way for media personnel to get into the disaster areas is courtesy of the aid organisation … The reporters get powerful stories, dramatic pictures. The NGOs get their message about the suffering through to millions of viewers and readers in the North, which again generates millions of dollars for the NGOs and their operations.' As a result critical questions remain unasked, and the people 'who live and die in African societies' are not heard, says Rønning.

In some cases, news organisations have thrown their weight behind particular organisations or campaigns. Titles in the Independent group routinely ran the phone numbers of the anti-Aids group LoveLife next to any reports on Aids. It is a difficult area, because publishing the phone numbers may have been a real public service. At the same time, LoveLife was not uncontroversial.

> "There is nothing like a disaster to boost an aid agency's profile, and they needed to have the media cover the existence of the [famine in Sudan]."[22]
> *Greg Marinovich and Joao Silva, photographers*

Creating such a close association with one organisation may make it more difficult to report critically on it.

It's as well to keep a critical distance even from people we regard as angels.

●●●

Independence:
a test of three questions

Journalists should ask these questions to check their reporting:
1. Do you stand to benefit in any way from this report?
2. Could anything lead to a perception of conflict of interest?
3. Are you prepared to disclose any interest?

●●●

TALKING POINT

Easy spinning
Chris Vick

'Without contradictions, there is no development.' I can never quite remember who said that. Lenin? Gramsci? Trotsky, maybe? It's not that important – but the concept is, particularly in a media environment that is, on the one hand, celebrating the conversational space that exists in our democracy, but on the other is feeling the resource crunch of media commercialisation.

Being a spindoctor with a conscience (yes, we do exist) in a democracy, during an era of rampant commercialisation, means life is full of contradictions. One moment you are celebrating the fact that, yet again, you have been able to get a press release into print, verbatim. Or you've been able to ensure that the position expressed by the company CEO or social activist has been swallowed – hook, line, sinker *and* fishing rod. But, simultaneously, you're mindful that the press release has been published without anyone noticing what was left out, or without any of the obvious questions being asked.

Of course, this doesn't happen all the time. We still bump heads with a fair number of inquiring, inquisitive and proving minds, and celebrate the integrity and vigour with which they go about their work.

But when it does happen, and you get one through the net, there's that contradiction again. The spindoctor in you celebrates: Another happy client. But the democrat in you wonders: If it's this easy, who else is doing it?

It's a difficult situation, brought about partly because of the increased attention that is paid to 'reputation management' and the fact that the public and private sector are putting more skills and resources into 'spin' and all that goes with it.

But the situation is aggravated by the skills and resources that are *not* put behind quality journalism – or at countering 'spin' – and the blurring of the line between editorial and advertising. How has it come to this?

I once ran a training programme for news editors, during which they were asked to illustrate the dominant culture in their newsrooms. The best group came up with a graphic that was simplistically vivid: a drawing of a red line across the bottom of the page.

'It's all about the bottom line,' they declared. 'Nothing else counts. Nothing else matters.' As one news editor put it more bluntly later (in the bar, obviously): 'Fuck quality. They only want quantity.'

The double-bind of a lack of resources to increase staff, and a lack of resources to increase the skills of staff, could be one of the greatest threats to 'editorial independence', or to any form of editorial integrity.

A similar threat is posed by 'advertorials'. Information that is paid for is perceived differently to information that has been subject to editorial scrutiny. Readers/viewers/listeners have a right to know when information has been paid for – and that means more than a headline in 14 point that says 'Advertisement'. But, as spindoctors, we find that advertising departments regularly undermine the integrity of editorial – promising various forms of airtime or space in editorial slots that should be a distinct 'no-go' area, and getting 'journalists' to write editorial copy.

The reality, from a spindoctor's point of view, is that the going will get easier unless there's a better understanding of the role of 'reputation managers', a serious reinvestment in the quality and quantity of journalists, or a serious rethink of the boundaries between editorial and advertising.

This includes recognising that, in a democracy such as ours, the greatest threat probably comes from commercial interests, not the state.

The more you cut back on training budgets, the more you confine journalists to e-mail journalism, the more you 'downsize' your newsroom teams, the more you blur the line between advertising and editorial, the easier you make the task of the spindoctor – and whoever pays their fees.

(Chris Vick is director of Spinmedia,
a communications consultancy)

Case study 8
Stopping the messenger

A Durban tow-truck operator, Colin Govender, had a grievance against the police. So on 28 August 2002 he fetched his girlfriend, Tashnee Govender, from the school where she was a teacher, took her to his flat in Phoenix and declared he was holding her hostage.[23]

He phoned a number of media organisations to plead for media attention, as police surrounded the flat and negotiators began engaging him. The standoff continued for most of the day, with Govender threatening to shoot his hostage. The police accepted his demand to be allowed to speak to a reporter, but would allow only one reporter onto the premises. SABC radio's Kas van Dyk agreed to do the interview, on condition that other reporters present would be allowed to listen to his tape afterwards.

During the interview, Govender made allegations of corruption at three Durban police stations, giving names and other details. He said he had been forced to pay bribes to police officers, including senior ones, in order to be allowed to tow vehicles away from accident scenes.

After Van Dyk emerged, police demanded to be allowed to listen to his tape. They then warned him not to share the contents with other reporters, and finally took it from him. Minutes later, a police sniper shot Govender through the neck, and he died.

The SABC immediately demanded the tape back. The head of SABC radio news, Pippa Green, said it was direct interference with media freedom.[24] From a journalistic point of view the tape was very valuable, she said later. Aside from the detailed claims against the police, the tape showed Govender taking business calls on a phone borrowed from a policeman, and his girlfriend taking calls, too. 'I wanted this on radio, I wanted the top dogs to hear,' she said.[25]

But police claimed information that was vital to their investigation was on the tape and only handed it back some weeks later, after the SABC's lawyers had threatened to go to court.

The police were clearly out of line in confiscating Van Dyk's tape. Questions about their motives have to be asked: after all, Govender was making allegations of corruption against them. Also, the order not to share the information with other journalists – despite the earlier agreement – and the swift shooting of Govender combine to leave an impression that the local police may have been acting to protect their own reputation.

Under the circumstances, Van Dyk was wrong to agree to surrender the tape. It broke an undertaking to a source – Govender was speaking to him on the basis that this would be a pool arrangement, and that his story would be shared with other journalists.

It turned him into a functionary of the police, and infringed media independence. Thloloe said his organisation was approached later for some material it had gathered at the scene.[26] He said his response was that e.tv was prepared to supply a tape of the report as it was broadcast, but nothing else. 'They were there so they should have gathered their own evidence. There is absolutely no reason why they should be coming to us for evidence.'

But the SABC did well to demand the tape's return immediately. It sent a strong signal of independence.

Case study 9
The public relations editor

The editor of *City Press*, Vusi Mona, stared pensively across a cafeteria table, his lips slightly pursed. He was in an unenviable position – looking out of the front page of another newspaper, *The Star*, under the banner headline 'Editor in jam over PR role'.[27]

The September 2003 story accused Mona of involvement in public relations firms that were doing work for the much-criticised provincial government of Mpumalanga. It said he had been a director of a company trading under two names, Rainbow Communications and Rainbow Kwanda Communications. The companies had placed an advertisement in his own newspaper in the name of the Mpumalanga premier, Ndaweni Mahlangu.

The advertisement, which appeared earlier in the same month, consisted of half a broadsheet page of dense type, accusing the media of dishonesty and the theft of documents in its reporting of the province. The rambling and poorly written diatribe asked: 'What is the naked truth in the land where the sun never sets? Is it what the media said or is it perhaps something else, is the media innocent or are there hidden agendas somewhere.'[28]

The Star report also said Mona and his business partner, Dr Moss Mashamaite, had successfully tendered for a contract from the Mpumalanga Parks Board 'to correct the negative perception the public holds about [the board] following a number of media reports on corruption, mismanagement and misappropriation of funds and nepotism by its previous senior employees.' In the minutes of the board's meeting with Rainbow, Mona was quoted as saying the public relations campaign would involve 'negotiating with journalists, pitching of stories to the media, booking of space and press events'.

Mona had met the newspaper's reporter to discuss the claims – which was where the picture was taken – but refused to comment on the record. He did respond in a statement carried in the next edition of his own newspaper.[29] 'I have not been involved in any wrongdoing or corruption,' he said. He stressed he was neither a shareholder nor director of the Rainbow companies, and added: 'I am not part of any consortium doing work for the Mpumalanga government.' He had always taken care to avoid conflict of interest situations, he said.

At his suggestion, Mona stepped aside from the newspaper's editorship while the company's owners, Media24, launched an investigation. 'The integrity of Media24's editors is of paramount importance to our company,' said Salie de Swardt, the company's managing director.[30]

Two months later, Mona resigned as editor. In a joint statement he and Media24 gave the findings of the probe.[31] It said that from 2001 to September 2002 Mona had had a 50 per cent member's interest in Zan Moss Technologies CC, which traded as Rainbow Communications and also as Rainbow Kwanda Communications. This constituted a conflict of interest with his duties as editor, the statement said. 'He did not disclose the details of his interests at the time as he should have, but realising the conflict, decided to dispose of his interests and signed an agreement to this effect on 4 September 2002,' it added.

During the time of his involvement, the company did training for a trust connected to the Mpumalanga government, and the probe confirmed that Mona had helped make a successful bid for work from the province's parks board. The probe found him not to have been involved in Mpumalanga's 'naked truth' advertisement. 'The investigation could not find specific evidence that the conflict of interest alluded to in fact led to Mr Mona favouring any of the customers of Zan Moss Technologies CC in *City Press*,' it said.

So much for the facts of the case. The conflict of interest issues it demonstrates are crystal clear. No journalist can play both sides of the field, reporting the news and taking money for spindoctoring on behalf of an entity that is in the news. It dramatically undermines any claim to independence and sets up fatally divided loyalties. Where the entity is as controversial as the Mpumalanga government, the dangers are particularly acute. The deputy head of Rhodes University's journalism department, Anthea Garman, said: 'Newspapers position themselves in a watchdog role. If you're going to take up the watchdog role, you have to make sure you don't compromise yourself.'[32]

The more senior the journalist is, the greater the responsibility. An editor behaving in this way puts the reputation of the entire newspaper at risk.

It is worth noting Mona's first statement in the light of the investigation's findings, which he agreed to have released. His statement that 'I am neither a shareholder nor director' was technically truthful. But only just: he used the present tense, having disposed of his interests a year beforehand. Omitting mention of his previous involvement was clearly misleading.

The Mona case also once again points to the issue of perceptions versus reality in conflict of interest situations. The company found there was no evidence that he had actually favoured any of the clients of the Rainbow companies. But journalists should avoid any connections that may lead their audiences to mistrust their reporting. Suspicion can arise even if actual reporting remains as pure as the driven snow. Even if Mona did not allow his business interests to influence his journalism, the arrangement still shredded his credibility. In any event, his participation in the presentation to the parks board showed he was quite willing to take the extra step and bend his newspaper to the interests of his clients.

There is a final intriguing aspect of this case. *The Star*'s report appeared soon after *City Press* ran a report claiming that the national director of public prosecutions, Bulelani Ngcuka, had been an apartheid spy. (This has been fully discussed as Case Study 1.) Mona hinted that the story about him might have been leaked by Ngcuka's special investigating unit, the Scorpions, because of this report. He said: 'I do not rule out the possibility that this has a lot to do with the editorial stance I have taken.'

There was never any evidence to support Mona's claim that he was the victim of a leak by the Scorpions. If there had been, it would have reflected poorly on *The Star*. But Mona's story was clearly intertwined with the Ngcuka saga. Even though it is hardly possible to separate it out, the ethical issues arising from one editor's venture into public relations are separate, and deserve separate consideration.

Case study 10
Bearding the boss

It was 1984, and the editor of *The Observer*, Donald Trelford, was in Zimbabwe to interview President Robert Mugabe to mark the fourth anniversary of independence. The interview was not very interesting, but while he was in the country he came across evidence of terrible atrocities being committed by the army against dissidents in Matabeleland. In an account published years later, he described the cloak and dagger way in which he was spirited out of his hotel one night and taken to a remote mission to be presented with a catalogue of eye-witness accounts, signed statements and sworn affidavits, many of which focused on the army's Korean-trained Fifth Brigade.[33]

The Observer's owners were Tiny Rowland's Lonrho, which had been founded in Rhodesia, as it was called at the time, and still had substantial interests in Zimbabwe. Trelford described his dilemma: 'Should I publish an anodyne interview with Mugabe or tell the truth about Matabeleland, thereby damaging the interests of my proprietor?'

He decided to go ahead, informing Rowland when it was too late to do anything about it. 'He slammed the telephone down after threatening the direst revenge,' wrote Trelford. 'Next morning I turned on the BBC eight o'clock news to hear my story condemned as lies in an official statement by Mugabe, supported by a letter of apology from Rowland: "I take full responsibility for what in my view was discourteous, disingenuous and wrong in the editor of a serious newspaper widely read in Africa." He described me as an incompetent reporter and announced that I would be dismissed.'

For two weeks there was a furious public row between the two men. There was an exchange of open letters, and Rowland insisted that Trelford should go back to Zimbabwe for a longer investigation. 'I refused, on the grounds that I had already established the truth of my story, and to do so would have endangered the lives of my sources.'

Rowland demonstratively met with the owner of the Mirror group of companies, Robert Maxwell, to discuss selling him the paper, and announced the withdrawal of Lonrho's financial support for the paper. 'On this occasion, brinkmanship failed,' writes UK academic Bruce Hanlin. 'The editor was backed unanimously by the journalistic staff, while the paper's five independent "watch-dog" directors denounced

Rowland for "improper proprietorial interference" and gave Trelford their full support for "vigorously maintaining his editorial freedom and defending his professional integrity."[34]

Finally he offered to resign the editorship in the interests of the newspaper, and Rowland 'seized the olive branch', Trelford wrote. 'We made up over an edgy lunch in the incongruous ambience of one of Lonrho's London casinos. Undeterred by the pop music and scantily dressed females, we concocted a priceless statement that we shared an affection for three things – Africa, *The Observer* and each other.'

The conflict about *The Observer*'s Matabeleland report is one of the most prominent fights between editor and proprietor, and demonstrates the fact that threats to independence can quite easily come from inside.

Freedom of the press, we should remind ourselves, was originally about the right to own a printing press. The press barons that have been such a prominent part of the media landscape in Britain and elsewhere saw their investments not simply as commercial. Owning a newspaper was about prestige and power, too. For most of them, interference in editorial decisions was second nature. Robert Maxwell, the larger-than-life owner of the Mirror group of companies, famously once referred to the London *Daily Mirror* as his 'megaphone'.

The Trelford story provides a rare example of an editor taking on his boss, and winning. But only a few years later, he published a special Thursday edition of *The Observer* (a Sunday newspaper), devoted entirely to a court case Lonrho was fighting around the acquisition of Harrods, the famous London store. Only a few hundred copies were sold before the paper was declared in contempt of court. Hanlin says it was 'a blatant publicity stunt', adding: 'The episode can hardly be seen as anything other than proprietorial abuse of the newspaper's name and reputation.'[35]

. . . .

NOTES

1   Jay Black, Bob Steele and Ralph Barney, *Doing ethics in journalism: a handbook with case studies*. Needham Heights, MA: Allyn & Bacon, 1995. 91.

2   Ibid. 91.

3   *Rhodes Journalism Review* 4, July 1992. 91.

4   *Rhodes Journalism Review* 4, July 1992. 21.

5   SABC, 'Editorial policies'. Johannesburg: SABC, 2004. 19.

6   Interview, 15 October 2002.

7   Interview, 2 December 2002.

8   BBC, *Producers' guidelines*. London: BBC, 1996. 92.

9   Johan Retief, *Media Ethics: An introduction to responsible journalism*. Cape Town: OUP, 2002. 137.

10   Interview, 2 September 2002.

11   Interview, 8 November 2002.

12   Quoted in 'Journalists in dock'. Posted at http://www.epnworld-reporter.com on 19 September 2002.

13   Interview, 2002.

14   Sapa report, 5 September 1993.

15   For full details of the case, see Retief, *Media ethics*. 130–2.

16   Canadian Broadcasting Corporation Journalistic Standards and Practices, 2001. Accessed at http://cbc.radio-canada.ca/htmen/policies/journalistic/index.htm on 6 December 2003.

17   Interview, 8 November 2002.

18   Interview, 2 September 2002.

19   Bruce Hanlin, 'Owners, editors and journalists' in Andrew Belsey and Ruth Chadwick (eds.), *Ethical issues in journalism and the media*. London and New York: Routledge, 1992.

20   Quoted in Guy Berger, 'Fourth Estate needs a fourth bottom line', *Mail&Guardian Online*, 18 August 2004. Posted at http://www.mg.co.za/Content/l3.asp?cg=Insight-Converse&ao=120609&sa=58, accessed on 6 October 2004.

21   Helge Rønning, 'The unholy alliance', *Rhodes Journalism Review* 18, December 1999.

22   Greg Marinovich and Joao Silva, *The bang-bang club*. London: Arrow, 2001. 145.

23   *Daily News*, 30 August 2002.

24   SABC radio report, 30 August 2002.

25   Interview, 2002.

26   Interview, 2 September 2002.

27   *The Star*, 26 September 2003.

28   *City Press*, 21 September 2003.

29   *City Press*, 28 September 2003.

30   Ibid.

31   'Joint statement by Media24 and Mr Vusi Mona, editor of *City Press*', 12 November 2003.

32   *The Star*, 26 September 2003.

33   Donald Trelford, 'The patter of Tiny's feet', 12 March 2000. Posted at http://www.gem.stir.ac.uk/corpus/guardian/zimbabwe_pages/zimbabwe/article/0,2763,145770,00.html, accessed on 5 January 2004.

34   Hanlin, 'Owners, editors and journalists'. 43.

35   Ibid. 43.

Die Burger encourages racial harmony and seeks to advance the welfare and progress of all sectors of the population through its reporting.
Die Burger: Ethical Code

A journalist shall not originate material which encourages discrimination on the grounds of race, colour, creed, gender or sexual orientation.
South African Union of Journalists: Code of Conduct

Sunday Times staff will not use language or pictures which are offensive, reinforce stereotypes, fuel prejudice or xenophobia.
Sunday Times: Charter

7

WRITING RACE

Race is largely an artificial construction. Around the eighteenth century, European scientists tried to categorise various kinds of human beings according to essential attributes that were held to belong inescapably to every member of a particular 'race'. A pseudo-scientific argument was built to show that whites were superior – and this helped justify the European conquest and colonisation of the rest of the world.

Even though genetics and a host of other disciplines debunked these ideas several generations ago, they retain extraordinary power. Apartheid, as a system of institutionalised racism, may have been removed, but the ideas on which it was based are still widespread. What's more, many areas of our society remain shaped by their history of racism: party support, residential areas, the division between poor and rich and many others still reflect racial divisions.

In that sense, racism is much more than a question of stereotyping. The Rhodes University academic, Lynette Steenveld, defines it as 'the system of *beliefs and practices* that people can be classified into groups on the basis of presumed differences which justifies the unequal allocation of power and privilege' (my emphasis).[1] In other words, it's about what is in people's heads, but it is also importantly about what they do.

Her definition also indicates the connection between racism and power. In their submission to the Human Rights Commission (HRC) inquiry into racism in the media, the political analyst Dumisane Hlophe and lawyer Christine Qunta make the connection even more explicit: 'Racism is constituted when racial prejudices are matched with power to act on such prejudices.'[2] It should be noted that power is not just political. In modern societies, many institutions outside government have power of various kinds. Companies have economic power, for instance, and even an insult thrown out during a bar-room argument involves the exercise of power: the power to hurt.

Why is racism an issue of ethics?

Racism contravenes several basic principles of journalistic ethics. It is unfair to the group being stigmatised. Stereotypes distort the reality of individuals and of society as a whole, and are therefore both inaccurate and harmful. Racist writing is simply bad journalism.

During the HRC inquiry into racism in the media, there was much debate about whether particular instances of racism found in print or on the air could be explained away as mistakes or errors of journalistic judgment. In its final report, *Faultlines*, the commission emphatically rejected this view. 'We are concerned that a too easy resort to an explanation of bad journalism might be another form of evasion and denial of racism.'[3]

That is not the argument being made here. Rather, I am arguing that racism is inimical to the principles of good journalism. Some instances of racist reporting may indeed be the result of slipshod work, but that is not enough to explain the phenomenon as a whole. Sometimes a bad decision made in haste reflects stereotypical assumptions that the journalist or editor may not be fully aware of.

More heat than light

In a class at the University of the Witwatersrand, students were asked whether the South African media were still racist. The responses fell neatly into racial categories. Black students generally said Yes, they were. White students said No, they weren't. Significantly, though, both sides struggled to move beyond the mere assertion of the view by finding real arguments to back it.

The discussion about race in the media is a very emotional one, and rarely moves beyond attack and defence. 'You are a racist!' is countered with 'You're playing the race card!' The HRC inquiry did not help much in moving the discussion along. The hearings were marked by bitter arguments that generated more heat than light, and after the *Faultlines* report appeared, the issue dropped from public view.

There has been hardly any attempt at identifying the areas in which racism may occur, in a way that would be useful to working journalists. A considerable amount of academic work has been done in the field, but it often remains dense and inaccessible.

One would expect the industry codes to provide some useful signposts, but they also reflect South African journalism's inability to engage with the issue.

Astonishingly, the Code of Conduct for Broadcasters says almost nothing about race. In its preamble it refers to the constitutional guarantee of free speech and the provision that excludes hate speech from protection. It rules out material which approves or promotes violence based on race, gender, religion or the like. And that is all. The section on news makes no mention whatever of race.

The press code goes a little further: it says the press 'should avoid discriminatory or denigratory' references to race, colour and other characteristics, and should refer to race only when it is strictly relevant. Finally, it emphasises the right 'and indeed the duty to report and comment on all matters of public interest', but – borrowing from the Bill of Rights – it says this must be balanced 'against the obligation not to promote racial hatred or discord in such a way as to create the likelihood of imminent violence'.[4] Although it remains at a very general level, the South African Union of Journalists code goes furthest with its provision that journalists should not 'originate material which encourages discrimination' (see extract on p. 115).

POTENTIAL PROBLEM AREAS

Drawing on written commentary, interviews conducted with editors, and international experience, I will in the following try to identify some areas in which racism may emerge in journalism. Rather than remain with the endless discussion of whether the South African media are racist or not, the intention here is to seek to develop some categories that can be useful in discussing concrete stories and situations that newsrooms may confront.

In general, one has to go to the small right-wing media to find examples of explicitly racist reporting. The head of news at e.tv, Joe Thloloe, says race is no longer such an obvious issue in the mainstream media. 'The days of very overt references to race are gone,' he says.[5] But he adds: it hasn't disappeared, it's simply become more subtle.

Issues of racism are bound up with belief systems that can be quite unconscious. We all operate with deeply held systems of value and belief, and it would strain credibility to expect such powerful ideas and preconceptions as those surrounding race not to play some part in the world-view of all journalists, white and black. (Of course, the present text and its author are not immune from these either.)

Racism is a subject that evokes strong emotional responses, and it is very difficult to scrutinise and discuss. Nevertheless, we need to be prepared to discuss particular stories and situations, and particularly the perceptions they may evoke. It seems a more productive approach than to stay in the mode of attack versus defence, or to shy away from the discussion entirely.

Tim du Plessis, the editor of *Rapport*, says his Afrikaans readers often criticise the paper for being inconsistent in identifying the race of attackers. "If you have a farm attack, you never say three black men entered the house, tied up the husband, raped the woman and shot them dead, you just say three men/intruders," he says. Many people in farming communities regard such attacks as racially motivated, but Du Plessis says he would attach a racial label to the attackers only if the police said it was racial.[6]

Labels

This is an easy issue to address. Conventional practice is to limit racial identifiers to cases where they are important for understanding the story. Where a white man gets onto a bus full of black commuters in order to shoot as many as he can, the race of both perpetrator and victims is clearly important to the story. Leaving that detail out would distort it.

It is worth remembering the background to this aversion to labels. In a frequently reprinted column,[7] the Poynter Institute's Keith Woods says they were used to tell white readers that a particular story wasn't about them. If nothing was said, the subject of the story was assumed to be white. He writes: 'Racial identifiers were used to selectively support beliefs in white supremacy. They were used to call attention to the criminal, immoral, or threatening acts of other racial and ethnic groups to demonstrate that the stereotypes about those groups were true.'

The use of racial labels in this sense is now uncommon. They have been driven underground. If you read about 'an 18-year-old suspect from Atteridgeville', you will immediately understand the person to be black, unless you don't know that Atteridgeville is a black township in Pretoria. Of course, it would be ludicrous to suggest that areas should no longer be named on the grounds that people will associate them with particular groups. It simply shows how deeply race has entered into language.

Some words with racial baggage:
- Suburb
- Township, township dweller
- Squatter camp
- Community
- Previously disadvantaged
- Gang of youths
- Ratepayers
- Informal settlement
- Minibus taxi
- Empowerment

There is a danger in developing such a nervousness about labels that we end up hiding an important factor in our society. Woods writes: 'The mangled language of race is punctuated with descriptions that underscore ethnicity but describe nothing. It is mired in euphemisms and the tortured, convoluted syntax that betray America's pathological avoidance of straight talk about race relations.' If race is a factor, write as clearly and directly as you can.

Diverse sourcing

Most media organisations now have a deliberate policy to reflect the diversity of the society in their sourcing. Of course, there are many instances in which journalists have no control over which source to use. If the minister of trade and industries makes an announcement, then that is who gets quoted. But there is discretion when it comes to the selection of experts and commentators or the compilation of vox pops. Thloloe says: 'When you look at things like comments on the economy, you will always get white columnists giving their version.' E.tv and most other groups have a policy to seek out black and women commentators.

Similarly, efforts are made to ensure that images used with stories do not reflect racial bias. It is too easy to have articles on management always illustrated with pictures of white men, for instance, and it requires only a little effort to break that particular habit.

Conversely, the criticism is often made that Aids is portrayed as a black disease – feeding damaging prejudices. The former editor of the *Sowetan*, John Dludlu, says it has become a 'clubbing stick' against blacks.[8] Although simple demographic realities determine that most people with Aids are black, it doesn't mean that all are. Accuracy demands that the full range of people with Aids is reflected in pictures and stories.

Blind spots

One of the biggest criticisms of the mainstream media under apartheid was that it did not tell the story of black people. In the early 1980s, East London was an important centre of resistance to apartheid, with an active and powerful union movement flexing its muscles. The city's only daily paper, the *Daily Dispatch*, paid scant attention to this development. On one memorable occasion, a mass stayaway that emptied the city of black people was relegated to a blob paragraph on the end of another story.

This kind of deliberate suppression of news is no longer possible. No news medium today can ignore the concerns of black people, and the new black elite is reported extensively. But there are still silences in the reporting of township concerns and developments. Referring to the growth of People against Gangsterism and Drugs (Pagad), the editor of *The Star*, Moegsien Williams, says 'the Pagad phenomenon' in the Western Cape surprised the media. He goes on: 'If we were doing our job well, if we were in tune with what was happening on the ground, maybe we would have picked up there was a rising tide of unhappiness and dissatisfaction.'[9]

The editor of *City Press*, Mathatha Tsedu, says economic constraints on most media cause such silences. To attract advertising, they have to show they are read by the wealthy end of the market. And that means dealing with their issues. 'It's not about whether there is water in Zola today, it's about whether there's water in Blairgowrie where I live. And so the issues of Zola are getting relegated, not because Zola is a black area, but because Zola is a poor area.'[10] Also, many black journalists have moved out of the townships, and now report as outsiders. These trends have meant less coverage for poorer areas than before, says Tsedu.

Journalists have an ethical duty to see beyond their backyards, to seek out stories from the other side of town.

Xenophobia

While South African journalists have become very cautious about identifying people's race, the use of national labels is still common. Often taking a cue from the police, crime reports often refer to Nigerians being arrested, or Chinese abalone smugglers, or Zimbabwean illegal immigrants. And yet the function of this kind of labelling is exactly the same as racial labelling. It feeds off and into a stereotype of foreigners as being criminals. 'Crime is not only "racialised", it is also "Africanised,"' write Ransford Danso and David McDonald of the Institute for Democracy in South Africa (Idasa).[11] Labels of this kind have a place in reports only if they add significantly to the story.

Williams says the growing African immigrant communities in Johannesburg constitute a blind spot in reporting. He comments: 'I'm worried about our inability to get into the immigrant community. We like to speak about the Nigerians in Hillbrow, [but] I'm worried that we're not covering them.'[12]

Value and authority

Possibly the most significant area of concern involves giving different weight to members of different groups. White victims of crime or other mishaps still often seem to matter more than black ones. Dludlu says this kind of bias shows in the coverage of Zimbabwe. 'We always talk about the victims of the misrule in Zimbabwe and those victims are always white but more people who have died and are continuing to die are black people,' he says.[13]

On similar lines, the editor of the *Sunday Tribune*, Barney Mthombothi, says newspapers are quick to run pictures of dead black people but much more cautious about intruding on the grief of white people in this way.[14] He says there were no pictures of bodies after the 9/11 attack, for instance.

> "What is the psychological explanation for the depth of compassion exhibited by [white] people towards animals and the indifference to the incredible human suffering in their midst? ... For those outside a European cultural milieu, the revered place that animals occupy is perplexing."[15]
>
> Christine Qunta, lawyer and columnist

A former parliamentary editor of the Independent Group, Zubeida Jaffer, says she saw related prejudices played out when the then minister of safety and security, Steve Tshwete, announced a moratorium on the release of crime statistics. She says he was given a very hard time by journalists, but then called a white civil servant whose explanation was accepted by the media corps. 'I felt so humiliated because I thought, here he has to bring some junior civil servant to come and explain and everybody accepts it, but when the minister explains, it must be pulled to pieces.'[16]

One may argue with particular examples given, but it is difficult to dispute that stories are sometimes handled differently because of the race of the people involved. As working journalists, we should get into the habit of asking ourselves a simple question: would we run the story differently if the racial picture was different? If in doubt, the best solution is to discuss the issue with colleagues – particularly with those who have a different background to our own.

'Fishers of corrupt men'

Coverage of corruption has become a major theme in the accusation that South African media are racist. Even President Thabo Mbeki has said that the reporting of corruption is driven by a racist desire to prove that blacks can't run South Africa. Some journalists had become 'fishers of corrupt men', he wrote in his online column 'Letter from the President' in June 2003.[17] There were 'insulting campaigns further to entrench a stereotype that has, for centuries, sought to portray Africans as a people that are corrupt, given to telling lies, prone to theft and self-enrichment by immoral means'.

Most editors reject the accusation. In an editorial comment, the *Mail&Guardian* wrote: 'The simple fact is that this country is run by black people … It is, therefore, demographically logical that its successes are directly attributable to black people at the helm. And it is also demographically logical that when wrongdoing takes place in the ranks of government, the probabilities are that it will be the black people running the show who will be fingered.'[18]

Mthombothi rejects the argument that there is racism in the fact that the media uncovered less corruption involving the previous government. 'Corruption is corruption,' he says, 'The fact that it wasn't discovered before doesn't mean that we should turn a blind eye when it is discovered now.'[19]

Reporting race and racism

Race remains a major story in South Africa. Whether it manifests itself about black economic empowerment or tensions between children at newly integrated schools, it needs to be told fully and honestly.

South African media do a reasonable job in covering racist attacks, as when a young shoplifter is painted white, or policemen set dogs on immigrants as a training exercise. Those are easy stories, but many of the subtle complexities of shifting race relations remain unexplored. The journalist Jonny Steinberg has written about the refusal of white farmers to participate in an agricultural census, for fear the government will use the information to expropriate their land. Their act of passive resistance recalled a 1904 census. Then, black peasants were deeply suspicious of the motives of the colonial authorities, who, indeed, used the information to impose a poll tax. This is still remembered with bitterness as the moment they lost their land to the white farmers – who are now suspicious of another census.[20] Reporting like this contributes to our understanding of the rich texture of the story of race in South Africa. It is very rare.

> "When I heard … the word 'nigger', I heard a lynch mob. I saw the grim and gleeful faces of murderous white men. I felt the coarse, hairy rope. I smelled the sap of the hangin' tree and saw Billie Holiday's 'strange fruit' dangling from its strongest limb. What a wickedly powerful word, nigger. You just can't convey that definition with n-dash-dash-dash-dash-dash. You can't communicate it with bleeps or blurbs or euphemisms. The problem is that sometimes the only way to do your job as a journalist is to say or write the word that furthers the mission of racists."[21]
>
> *Keith Woods, Poynter Institute*

In reporting racism, journalists will sometimes have to deal with racist slurs or even hate speech. In South Africa, racist vocabulary is usually treated like four-letter words. Reference might be made to 'the k-word', for instance. Hate speech is of course prohibited by the Constitution. Nevertheless, there may be situations when accuracy demands that highly offensive statements should be reported fully.

Segmented audiences

In the past, audiences were defined by race, and editors tailored their content according to the perceived interests and preferences of those audiences. Black newspaper readers were given 'extra' editions that concentrated on sex, soccer and pictures of black models, leaving the rest of the paper largely white. Some of these extra editions – notably those of the *Sunday Times* – survived long into the new South Africa, since they were often highly profitable.

In general, the practice is dying out. Williams says when he arrived at *The Star*, there was a tendency to change the sports lead for the paper's different editions, depending on whether it was bought mainly by white or black readers. Soccer was preferred for black readers, rugby and cricket for white. But he says he put a stop to it. Now 'it's purely a news judgment on what in our view is the strongest story to lead the page.'[22]

He warns that making assumptions about buying patterns is dangerous. Just because an edition goes mainly to Sandton does not mean it is mainly bought by whites, he says.

Diverse newsrooms

The days when newsrooms were overwhelmingly white are long gone. The Soweto revolt of 1976 has been identified as a key impetus in bringing black reporters into mainstream newsrooms: white editors suddenly found themselves unable to cover a major story properly, since their white reporters had all sorts of difficulties in gaining access to the scene.

Still, until the 1990s the senior levels of the profession remained overwhelmingly white. The ranks of editors began changing in complexion with the coming of democracy, but a key element of the complaints that led to the HRC inquiry was that there were still too few black people in positions of authority. Even those black journalists who had been appointed to senior posts felt unable to change a dominant white world-view. The then editor of the *Sowetan*, Mike Siluma, told the HRC: 'I think we need to understand that as a black editor or in particular as an African editor, you can either be assimilated and become part of the whole system or you can try to introduce that diversity and bring into play your own thing, your own experience and try to introduce that into the mainstream but that is a difficult thing because if you play along you will be fine.'[24]

> "Everyone spoke about the incompetence of black reporters and their advocacy. Even then what was happening was the black guys would get the stories and feed in to some white journalist who would write the story."[23]
> *Former Sowetan editor, Joe Latakgomo*

Since then, the picture has changed further. Tsedu points out that in Gauteng, the country's media powerhouse, a clear majority of editors at major news organisations are black. The newer generation of editors don't share the view that they have been appointed as mere tokens, unable to make real changes. Tsedu says editors do have power: 'If you don't exercise it, don't blame it on somebody else.'[25]

The benefit of a diverse newsroom is that a range of perspectives is brought to bear on the reporting of news. There are sharp racial divisions in journalists' own attitudes to many issues. Tsedu highlights differences about the reporting of Zimbabwe, and there are many others. Varied attitudes must lead to differences in approach to reporting.

If a range of viewpoints can be discussed openly, then a diverse newsroom is a huge asset. But if those differences are left undiscussed and become sources of tension and conflict, then real problems arise. Few South African newsrooms have the maturity to use their diversity in the most productive way.

Race:
a test of five questions

Journalists should ask these questions to check their reporting:
1. Does the story reinforce racial stereotypes?
2. Is race an issue in the story? If not, have you stripped out obvious or hidden labels?
3. If it is, have you written about it clearly and honestly?
4. Are the voices in the story diverse?
5. Would the story, or anybody in it, have been treated differently if the racial context was different?

The value of a life still needs weighing
Justice Malala

On 7 May 2004 I came under fire, on the pages of my newspaper, *ThisDay*, from one of my reporters.

Carien du Plessis, a young, feisty reporter working out of our Cape Town office, had never written anything that cried out for an answer as much as the piece she produced that day. And what did she get in response? My shameful silence, and the silence of all the editors she fingered.

She had recently covered two court cases and had found my treatment of the stories appalling, to say the least. My colleagues at other newspapers did not come off lightly either. This is how she described the two cases and the stories that appeared in the newspapers over time:

> The first was the celebrated Sizzlers trial. Two men were convicted of killing nine (white) men execution-style, attempting to kill another, and robbing them in a gay massage parlour last year.
>
> In the second case a young man named Asanda Baninzi got 19 life sentences (regarded by some as a record for this High Court division) for killing 14 (black) people, raping four others, and committing 33 other crimes over a three-month period in 2001. In these cases, all the victims were young, not particularly rich and not particularly well known.
>
> Nor were the accused wealthy or high-profile individuals. [Yet] court reporters talked about the Sizzlers trial weeks before it started and wrote previews in gory detail. On the first day of the trial, and throughout, we sat like sardines in the press benches, lapping up each tear. We irritated the relatives of the victims and invaded their privacy in an attempt to get the best story.
>
> No such problem with the Baninzi trial. Even when journalists eventually caught on, and editors in Cape Town began placing the story on page one, there was still enough arm space in the press benches to take notes comfortably. The families of the victims approached any journalist who bothered to listen to get their stories told.

126

As a young reporter on *The Star* in the early 1990s I used to point out these injustices often. I would rail against the wanton usage of dead black bodies and the strict refusal to show dead white bodies; the assumption that it is fine to show black breasts but indecent to show white ones.

What I was railing against was really the surface of the problem. The heart of it was mindsets and changing them. It was a push to acknowledge all humanity instead of just white humanity. It was a cry to change the colour of newsrooms and newsroom leadership. And here I am, 10 years after our uhuru, accused – rightly – of the same thing.

I am black, at the time of covering these trials our news editor was black, and we are a black-owned newspaper. In a black country. What went wrong, then?

As I write, a South Korean hostage has just been beheaded by alleged Iraqi militants. He is not the first – two Americans met the same fate recently. Their stories were on the front pages of newspapers across the world. The South Korean man's story was on page seven of my newspaper and his name was in the second paragraph.

What is a life worth? Is it as valuable as its skin colour or its nationality, as the reporter Du Plessis claims? What do I, an editor of a newspaper that was launched specifically to get out of the rut of this crass, tired, offensive kind of journalism, have to say in reply? I look at my newspaper and say we have tried to do away with the *swart gevaar* mentality, where everything that was a black initiative was immediately regarded with suspicion.

I feel that many of our competitors are trying to do things better and differently. But in general we have failed. I say the battle to be vigilant and stay vigilant has to be fought every day. In every management meeting and at every news conference.

I know. As Du Plessis's piece showed, I lose it every day. But I have not lost hope yet. Although sometimes it feels like we are moving backwards, in 10 years we will hopefully not even recognise the quagmire we find ourselves in today with regard to reporting race. Ten years ago many would not recognise that the media had problems; today we fail to rectify the problems we openly admit to.

That is a victory in itself.

(Justice Malala is editor of ThisDay)

Case study 11
Sing a song of prejudice

Oh men! Oh virulent men! We need a courageous man
    to delegate to the Indians
For this matter is complicated and now needs to be
    reported to men
Indians don't want to change, even Mandela has failed
    to convince them
It was better with whites, we knew then it was a racial
    conflict
Even our leadership is not keen to get involved in this
    situation
Your buds are watering for roti and bettlenuts
Indians are not interested to cast their vote but when
    they do so they vote for whites
And their numbers fill up the Parliament and in the
    Government mould.
What do you say, Buthelezi, you're so quiet yet the
    children of [your] *Ngqengelele kaMnyamana*
    [Buthelezi's clan hierarchy]
Being turned into clowns by Indians
Zulus do not have money and are squatting in shacks
    as chattels of Indians.

Beginning of AmaNdiya,
in the translation used by the BCCSA

In early 2002, the playwright and musician
Mbongeni Ngema released a CD with the song *AmaNdiya* – The Indians.
Its Zulu lyrics were a litany of complaints against Indians. 'We struggle so
much here in Durban, as we have been dispossessed by Indians who in
turn are suppressing our people,' said one line. Some saw a few references
as disguised calls to action against Indians as a group.

The song drew strong reaction, which showed how deep tensions
between Indians and Africans still ran. The sociologist Fatima Meer called
it hate speech, and accused Ngema of making money from people's emotions.[26] Meanwhile the CD sold very well, and thousands of people attend-
ed a Durban meeting in Ngema's support, according to *City Press*.[27]

Several initiatives were launched to have the song stopped. A filmmaker, Ramesh Jethalal, obtained an interim interdict preventing the sale and distribution of the CD. He argued that the song constituted hate speech. Ironically, his argument was itself racist. In his court papers, Jethalal said Africans were criminals, carriers of HIV, and uneducated.[28] The interdict was later lifted, although the Film and Publications Board ruled it could only be distributed to people over 18.

The Human Rights Commission (HRC) lodged a complaint with the Broadcasting Complaints Commission of South Africa (BCCSA) on the grounds that it contravened the constitutional ban on hate speech, and therefore fell foul of the broadcasting code. The specific broadcast cited in the HRC complaint occurred in an evening current affairs programme on Ukhozi FM, the SABC's Zulu language radio station, and was used to start a discussion of the issue.[29]

The BCCSA took a different view from the Durban High Court. The BCCSA tribunal:
- accepted Ngema's bona fide intention to begin a debate;
- but found that the song demeaned Indians;
- ruled that the song's language went further than allowed in the Constitution and broadcasting code, since it
  — 'promoted hate in sweeping, emotive language against Indians as a race';
  — 'constituted incitement to fear for their safety'; and
  — violated Indians' right to dignity, as protected in the Constitution; and
- found that the song's use by Ukhozi to start a discussion did not contravene the code, since it was done to 'inform the debate'.[30]

The decision was widely reported as constituting a ban on the broadcast of the song, even though the BCCSA has no such powers.[31] Ngema denounced the BCCSA's hearing as a kangaroo court,[32] but later gloated that all the controversy had given him millions of rands' worth of free publicity.[33]

There is no question that *AmaNdiya* is a deeply offensive song. But as the various hearings highlighted, that is not enough to bring it within the constitutional provisions on hate speech. That requires 'incitement to cause harm'. The Durban High Court said there had been no incidents of violence between Africans and Indians as a result of the song, and therefore allowed the song's distribution.

But the BCCSA took a different view. Taking its cue from some Canadian and German precedents on hate speech, it said a legal limit should be placed on sweeping racial slurs in 'our young democracy, where we are still building unity amongst diverse groupings'. The BCCSA also found it was irrelevant whether there was a likelihood of real attack. It was enough that there was a likelihood of fear.

As heated as it was, the debate on Ngema's song did not settle the question of where the South African courts will draw the line between offensive, but not illegal, statements and constitutionally proscribed hate speech. Dealing with the CD's distribution, the Durban High Court initially took one view. Dealing with the song's broadcast, the BCCSA took another view. But from the point of view of journalism ethics, the last finding by the BCCSA is the most significant.

The commission said that for purposes of journalism and stimulating debate, it was acceptable to play the song – even though it deemed it to be hate speech, which is several degrees worse than simple racist speech. The BCCSA also found that Ukhozi's use of the song was bona fide, and not 'a veil'.

It is indeed important to write clearly about racism, and that may include repeating offensive material. Of course, each case should be judged on its merits. Such material should not lightly be repeated, but it is justified if it is necessary for audiences to understand the story properly. In this case, there was no question: much of the sentiments of Ngema's song were tucked into fairly subtle language, which needed to be seen or heard in full in order to be understood.

Case study 12
Hey there, big spender!

Barney Pityana has had several clashes with the media. As chairperson of the HRC, he presided over its fractious inquiry into racism in the media. After leaving the commission, he took over as vice-chancellor of the troubled University of South Africa (Unisa), the giant distance-learning institution. In May 2002 the *Mail&Guardian* published a report containing a litany of allegations of overspending against Pityana.[34] The report was headlined 'Barney's binge spending', and the front page was turned into a poster with the headline 'Hey there, big spender!'

The most important claims were that:

- the university had spent R1.7 million to reverse the sale of Cloghereen, the official residence of the vice-chancellor, and was planning to spend millions more to refurbish it so that Pityana could move in;
- R1.5 million was to be spent on refurbishing his offices; and
- Unisa was flying top management and council members to Mauritius to hold a graduation ceremony.

The report also said Pityana had refused to answer questions on the issue.

A few days after the report appeared, Pityana called a media conference. He claimed the *Mail&Guardian* had allowed itself to be used by dissatisfied members of the university to further a 'not-so-veiled racist plot'.[35] He singled out the paper's reporter at the media conference, and accused him of behaving like the old security police by using anonymous sources. 'I will expose him for the fraud he is,' Pityana said.

He defended the decision to cancel the sale of Cloghereen as it had been sold on unfavourable terms. The university would not have been able to replace it for the money its sale had brought, he said. He also defended the refurbishment of his offices, saying Unisa needed to be given an '*ubuntu* feel', and confirmed that a graduation ceremony would be held in Mauritius. He also said that it was 'a lie' to say he had refused to answer questions on the claims, saying he had asked for further clarification before responding.

It later emerged that the return fax to the *Mail&Guardian* had not been sent off before the publication's deadline.

So was the report a racist plot, as Pityana alleged, or was it legitimate exposure of corruption? Of course the paper rejected the accusation out of hand. Under the headline 'Pityana won't trump us with race card' it argued: 'Underlying Pityana's behaviour is the same assumption that underpinned the Human Rights Commission's notorious probe into media racism, Pityana's baby. It is that the dignity (read immunity from harsh criticism) of black public figures is sacrosanct and that white critics should keep their traps shut.'[36]

Certainly Pityana's personal attack on the reporter was outrageous, and he needs to take responsibility for his organisation's failure to get his answering fax off in time. But the paper's statement that he had 'refused' to answer the questions was not accurate either. It would have been better to set out in more detail what efforts had been made to get his comment.

The report relies almost entirely on unnamed sources. In the light of the notoriously bitter infighting raging at Unisa at the time, it seems likely that at least some of those sources were pursuing their own agendas. That is not enough on its own to disqualify the information, but it does increase the need to corroborate it. While this may have been done, the report does not demonstrate clearly enough what steps were taken to check the claims.

Pityana did afterwards acknowledge several of the most important claims, but his core defence was that they constituted justified spending. The paper did not do enough to establish whether the spending was reasonable or not. Certainly the claim that Cloghereen had been sold for too little seems to justify the decision to cancel the sale. Local estate agents would most likely have been able to corroborate or dispute the property's valuation.

The tone of the report attracted criticism. Particularly the front-page headline, 'Hey there, big spender!', seemed to stray into gotcha journalism. Thloloe says it was 'the tone of the writing that was offensive to many people, not the facts. Exposing the facts isn't the issue, but if we adopt a tone that seems to say that the new leadership, the new elite [can't be trusted], somehow it smacks of racism.'[37] And Mondli Makhanya, who took over editorship of the paper later, said that although the facts were true they did not necessarily justify characterising Pityana as a spendthrift.

Weaknesses in the report and its handling can be identified, but do they support Pityana's charge of a racist agenda? Because it is so hard to prove racism, judgments of cases like this remain subjective. Some people will see no other possible explanation for the tone of the *Mail&Guardian* report than a deep desire to prove the corruption and inability of the new black elite. Others will see it as journalists doing their job.

Perhaps the most definitive statement one can make is that race can never be a reason to cover up real cases of corruption. But where race is a factor, there is a particular duty to be careful with the facts and the tone of the report.

Case study 13
Arms, race

The minister of defence, Joe Modise, was furious. He was setting off to the Middle East to try to rescue a R7-billion arms deal. 'My chances are very, very, very slim. I'm going to go down on my knees to try to persuade them. But I am doubtful the deal will be signed.'[38] He had promised confidentiality to the country involved, Saudi Arabia, but details had been published in overseas media and then, in July 1997, in the *Sunday Independent* and its sister newspapers.

An angry Modise said: 'We were placed in this humiliating position because of our own press, which is supposed to be working in the interest of the South African public.' The leak had been a deliberate ploy to undermine the government's business. Modise rejected the argument that the public had a right to know who South Africa was selling arms to. 'I don't think our people want to know. Not at that price. I don't think our people want to see thousands of people jobless in the streets just because we could not meet the conditions of the deal.'

The arms manufacturer Denel had made concerted attempts to block publication, obtaining a court interdict and even laying criminal charges under an apartheid-era secrecy law that was still on the statute book. But these had failed. The newspaper justified its decision to publish on the basis of public interest. The editor, John Battersby, said in reference to the court interdict: 'We will abide by the decisions of the court, but we will do everything in our power to defend the public's right to know.'[39]

The issue quickly turned into a wider row about race and the role of the media. Support of the government's position came from two prominent black journalists, the publisher of Mafube Publishing, Thami Mazwai, and the veteran journalist Jon Qwelane, at the time editor of *Enterprise*, one of Mafube's titles.

Calling for a patriotic media, Mazwai suggested in various columns that the national interest – in this case the benefit in terms of investment and jobs – should take precedence over the public's right to know. 'That no black editor has come out in support of disclosure of Saudi Arabia as the destination for South African arms speaks volumes. It is not surprising that we are not caught in an identity crisis in which we have to be South African, Irish, American and European all at the same time.'[40] Elsewhere, he said the case showed up the problem of continuing foreign and white ownership. The decision to identify Saudi Arabia 'did not take our national interest into account, it looked at British national interest'.[41]

There they were, the big issues of the post-apartheid media, all on the table because of an arms deal: transformation, role, and race. For our purpose, we should first consider whether the *Sunday Independent* was justified in publishing details of the deal.

Selling arms is a profoundly political matter, and has to take into account where and how those weapons are likely to be used. Even aside from the moral questions that arise, supplying weapons to a particular country is a gesture of support, and is used in this way in international diplomacy. Presenting the potential deal with Saudi Arabia as simply a matter of business and jobs, as Modise did, was disingenuous.

The deal could have had major implications for South Africa's foreign relations. This is not the place to assess them, or to suggest that the deal would have been a bad one for the country. Perhaps it would have been a very good thing. But negative or positive, such matters deserve full public scrutiny in a democracy. In any event, the fact that the deal was being reported abroad made it just silly to try to keep it secret within the country. The *Sunday Independent* was quite right to run the story.

The debate served as a particularly neat illustration of why the media prefer to think of themselves as serving the public rather than the national interest, as discussed in Chapter 2. The case showed how those with political power also have the power to define the national interest. The minister defined the deal as being about commercial and employment benefits, ignoring all the other ramifications. In the concept of public interest, on the other hand, citizens are the starting point. When we use this idea, it becomes much harder to find good reasons to keep things secret and out of the public domain. If citizens matter most, as they should in a democracy, there can't be many situations when it's better for them to be kept in the dark.

But what about race? Mazwai cast the dispute as one between the new, democratic government and white journalists who had difficulty in accepting its authority. Researcher Sean Jacobs says Mazwai's 'developmentalist' view of the media's role was set against a 'liberal-humanist' view, articulated mainly by white editors and journalists.[42]

It is undeniable that there are different traditions in the South African media, which often – but not always – coincide with racial divisions. But the row needs to be understood in the context of its time. In 1997, tensions around race and the media were high. Then President Nelson Mandela had launched several attacks on an industry where white interests were still dominant. Soon afterwards – in late 1998 – the HRC launched its inquiry into racism, discussed in Chapter 2.

The industry was undergoing massive change in those years. By 2004, black editors were no longer a rarity. Mazwai was later appointed to the

SABC board and continued to argue for a patriotic media. But his position was an isolated one. The mainstream view among white and black editors was that a healthy independence of government should be maintained. This could be done while still embracing the new South Africa and its values and projects: non-racism, democracy, the fight against poverty, and others. Loyalty to the Constitution as the expression of the national compact was fine, but appeals to patriotism should be treated with caution.

. . . .

NOTES

1   Lynette Steenveld, 'Defining the undefinable' in *Rhodes Journalism Review* 19, August 2000. 11.

2   Quoted in ibid.

3   South African Human Rights Commission (SAHRC), *Faultlines: Inquiry into racism in the media*. Johannesburg: SAHRC, 2000. 80.

4   Press Ombudsman of South Africa, 'Press code of professional practice'. Johannesburg: Press Ombudsman of South Africa, 2001.

5   Interview, 2 September 2002.

6   Interview, 15 October 2002.

7   Keith Woods, 'The language of race', July 1999. Posted at http://www.poynter.org/content/content_view.asp?id=5468, accessed 20 March 2004.

8   Interview, 18 October 2002.

9   Interview, 2002.

10   Interview, 11 December 2002

11   Mansford Danso and David McDonald, 'Writing xenophobia: immigration and the press in post-apartheid South Africa'. Cape Town: Idasa (Institute for Democracy in South Africa), 2000. 17.

12   Interview, 2002.

13   Interview, 18 October 2002.

14   Interview, July 2002.

15   Christine Qunta, 'Of penguins and pigment', *Business Day*, 4 August 2000.

16   Interview, 7 November 2002.

17   Reprinted in the *Mail&Guardian*, 6–12 June 2003.

18   *Mail&Guardian*, 6–12 June 2003.

19   Interview 17 July 2002.

20   Jonny Steinberg, 'Census rumours grist to farmers' mill again', *Business Day*, 10 October 2002.

21　Keith Woods, 'An essay on a wickedly powerful word', November 1995. Posted at http://www.poynter.org/content/content_view.asp?id=5603, accessed on 20 March 2004.

22　Interview, 2002.

23　In the Independent Newspapers' submission to the TRC.

24　SAHRC, *Faultlines*. 19.

25　Interview, 11 December 2002.

26　*City Press*, 30 July 2002.

27　*City Press*, 23 June 2002.

28　*City Press*, 16 June 2002.

29　BCCSA ruling, case no 2002/31, SABC – 'Ngema song'.

30　Ibid.

31　However, any broadcaster would understand the strong statement of its undesirability as a warning that its use would be frowned on by the BCCSA.

32　*City Press*, 30 July 2002.

33　*The Independent on Saturday*, 28 June 2002.

34　*Mail&Guardian*, 23–29 May 2002,

35　*Daily News*, 29 May 2002.

36　*Mail&Guardian*, 31 May – 6 June 2002.

37　Interview, 2 September 2002.

38　*Cape Times*, 8 August 1997.

39　Quoted in Sean Jacobs, 'Tensions of a free press: South Africa after apartheid'. Research paper R-22, Joan Schorenstein Center on the Press, Politics and Public Policy, Harvard University. Cambridge, MA: Joan Schorenstein Center, June 1999. Footnote 31

40　*Business Day*, 15 August 1996, quoted in Jacobs, 'Tensions of a free press'. 6.

41　Thami Mazwai, 'Address to the Black Management Forum's 2001 annual conference'. Posted at http://www.bmfonline.co.za/thami.htm, accessed on 15 January 2004.

42　Jacobs, 'Tensions of a free press'. 6–7.

Our use of language should reflect not only changes in society but also our values as a progressive news organisation. Phrases still abound which suggest that certain activities are the preserve of males only.
E.tv: Ethical Code

Broadcasters shall not broadcast material which, judged within context, sanctions, promotes or glamorises any aspect of violence against women.
Icasa: Code of Conduct for Broadcasters

Broadcasters recognize the changing interaction of women and men in today's society. Women and men shall be portrayed, in programming, in a wide range of roles, both traditional and non-traditional, in paid work, social, family and leisure activities.
Canadian Broadcast Standards Council: Sex Role Portrayal Code for Television and Radio Programming

8

THE NEXT FRONTIER: GENDER

The story described an incident in which a policeman had shot his girlfriend twice, killing her. He then turned the gun on himself, but was only injured. The *Sowetan*'s headline: 'Suicidal cop fights for life.'[1] The woman who died rated no mention in the headline. Another story described an incident in which a husband came across his wife and a policeman at a braai. He shot both of them and then himself. All three died. *The Star*'s headline: 'Policeman among 3 killed as lovers' tiff ends in tragedy.'[2] Again, the woman did not make it into the headline. And does the expression 'lovers' tiff' properly describe an incident in which a man kills three people?

This kind of reporting removes the women from the picture as if they didn't matter, and trivialises a major crisis in South African society. The country has very high rates of rape, domestic violence and of women being murdered by their intimate partners. The issues deserve more serious and thoughtful treatment than shown in these examples.

Gender issues remain a blind spot in our journalism. Racism also remains a deep-rooted problem, but it has become seriously unfashionable to admit to racial prejudice. Newsrooms have developed an acute awareness of racism, and often have clear guidelines on how to deal with the issue, at least at an overt level. Much of the debate now focuses on unconscious forms of racism.

But the discussion on gender is much less well developed. It is generally regarded as the concern of gender activists and NGOs, something to be smiled about indulgently. Chris Vick, at the time group editorial training director of Independent Newspapers, calls it the 'fringe' issue. He cites *The Star*'s extensive coverage of the Truth Commission's media hearings, which left out just one presentation, the only one that dealt with gender issues. 'Is it not newsworthy when one of the country's few black women journalists [NomaVenda Mathiane] declares: "For years, editors and news editors have relegated black women journalists to fill the women's pages. Women were kept down." ... Maybe it's not newsworthy if you're a man.'[3]

Of course the dismissive attitude to gender that is common in newsrooms is itself a reflection of the broader problem. In that sense, gender is the next area of prejudice and discrimination to be conquered – the next frontier.

In 2003 the South African National Editors' Forum (Sanef) decided to focus its annual general meeting on the issue. Several groups and individuals gave input, and as a result the organisation decided on a number of steps. It said it would facilitate workshops to improve coverage of gender issues; develop a database of women experts; and called for gender-sensitive style guides and procedures.[4] These decisions marked an important step forward, although much remains to be done.

Race and gender are often lumped together, and indeed there are many similarities between the issues that arise in the two areas. But there are enough significant differences to warrant a separate investigation of gender coverage from an ethical perspective.

"What, in the end, could be more central to free speech than that every segment of society should have a voice? And what more fundamental and cross-cutting faultline is there in every one of our societies than that between men and women?"[5]

Athalia Molokomme, head of the Southern African Development Community's Gender Unit

Just as we have seen in the context of race, gender is clearly an issue of ethics. The argument is worth repeating in this context. It involves questions of *accuracy*, since stereotypes distort reality, both at an individual and at a social level. It involves *fairness*, since reporting that ignores women's perspectives leaves out a critical perspective. It involves *independence*, since it often shows an inability to distance ourselves from our own deep-seated prejudices. It involves *harm*, since stereotypes reinforce habits of mind that lead to harmful practices of various kinds. And it involves *accountability*, since it ignores about half of almost every audience.

For many, the responsibility goes a step further, to play an active role in challenging and changing harmful practices and beliefs. The gender policy of the Media Institute of Southern Africa (Misa) says: 'As an agenda setter, the media has a duty to portray not just what is, but what could be.'[6] This means that journalists have a duty to challenge stereotypes when they come up, for instance, not just report them.

Gender or sex

Sex refers to the biological differences between men and women. It is not to be confused with gender, which the gender activist Colleen Lowe Morna defines as 'the way in which society assigns characteristics and social roles to men and women'.[7] She points out that almost all societies have attached greater value to the roles, functions and characteristics attributed to men. 'Gender inequality creates power imbalances in society, and limits the potential of both men and women,' she writes.

Her formulation highlights an important point: gender issues are not only about women. Where men are typecast as tough and aggressive, they are just as unfairly treated as when women are typecast as meek and submissive. Elsewhere, Lowe Morna makes this comparison: 'Just as the ending of apartheid benefited black as well as white South Africans, gender equality has advantages for men, for the economy, for democracy, governance, participation etc.'[8]

POTENTIAL PROBLEM AREAS

Lowe Morna describes a 'triangular test' for measuring the extent of gender awareness in coverage.[9] This looks at:
• the **breadth** of coverage: whether the full range of stories affecting women is dealt with;

- the **depth** of coverage, which includes the sources consulted, and the revelation of hidden stories; and
- the **angle** from which a story is told.

It is an interesting tool, which neatly summarises the possible problem areas.

The problem of stereotypes

Journalism is vulnerable to stereotypes, partly because of the speed with which the daily 'first draft of history' has to be compiled. When deadlines loom, it is easier to fall back on tried and tested assumptions and patterns of thought. It needs effort and time to break away from established formulas like stereotypes.

Ironically, journalism is vulnerable in a deeper sense because one of its core values is the search for the unusual. Stories become interesting because they deal with things that are unexpected or surprising. A famous and often repeated example demonstrates the principle: dog bites man isn't a story; man bites dog is. But every time we single out something as unusual, we simultaneously demonstrate our view of what is normal. For instance, crime is a story because it disrupts our expectation of a normal, stable society. Similarly, when we describe a rape survivor as 'conservatively dressed', for instance, we expose our own belief that it is more usual for women to be raped if they are 'provocatively dressed'. And that in turn is based on a whole set of fallacious assumptions about the nature of rape.

As the Stellenbosch University ethicist Johan Retief points out, many different groups are stereotyped. Unfair labels apply to 'fat people (they are "lazy"), politicians (thought to lack moral principles), the elderly ("slow, forgetful, childlike, stubborn"), the handicapped ("helpless, vulnerable"), and to teenagers, teachers, construction workers, farmers, clergymen, lawyers, doctors, homosexuals and bankers. The list is seemingly endless.'[11]

Some prejudices are more harmful than others. The more profound the discrimination a group suffers, the more harmful are the attitudes that feed these practices. Groups in this category include gays and lesbians, the disabled (a better word than handicapped) and some national and religious groups. We have already investigated the issue of racist stereotypes,

> "P3's titillating tit-bits are just what the doctor ordered – as a tonic against all the world's gloomy news. Research has shown that the *Sun's* famous glamour pictures are a vital bit of cheer for readers depressed by strikes, deaths and disasters."[10]
>
> *The British tabloid Daily Sun on its daily use of a topless young woman's picture on page three*

and will here concentrate on gender issues. However, much of the discussion can be applied to other areas of stereotyping.

Women generally appear in the media in a limited range of roles: they are housewives, victims or simply decoration. The Gender and Media Baseline Study analysed 25 South African news media and found that women outnumbered men in only three occupational categories: beauty contestants, sex workers and homemakers.[12] Even though women are involved in every aspect of life, they rarely appear in these roles.[13] Professor Lizette Rabe of Stellenbosch University points out that the media identify women in terms of their family or marital status, while men are identified by their professional status.[14]

Women are commonly used in advertisements as decoration – the clichéd picture of a beautiful woman draped over the hood of a car springs to mind. The famous 'page three girl' has found its way from British newspapers like *The Sun* into South Africa's new tabloid press.

Even in the news pages, fashion or similar photographs are common, and stories are often used simply because they provide an opportunity to use a picture of a beautiful young woman. The photographer Peter McKenzie says: 'Negative gender images on billboards, newspapers, television and magazines can significantly contribute to sexist attitudes and behaviour.'[15] Related to this is the practice of describing a woman's physical appearance in copy when it is not really relevant to the article.

Profiles of women in public life illustrate the problem with stereotypes. There is often significant focus on the woman's ability to be a homemaker and mother as well as follow a career. Some people take offence at this, arguing – correctly – that nobody asks a man about his domestic arrangements.

The problem is that women still often have to do much more juggling of career and family than men do. In that sense, a rounded picture of a successful woman can justifiably sketch this aspect of her life. Perhaps profiles of men should be criticised if they ignore the question of who is keeping the home fires burning while he builds a career.

"Too frequently we have negative images of women, when they are victims ... We started putting pictures in the paper which very often were sleazy pictures, someone with their boobs hanging out. And I felt we were being a bit degrading and we needed more positive images. Most of our images of women in the past have been sufferers of abuse, victims of violence, which is really not the image we should be pushing for. We need to go out and find successful people, or people who are making a difference, and portray them in a very positive light. Something people can aspire to."[16]
Robin Comley, pictures editor at The Star

The other very common stereotype is that of the woman as victim. A researcher at the Media Monitoring Project, Phumla Mthala, writes: 'There is near invisibility of black women in the news, and where they do appear, it is still mostly in the following stories: underdevelopment, oppressive traditions, high illiteracy and urban poverty, religious fanaticism, overpopulation, disasters (burning of shacks) and violence against women. In these items, they mainly appear as victims and people who have absolutely no control over their destinies.'[17]

She says it is true that black women are 'largely uneducated, are victims of violence and live in abject poverty'. But that does not justify the stereotype. The challenge, she says, is not merely to reflect society but to change it. 'The structures and social practices of racism are starting to be challenged by the media, but journalists have the added challenge and responsibility to represent black women in all their diversity,' she writes.

Language

The language we use reflects some very ancient prejudices. For instance, the use of 'man' as a synonym for the human race clearly identifies humanity as essentially male, which relegates women to a secondary status. *The new word power* says: 'Just as there is no longer any justification for perpetuating racist stereotypes and bias in one's use of language, so sexist language is increasingly being regarded as indicative of lack of education or extreme subjectivity on the part of the speaker or writer.'[18]

Many newsrooms have some level of awareness of these issues, and will discourage the use of discriminatory language. Areas to watch out for include the following:

Perhaps the most difficult challenge to solve elegantly is the generic male pronoun. Misa's head of broadcasting, Tracey Naughton, writes: 'By using he, his, or him as a generic pronoun when the referent's gender is unknown or irrelevant, the writer misrepresents the species as male.'[19] She suggests four possible solutions:

- restructure the sentence to avoid pronouns;
- use plurals;
- use a first-person perspective; or
- use the passive voice.

Another set of difficulties arises because English has many compound

"At one lively meeting I questioned the double standards when the *Daily News* referred to a woman who owned a brothel that had been raided as a 'sex queen', while her clients were referred to as 'businessmen'."[20]
Reyhana Masters-Smith, former deputy features editor at the Zimbabwean Daily News

words that use the suffix -*man*. With a little thought, alternatives can generally be found. Style guides would do well to build up a list of preferred equivalents. Some examples are:

- executive, instead of businessman
- labour, instead of manpower
- average person, instead of man in the street
- police officer, instead of policeman (in South Africa, the police's own usage of 'member' sometimes creeps into general use. This is a particularly ugly choice, and best avoided.)
- chair, or chairperson, instead of chairman (some organisations prefer to retain chairman when a man is involved, but balance it with chairwoman otherwise)
- representative, or official, instead of spokesman

The suffix -*ess* is dropping away. Actor and author, for instance, now generally refer to both men and women, and the usage of actress and authoress has become rare.

The term 'rape victim' should be replaced with 'rape survivor'. The word 'victim' is held to underline powerlessness, whereas survivor emphasises the positive.

Another problem area arises in some terms used to refer to women. 'Girls' should be used only in the context of children, and 'chicks' and other demeaning or patronising terms should be avoided entirely.

Diverse sources

The Gender and Media Baseline Study found that women made up just 19 per cent of news sources in South Africa. This compared to a figure of 17 per cent internationally. Particularly low scores were found in sport (5 per cent), politics (10) and economics (9), while even on the subject of gender equality they were outnumbered significantly by men (36 compared to 58).[21]

These discrepancies are partly due to the real gender imbalance among newsmakers. As long as most economists are men, journalists will quote more men in economic stories. But this does not account for the discrepancy in politics: women accounted for only 10 per cent[22] of sources even though they make up 31 per cent of Parliament and of the cabinet.

In many cases, journalists have no choice in who to quote. If a male minister announces a new initiative, then that is who gets quoted. But in many other cases they do. Although most economists are men, there is a significant and growing number of women in the field who can be accessed with a bit of effort. Many organisations now have a policy of seeking out black and women experts. The news editor of YFM, Hope Mahlangu, says: 'We try to get female commentators for most stories, it's not an easy task.'[23] She says a directory compiled by the Commission on Gender Equality helps in this task.

Missing stories and perspectives

Closely linked to the discussion of sourcing is the question of the absence of female perspectives and stories. Men and women are affected differently by many developments, and too few stories deal with these differences. This has several dimensions. We have already discussed the need to include women commentators in stories of general interest. This may provide a different perspective on the story, but it need not.

The need to find additional perspectives becomes even more pressing when we are dealing with stories that have particular implications for women. In 1999, the Harare Supreme Court ruled that women could not inherit their fathers' estates if there were male children alive.[24] *The Herald* covered the court case, quoting at length from the judgment. No other sources were accessed. Either in the report itself, or in a follow-up story, there was an obvious need to canvass some commentary on the implications of the ruling.

The baseline study mentioned above refers to 'gender-blind reporting' – where obvious gender implications are ignored. Stories on poverty often refer to the effects on people, without dealing with the fact that men and women are affected differently. As a particular example, it points to an SABC 1 report on the end of the World Summit for Sustainable Development. The report summed up the summit's successes and failures. It quoted five men and no women, offered no gender perspective on the summit's main themes, and failed to mention an important dispute about the wording to be used on women's rights.[25]

In fact, when we begin looking in this direction we find that there is a wealth of valuable stories worth covering. Given a statistic on children's enrolment in

"It is a sad fact that one of the few profoundly non-racial institutions in South Africa is patriarchy. Amongst the multiple chauvinisms which abound in our country, the male version rears itself with special equal vigour in communities ... Patriarchy brutalises men and neutralises women across the colour line."[26]
Judge Albie Sachs

144

schools, for instance, teasing out the different figures for boys and girls could reveal an interesting story. It does sometimes take more work – this kind of investigation requires a willingness to move beyond a few phone calls to the obvious sources.

Violence against women is one area that has seen some greater attention in the media. But problems remain in the way in which the subject is treated. As we saw in the examples cited at the beginning of this chapter, incidents are trivialised or lack context, the women are ignored or are represented as having 'asked for it'. Other accounts draw heavily on the 'victim' stereotype, which also writes them out of their own story.

The word 'victim' itself is increasingly being seen as having too much stereotypical baggage. It is being replaced with the word 'survivor' – signalling a significant shift of emphasis.

> "Well, pre-affirmative action, when I was looking for jobs early on, people said, out loud and without any hesitation, 'We don't hire women to do that. We will not hire women to deliver the news. Their voices are not authoritative. We don't hire women as writers. Men would have to work for them, and we can't have that.' It was overt, and nobody was even embarrassed about it."[28]
> *ABC newscaster Cokie Roberts*

Diverse newsrooms

The gender baseline study also investigated the balance among those who report the news. It found that black women accounted for only 6 per cent of the media practitioners in the study.[27] Women were best represented in the category of TV and radio presenters, with a share of 44 per cent. It also found that men predominated in all beats, particularly in the 'serious' ones of economics, politics and sports.

Unfortunately the study has severe limitations in that it concentrates only on bylines. It is not clear how it deals with agency stories, or with those without a byline. It also concentrates only on the 'front-of-house' jobs – reporters and presenters. No account at all is taken of those often-influential job categories that operate behind the scenes – the producers, sub-editors, and so on.

Nevertheless, we can accept the basic point that men still dominate newsrooms. This is particularly true at senior levels. South Africa still has very few women editors. It is also true that the imbalance is greater on beats like politics and economics.

Women journalists sometimes face particular challenges. Shift times, the availability of transport and childcare facilities all impact on women journalists differently from their male colleagues. The former parliamentary editor for Independent Newspapers, Zubeida Jaffer, describes how easily politicians read normal friendliness as some sort of sexual signal. She says: 'You know, normally one banters and it gets the person relaxed, and then somebody wants to put their arms around you or something, you don't know what the hell to do!'[29]

Where organisations make the effort to create more diverse newsrooms, it is more likely that gender issues will be taken seriously. The rewards can be substantial. Perspectives are broadened by taking in voices, concerns and issues that otherwise would remain unexplored. Rather than being a threat, the challenge of gender represents an opportunity to do better journalism by telling more stories better.

Gender:
a test of five questions

Journalists should ask these questions to check their reporting:
1. Does the story reinforce, accept or challenge gender stereotypes?
2. Is there sufficient context?
3. Does the story contain sexist language?
4. Have you made an effort to include women's voices?
5. Are there gender perspectives on the issue that need exploring?

No change at the bottom of the pile

NomaVenda Mathiane

There was a time when African journalists used to complain that when two youths – a white and a black – join the newsroom, the powers-that-be see a future leader in the white boy, while the black one will be relegated to the newsroom forever.

I have always wondered what would have happened had Nat Nakasa not left the country and chosen exile. What were his chances of becoming an editor at the *Rand Daily Mail*? Why was Doc Bikitsha never given a prominent position at the *Sunday Times*? And why was Sophie Tema, who wrote for *The World*, elbowed out of journalism in spite of the contribution she made to that publication?

In order not to lose perspective, it is important to make a clear distinction between coloured, Indian and African journalists because the black generic term is often confusing and misleading. Coloured and Indian male journalists have always been next to power. These were succeeded by Indian and coloured women journalists. They are next to their white sisters.

With the political change of 1994, we have seen our African brothers become editors and managers. Alas, they have not taken their African sisters along. The African woman journalist is still in the newsroom reporting and nowhere near decision-making. Women journalists are still given soft stories such as covering health issues, education and social pages while the male journalists do hard-core beats such as covering Parliament, interviewing politicians and covering elections.

Newsrooms are still not welcoming to African women reporters. Women are not only marginalised, their opinion in most cases counts for nothing.

In my case, in 1997 I was assigned to cover the local elections at most rural areas in KwaZulu-Natal as well as townships around Cape Town and East London. The week before I set off, the editor in charge of those pages invited my fellow male journalists who were on the beat for a strategy meeting. I was not invited. They came out of the meeting and told me where I would be going and when.

There are those who argue that African women are not assertive and do not market themselves. To a large extent that could be true. Unlike our white sisters who grew up in a business environment, and learnt the ropes from their parents, the African girl was not raised to be assertive. Fortunately this is changing. We have raised our daughters differently.

In those newsrooms where there has been change, it happened because someone at the top wanted it to happen.

If newsrooms are to change and the quality of newspapers too, then the editors must stop giving lip service to diversity. As we start the new millennium with African editors at the helm, we are going to look up to them to right the wrongs of the past.

If the lot of women journalists, African women journalists in particular, is to change, then we are going to need all the help we can get.

(NomaVenda Mathiane is a journalist)

Case study 14
Classroom temptresses

In September 2002 *The Chronicle* in Zimbabwe published a report that the ministry of education, sport and culture was banning female teachers from wearing mini-skirts, tight clothes and trousers which 'revealed too much of their bodies' and dresses and skirts with 'long revealing slits'.[30]

The report quoted the circular issued by the ministry's permanent secretary as justifying the ban by the need to avoid exciting schoolboys. 'They can wear trousers with a jersey or jacket covering their backs. We don't want trousers that show the body too much … we are not saying there is anything wrong with a woman's body, but young boys will admire too much and become a problem.'

The unnamed male permanent secretary refers to community and cultural sensibilities as another reason for the ban: 'In general, women must at all times wear decent clothing, avoiding any dressing that may attract disapproval from the communities they serve.' A dress code is also imposed on male teachers, but it refers only to men wearing suits, jackets and ties during the appropriate season of the year.

The Gender and Media Baseline Study, which describes the case, notes that the issue of women's dress 'is linked to "decency" and suggestive behaviour, while the men's dress is seen in the context of "maintaining dignity and formality."' It adds:

> The story also sends out the message that women must dress with young boys in mind. Neither the circular nor the story questions the notion that young schoolboys are viewing their teachers as sex objects. It is inferred that this is 'normal male behaviour', and that women should change the way they dress. Women are therefore viewed as objects for the pleasure of men, regardless of age. Young boy students are in effect set out as superior to their older female teachers.

The study may be overinterpreting the story to some extent. It is perfectly normal for pubescent schoolchildren to weave sexual fantasies around their teachers. This is generally quite innocent, and involves both boys and girls. The ministry is at fault in thinking that girls don't develop crushes on their teachers. In that sense, there is a strong gender bias at work in the ministry's decision, as if girls and women don't think about sex.

Certainly, the ministry can be strongly criticised for making the women teachers responsible for the alleged predatory sexual responses of the boys they teach. If there is such a problem, then the responsibility should remain where it belongs: with the boys. The women should be free to choose how they dress. If there are any concerns about people dressing so informally as to undermine teachers' dignity, they should apply to men and women equally.

The study's commentary does too little to separate the report from its subject: the prejudices at the heart of the ministry's decision are not necessarily the reporter's. The story represents the reality of some very old-fashioned attitudes.

Having said that, though, the story misses an opportunity to subject the ministry's attitude to some critical scrutiny. The only source quoted is the ministry's own circular. Affected teachers, lobby groups and observers could be tapped to put the decision into a broader perspective. In that way, the report could have challenged stereotypes and prejudices rather than simply accept them uncritically. It would have made for a richer, better story.

Case study 15
Judging judges

Here's a case study where the media got it right. It is also different from most others in that it deals with the handling of a story by the media in general, not just a particular report in one outlet.

A Cape High Court judge, John Foxcroft, caused an outcry when he sentenced an Elsies River man to seven years in jail for raping his 14-year-old daughter. The sentence, handed down in October 1999, was widely seen as lenient, despite legal requirements that a life sentence be handed down in particular types of rape cases, including those involving a woman under 16 years of age.[31] Judges are allowed to impose lesser sentences if there are 'substantial and compelling circumstances'.

Foxcroft found grounds to be lenient in the fact that the community was not threatened since the rape had occurred within the family. He said: 'Although it is morally reprehensible to rape one's own child, the man's sexual deviancy was limited to his own family.'[32]

Reaction came swiftly. Rape Crisis called it 'absolutely appalling'.[33] A parliamentary committee said it would call him to explain his reasoning – although it later backtracked after concerns that the move might infringe judicial independence.[34] Even the minister of justice, Penuell Maduna, entered the row. 'I know that, as the father of two daughters, it would never be acceptable that my daughters are not safe from me as their father,' he said.[35]

The media participated vociferously in the criticism, devoting a good deal of space to the issue. Journalists actively sought out comment from critical groups and developed follow-up stories, columns were written about the wrong-headedness of the ruling and the need to transform the judiciary. The *Sunday Times* wrote in an editorial: 'Somewhere in Elsie's River a child weeps: betrayed by her father, who raped her; betrayed by the criminal justice system, which failed her.'[36]

The state appealed against the sentence, and the Appeal Court criticised Foxcroft's ruling and increased the sentence to 12 years (which was still regarded as inadequate by many groups). In the wake of the outcry, Cape Town judges reportedly handed down 'a steady stream of life sentences' in cases where fathers raped their children.[37]

It would be wrong to see the public furore around the issue as created by the media. It was the result of real public concern about rape in South

Africa. Parliament, the Commission on Gender Equality, NGOs and other groups took various steps quite independently of the media. But the discussion took place largely in the media, and journalists participated enthusiastically. They caught a popular mood, and used it to raise further awareness of an important issue.

The row around Foxcroft's judgment showed the media going further than simply reporting an event, and actively challenged old, harmful attitudes. It is difficult to say categorically that the outcry influenced judicial thinking on rape, but it is hard to imagine that it did not have some effect.

Case study 16
The judge, the activist and the husband

It had been a long, pleasant evening for South African delegates to the World Social Forum in Mumbai, India, with dinner, clubbing and drinks. Eventually, long after midnight, the group dispersed to their hotel rooms. But Salome Isaacs, an Aids activist from Bela Bela in Limpopo province, decided she needed to discuss the conference programme with another delegate, the Cape High Court judge Siraj Desai. Around 3 a.m., she sent him an SMS to that effect, she later said, and then went to see him in his room.[38]

What exactly happened there is a matter of some dispute, but very shortly afterwards, Radio 702 in distant Johannesburg received a call from Isaacs's husband. It was around 2.30 a.m. in Johannesburg, and a distraught Mark Isaacs asked for a reporter. When told there was nobody available, he told the DJ on air that his wife had been raped by Desai in Mumbai. He claimed to have phoned his wife regularly throughout the night because he had a sense of foreboding. He also claimed to have phoned Desai several times, urging him to admit the act and ask for forgiveness.[39]

In Mumbai, Desai was arrested. He proclaimed his innocence, saying through his lawyer that he was being framed because of a previous conflict with the family. By the next morning, the story was all over the local and South African media – probably the juiciest sex scandal in South Africa for many years.

Only the very early reports withheld the identities of the two people involved, as is normal in rape cases. By the end of the first week of coverage, only e.tv was not naming them. Joe Thloloe, the channel's head of news, said the lonely stand was not silly. 'If the majority of the media does wrong it does not mean we will follow,' he said.[40]

The media's decision to flout the normal rules that protect people in rape cases was greatly assisted by Mark Isaacs, who talked to anybody and everybody. Isaacs even allowed the publication of pictures of the couple's young children, which Anton Harber, professor of journalism and media studies at the University of the Witwatersrand, called 'sordid and distasteful'.[41]

Were the media right to identify Desai and Isaacs? This was one of those stories where interest really hinged on the identities of the people involved. A story about claims of rape involving two delegates to an international conference would have had far less impact. But that does not justify throwing the normal practice out of the window.

Legally there was no problem, since South African law did not apply. But the ethical problem remained, since both reputations were badly damaged by the incident. Questions were asked about Desai's ability to continue serving on the bench. As for Isaacs, many people were quite certain she had made the whole thing up. In a front-page column in *ThisDay*, the journalist Marlene Burger wrote: 'I am both a woman and a seasoned journalist, and a combination of intuition and instinct developed over many years tells me that, whatever happened in a hotel room halfway across the world, it wasn't rape.'[42]

Rape survivors often have difficulty having their claims believed, particularly when they know their attacker. Acquaintance rape is a very difficult area, involving, wrote the *Mail&Guardian*, 'the difficult and confusing space between yes and no'.[43] Much of the coverage of this case was informed by old attitudes that are quick to blame the victim.

Many people soon decided that a man who was a respected judge should be believed. Others – far fewer in number – assumed that a woman who claims rape must always be believed. In fact, it is unlikely the full truth will ever emerge about what happened in that hotel room. Even though Isaacs later withdrew the charge, she stood by the claim that there had been sex she did not agree to.

Under the circumstances, journalists should have been far more cautious in their handling of the story.

. . . .

NOTES

1   *Sowetan*, 12 August 1997, cited in *Rhodes Journalism Review* 16, July 1998.

2   *The Star*, 25 August 1997, cited in *Rhodes Journalism Review* 16, July 1998.

3   *Rhodes Journalism Review* 15, November 1997.

4   Sanef press statement, 29 July 2003.

5   Quoted in Colleen Lowe-Morna (ed.), *Whose news? Whose views? Southern Africa: gender in media handbook*. Johannesburg: Gender Links, 2001. 35.

6   Media Institute of Southern Africa (Misa), 'Gender policy and action plan', October 2001. Posted at http://www.genderlinks.org.za/docs/2001/misa-draftpolicy-actionplan.pdf, accessed on 20 March 2004.

7   Colleen Lowe-Morna (ed.), *Whose news? Whose views? Southern Africa: gender in media handbook*. Johannesburg: Gender Links, 2001. 19.

8   Colleen Lowe-Morna (ed.), *Gender in media training: a Southern African tool kit*. Johannesburg: Gender Links and the Institute for the Advancement of Journalism, 2002. 57.

9   Lowe-Morna, *Whose news?* 65.

10 Quoted in Stuart Allan, *News culture*. Buckingham: Open University Press, 2001. 145.

11 Johan Retief, *Media ethics: an introduction to responsible journalism*. Cape Town: OUP, 2002. 193.

12 Media Institute of Southern Africa (Misa) and Gender Links, 'Gender and media baseline study'. Johannesburg: Misa and Gender Links, 2003. 32.

13 Lowe-Morna, *Gender*. 97.

14 Quoted in Retief, *Media ethics*. 196.

15 Lowe-Morna, *Gender*. 97.

16 Interview, 2002.

17 *Rhodes Journalism Review* 19, August 2000.

18 David Adey, Margaret Orr and Derek Swemmer, *The new word power*. Jeppestown, Johannesburg: AD Donker, 2002. 259.

19 Tracey Naughton, 'English as a medium of discrimination' in Lowe-Morna, *Gender*. 116–18.

20 Quoted in Lowe-Morna, *Whose news?* 61.

21 Misa and Gender Links, 'Gender and media study'. 11. The figures don't add up to 100 per cent because the sex of some sources could not be determined.

22 Elsewhere, the study gives the figure of 8 per cent.

23 Interview, 2002.

24 Cited in Lowe-Morna, *Whose news?* 72.

25 Misa and Gender Links, 'Gender and media study'. 48.

26 Quoted in Colleen Lowe-Morna (ed.), *Gender in media training: a Southern African tool kit*. Johannesburg: Gender Links and the Institute for the Advancement of Journalism, 2002. 123.

27 Misa and Gender Links, 'Gender and media study'. 36–40.

28 Quoted in Allan, *News culture*. 139.

29 Interview, 7 November 2002.

30 The case is described in the Southern African regional overview of Misa and Gender Links, 'Gender and media study'. 42–3.

31 Dirk van Zyl Smith, 'Foxcroft's rape sentence is seriously flawed', *Sunday Times*, 17 October 1999.

32 *Mail&Guardian*, 8–14 October 1999.

33 *The Mercury*, 5 October 1999.

34 *The Sunday Independent*, 16 October 1999.

35 *The Star*, 7 October 1999.

36 *Sunday Times*, 10 October 1999.

37 *The Star*, 5 November 2001.

38 *The Star*, 19 January 2004.

39 *Cape Argus*, 23 January 2004.

40 *Mail&Guardian*, 23–29 January 2004.

41 *Business Day*, 30 January 2004.

42 *ThisDay*, 20 January 2004.

43 *Mail&Guardian*, 23–29 January 2004.

A journalist should not present lurid details, either in words or picture, of violence, sexual acts, abhorrent or horrid scenes.
Nigerian Press Organisation: Code of Ethics

Licensees shall not broadcast any material which judged within context – (i) contains gratuitous violence in any form, ie violence which does not play an integral part in developing the plot, character or theme of the material as a whole; (ii) sanctions, promotes or glamorises violence.
Icasa: Code of Conduct for Broadcasters

Children's programmes should be wide ranging in genre and content, but should not include gratuitous scenes, and sounds of violence and sex through any audio or visual medium.
Commonwealth Broadcasting Association: Africa Charter on Children's Broadcasting

9

STEPPING ON TOES: PUBLIC SENSITIVITIES

Sixteen seconds of television in early 2001 sparked a major discussion about morality in the media. An episode of *Yizo Yizo* showed one of the characters, Chester, being sodomised in jail by an older inmate. The popular series was already controversial for the gritty realism it used to explore rape, drugs and other problems in South Africa's schools. The sodomy scene caused an immediate outcry, and ANC MPs tabled a motion in Parliament calling for the series to be scrapped. The MP Thandi Modise said the programme negatively influenced children who watched it and violated the culture, standards and dignity of black South Africans. A member of the Film and Publications Board testified that he would have banned the series as child pornography if the board had authority over television.[1]

The SABC defended the series. Siven Maslamoney, editor of youth, adult and public education programmes, told a parliamentary committee: 'We feel we had to be very direct with young people about prison not being a place to be.' The series put previously taboo subjects in the public domain as part of its educative mission, he said.[2]

The issue of morality in the media is hugely controversial among large parts of the public. The chair of the Broadcasting Complaints Commission of South Africa (BCCSA), Kobus van Rooyen, says most of the complaints received about television programmes fall into this category.[3] Some viewers are very sensitive to depictions of:

- sex
- nudity
- offensive language
- blasphemy, and
- violence.

Television, with its ability to imitate reality, is particularly vulnerable to complaints of this kind, while newspapers and radio more rarely face them. Nevertheless, it is an issue for all media.

'Causing moral decay'

People object to such material for a range of reasons. For many, it should not be tolerated simply because it offends their sense of morality. Many others believe that it is harmful because it encourages impressionable audiences to copy bad or dangerous behaviour. In a frequently quoted passage, the academics James Q Wilson and Richard Herrnstein write: 'If so many commercial and political interests invest so much money in media advertising, it would seem absurd to believe that the media have no effect on our behaviour, including, perhaps, our criminal behaviour. Otherwise, billions of dollars are being wasted by advertisers. And if the media changed only the noncriminal aspects of our behaviour, that would only be slightly less remarkable.'[4]

The argument seems eminently reasonable, and is supported by disturbing incidents that occur from time to time. Children have been known to get hurt by trying to imitate Superman. In early 1999, two students at Columbine High School in the US state of Colorado gunned down 13 of their classmates and then killed

"The prominence of farm attacks in the media will lead to an increase in these attacks because it over-emphasises the vulnerability of a specific group of the South African community."[5]

Neels Moolman, criminologist

themselves. In the soul-searching that followed, violence in the media was fingered as an important cause, being seen to have provided a breeding ground for the incident. A string of initiatives to research and deal with youth violence were launched, and Congress took up dozens of Bills designed to curb media violence.[6]

In the case of *Yizo Yizo*, the storm of criticism followed incidents of copycat behaviour reported after the programme's first series. In early 1999 a few children had imitated a scene from the opening episode, in which a bully flushed a schoolmate's head in a toilet bowl. Dlame Mndaweni, a 20-year-old Vosloorus pupil, boasted he would have made a better Papa Action than the bully in the series, adding: 'I got the idea [to flush a boy's head in the toilet] from watching the series.'[7]

The debate is not new. As long ago as the fourth century BC, the Greek philosopher Plato called for restrictions on unsavoury elements in epic and tragic poetry. In contrast, his pupil Aristotle suggested that violence portrayed in the theatre might have a cathartic effect. Rather than inspiring the audience to rush out and copy a stage murder, for instance, he said it might purge them of unruly emotions and make violence less likely.[8]

More recently, media sociologists have devoted considerable attention to the question of whether violent programming increases aggression among viewers. In the early 1960s one researcher conducted a series of experiments in which he showed groups of pre-school children films of people hitting a large, bouncy 'Bobo doll'. When given the opportunity, the children who had seen the films were more aggressive towards real Bobo dolls than children who had not seen the films.[9] Laboratory experiments like this one were criticised for using an artificial situation to make deductions about the real world. In an attempt to deal with this criticism, other researchers conducted field studies which tried to measure changes in behaviour after exposure to violent entertainment in real-world situations. Persuasive to some, these studies did not put the matter to rest either.

A third type of study looked for correlations between aggressive behaviour and a preference for violent entertainment. One set of studies, for instance, showed a correlation between the sales of men's magazines like *Playboy* and rape rates in various states of the US.[10] Of course, a correlation does not prove a causal link.

According to academic John Corner, the question of

> "When [the German poet Johann Wolfgang von] Goethe published his *Sorrows of Young Werther* in the eighteenth century … authorities in several nations worried that readers would commit suicide in imitation of the book's tragic hero."[11]
>
> *Louis A Day, ethicist*

how the media influence behaviour is the 'contested core of media research'.[12] It is a vast and complicated field, and it is not possible to do it justice here. But it should be noted that despite scientists' best efforts, and despite the apparent persuasiveness of particular incidents, evidence for the media directly causing antisocial behaviour is thin.

Sceptics have pointed out that for every person who copies bad behaviour from the media, there are thousands of others who don't. And there are almost always other factors at play. Referring to the shootings at Columbine High, the US lawyer Marjorie Heins writes: 'Instead of talking about the easy availability of firearms, about the mean social pecking order at Columbine High School, or about the personal demons that drove the two young criminals, many political leaders and political pundits focused on violent entertainment.'[13]

In any event, violence and sex have always been part of human storytelling, and occur prominently in children's games, fairytales, religious texts like the Bible, and elsewhere. It is a very old cultural reality.

Corner notes that the influence of the media on society as a whole is easier to see than at an individual level. (In dealing with race and gender stereotyping in Chapters 7 and 8, we have touched on the way consistent patterns of media messages can shape social values negatively). He writes: 'The search for the direct consequence of media upon individual consciousness and behaviour ... is largely futile.'[14] The British philosopher Matthew Kieran follows a similar approach. Rejecting the argument that the media cause direct harm by making people behave badly, he says: 'Even if we judge we have reason to do something because we watched a certain programme, the responsibility for what we do lies with us and not the television programme.'[15]

In dealing with all the complaints the BCCSA gets, Van Rooyen follows the more sceptical approach. He accepts that some children might be influenced by what they see, 'but the test cannot be the oversensitive child'. Aside from some research into violent forms of sex, he says there has been no convincing evidence that shows a clear correlation between media and deviant behaviour.[16]

Freedom of speech and the question of harm

Van Rooyen's caution is grounded in concern with limits being placed on freedom of speech, which is protected in Chapter 16 of South Africa's Constitution. Significantly, the right is not absolute. The Constitutional

Court has taken an attitude that all rights have to be balanced against each other, and the Constitution itself excludes propaganda for war, incitement to violence and hate speech from protection. Hate speech is described as the advocacy of hatred, on the grounds of race, ethnicity, gender or religion, that constitutes incitement to cause harm.

But that's as far as the limits go. Morality no longer justifies legal limits being placed on free expression. Similarly, the Films and Publications Act of 1996 places just five categories of material under its prohibited classification XX. They are child pornography, violent sexual conduct, bestiality, degrading sex, and extreme violence, where the last two also have to involve incitement to cause harm to fall foul of the provision.

The key concept here is harm. In the new South Africa, moral issues justify legal intervention only when they can be shown to cause real harm. This is an approach also followed by the BCCSA. Van Rooyen says that there's no legal basis for acting against blasphemy and other language that's offensive to religious sensibilities, for instance. It only becomes actionable when it strays into the category of hate speech. 'The test which we apply is advocacy of hatred, based on religion,' he says.[17] Similarly, the argument against child pornography is that it causes real harm to the children involved in its production, and may make it easier for paedophiles to operate.

In practical terms, adult audiences are given primary responsibility for deciding what they are prepared to watch. In the past, censorship imposed an official morality on viewers. Now, notices are attached to films that indicate whether there will be violence, sex, nudity or strong language. Viewers can then decide for themselves whether they want to watch or not.

Special provisions are made to protect children, however. The Icasa Code of Conduct for Broadcasters contains extensive guidelines on the issue, chief of which is the 'watershed period' between 9 p.m. and 5 a.m. Broadcasters are expected to be more careful in their programming at times when children are more likely to be in the audience, and more adult material should be kept for later at night.

Other provisions include:[18]

- Violence should be used in children's programmes only when necessary to the plot;
- Material dealing with issues like death, drugs, domestic conflict or crime should not threaten children's sense of security;

- Animated films should not invite dangerous imitation;
- Care should be taken in the portrayal of themes that could invite imitation, like playing with plastic bags or matches;
- Violence should not be presented as the preferred method of resolving conflict;
- The consequences of violence should not be glossed over; and
- Frightening or other excessive special effects should be avoided.

The ethics of causing offence

In the new dispensation, then, morality is no longer enough to limit freedom of expression. But does this legal approach also answer the ethical question? We have seen above that ethics and law are not quite the same thing. The law sets hard limits and punishes those who break them. It is appropriate to be extremely cautious about imposing legal limits on freedom of speech, which is a hard-won, precious and valuable right.

Ethics, in contrast, deals with standards people aspire to. The question is not 'What may I do?' It is 'What should I do?' Considering obscenity, blasphemy, screen violence and the like from an ethical perspective takes us in a slightly different direction.

It is clear that material of this kind offends some public sensibilities, as demonstrated by the reaction to things like the prison sodomy scene in *Yizo Yizo*. In modern South Africa, the law has nothing to say about that. But ethical questions may still be asked.

Causing offence is a kind of harm. Kieran cites the example of religious sensibilities:[20]

> "I remember a woman who was severely tortured in George. Her breasts were slammed in a drawer, and her nipples split open. That night they didn't use it in the news. I phoned and asked them why, and they said it was just too cruel. We complained, and they said I must send the news item again. I did, and they used it at 11 o'clock that night when nobody actually listened."[19]
> *The SABC radio journalist Kenneth Makatees, on covering TRC hearings*

Christians and Moslems may find their lives harmed in similar ways where a hostile secular culture is predominated by programmes and films that are derisive and mocking and deliberately set out to blaspheme against their religious beliefs and way of life. The perpetuation of programmes that cultivate the attitude that religious belief is no more than superstitious nonsense, and mock it merely as something akin to a sad and naïve faith in Santa Claus, fails to take religious claims seriously, and clearly makes it more difficult to live a religious life freely.

Recognising the potential to cause offence does not mean it is always unethical to do so. Sometimes, there is good reason to shock an audience. The SABC's defence of *Yizo Yizo*, as we have seen, was of that kind: the corporation argued that it was necessary to show young people very clearly how awful prison really is. Below, we will consider situations where there is an ethical duty to cause offence in the context of journalism.

Meanwhile, in journalism

So far, our discussion has dealt with the issue as it affects the media as a whole. In fact most examples have been drawn from the world of entertainment. But what of journalism?

The press code says: 'A newspaper has wide discretion in matters of taste but this does not justify lapses of taste so repugnant as to bring the freedom of the press into disrepute or be extremely offensive to the public.' It's not a very helpful provision, as it relies on the antiquated notion of good taste.

Even though it's clearly framed for entertainment formats, the Icasa code is more helpful (see the quote on p. 115). It makes a distinction between gratuitous violence and material that plays an integral part in developing plot, character and theme. That principle can easily be extrapolated to be relevant to journalism. Causing offence can usually be defended if there is a compelling *journalistic* reason to do so.

The pictures editor at *The Star*, Robin Comley, also uses the word 'gratuitous' to describe images of violence that should not be run. She says that the newspaper used to have a policy not to run pictures of dead bodies on the front page, but this fell away during the violence before the first democratic election in 1994. 'There was death and destruction every day and it was absolutely unavoidable. One had to tell the story, the country had to know what was going on. And the only way to do that was visually.'[22]

A discussion of a controversial photograph from the Persian Gulf War in *Doing ethics in journalism* uses a similar argument. The gruesome pho-

> Andrew Bolton, the news editor at *Cape Talk*, says some very graphic and intimate descriptions of the former first lady, Marike de Klerk, emerged during the murder trial arising out of her death, since rape charges also formed part of the trial. The station limited the use of the details since they did not add to the story. "Our reporting was quite graphic but it wasn't extremely graphic," says Bolton.[21]

tograph showed the charred remains of an Iraqi soldier who burned to death inside his armoured vehicle during Allied bombing. The photographer, Ken Jarecke, defended the photograph by saying: 'If we are big enough to fight a war, we should be big enough to look at it.'[23] Still, many newspapers refused to run the image.

Similar debates erupted in the US again during the Iraqi war of 2003. 'People look at their newspapers in the morning and we don't want to upset our readers' breakfasts,' wrote G Jefferson Price III, the editor of the 'Perspectives' section of the *Baltimore Sun*.[24] But then he went on to say that newspapers need to show their readers how 'inhuman and horrifying war is'. They must also reflect injury and death on both sides, not just their own side. 'People who believe that war is good and necessary need to see these images. People on both sides.'

If truth-telling is the core function of journalism, then that must at times include showing an unpleasant reality in all its graphic, horrifying detail. Sometimes the argument is taken a step further, and it is said that exposure to a nasty truth will cause people to do something about it. It is, really, the flipside of the fear that the media will cause bad behaviour. In both cases the potential for influence is often overestimated. Cases where people rush out and fix the problem being highlighted do occur, but are not that common.

Also, there is a real danger of overkill. The BBC cautions: 'With some news stories a sense of shock is part of a full understanding of what has happened. However, the more often viewers are shocked, the more it will take to shock them.'[25]

Much depends on the handling of potentially offensive material. A picture may be acceptable on a newspaper's inside pages, but not on the front page. The reasoning here is that children and adults may be exposed to images of this kind against their will if they are published on the front page, simply by noticing them on a newsstand. Television news bulletins will sometimes warn sensitive viewers of what is to come. Similar 'avoidance techniques' are routinely used to deal with obscene language. Newspapers will refer to 'the f-word'; television or radio may bleep out the offensive words.

As in so many areas, a decision to use offensive material is a very subjective matter. The former editor of the *Sowetan*, John Dludlu, says justi-

> "News media have, for years, run graphic photos of automobile accidents under the pretext that such photos would somehow let motorists know what awaits them should they become careless behind the wheel. But people continue to have auto accidents, and there is no evidence that conclusively demonstrates the deterrent effect of newspaper photos."[26]
> *Carl Hausman, ethicist*

fications for showing gory images like that of a woman killed by a train after being tied to a Soweto railway track can easily be constructed. 'Not to publish [pictures of the body] could be motivated by the fact that we don't want to encourage killers, but you could also publish them and say you want to discourage this. We want to shock the public in such a way that they stand up and all of them are morally outraged.'[27]

It is doubtful that a picture will cause a wave of moral outrage that stops killings of this kind, and the problem is that an argument justifying offensive material can be constructed a little too easily. Sometimes reasons can be found to justify usage that is actually just prurient. And because 'pushing the envelope' can attract audiences, we should be careful that justifications are real, not self-serving. Journalists will take good ethical decisions in this area if they consider carefully the nature and seriousness of the public sensibilities at stake, and make quite sure that there is a good journalistic reason for offending them.

Public sensitivities:
a test of five questions

Journalists should ask these questions to check their reporting:
1. Does the report include offensive language, blasphemy, references to violence, sex, or nudity that audiences might find offensive?
2. Who may be offended?
3. Is the use of the material necessary to achieve legitimate journalistic ends?
4. Are there alternatives that could mitigate the offence without detracting from the journalism?
5. Can you justify your decision?

The duty to offend
Jon Qwelane

Every 'given' should be tested to the limit, and that holds true for ethics as well as everything else. We have a duty to weed out the likelihood of self-censorship and hence a descent into the quagmire of keeping the populace in the dark (thereby violating the constitutional principle of the right to inform and be informed).

The Afrikaans press, to its credit, tested the limits during the apartheid days: at the risk of offending its audience's sensibilities, it regularly published without fear the horrific dismembered parts of human bodies which had been ripped apart in bombing incidents. (The truth, of course, is that the apartheid secret police had done the dirty in order to blame the 'terrorists', but that is another matter.)

In early 2004, a mini-furore exploded deliciously about a breast. During a live stage performance, the singer Justin Timberlake brazenly ripped off a boob cover to expose the breast of his co-singer, Janet Jackson. Janet, like the unconvincing moralists, played all shocked and embarrassed but most of the world just loved every salacious moment.

To my mind there are only three real questions. If you can answer them satisfactorily, go ahead and publish:

What's the public interest? Did Mrs Salome Isaacs, a married young mother, and Judge Siraj Desai do it when she paid him a visit at 3 a.m. in his hotel room to 'discuss a project' which apparently could not wait for a more civilised time of day? Publishing the story allowed us, as the public, to sit in judgment over the judge and his moral sense. A clear case of public interest.

Is it in good taste? So long as great care is taken not to offend the moral sensibilities and sensitivities of the greater reading and viewing public without good reason, then go ahead and publish.

Is it defamatory? It is far better to run the copy past a lawyer first than to deal with a letter from the lawyers of the offended party later. The rule of thumb is to look out for offensive words like 'kaffir', 'coolie', 'boesman'. 'chink', 'porra', and so on. Satire is a great minefield, and often testing the intention behind the use of the words – and taking the entire context of the piece into account – is a safe way out.

But in my opinion, there's sometimes a positive duty to offend people's small-minded sensitivities. Go ahead and test them to the utmost. We can only become wiser, and better, for it.

(Jon Qwelane is a broadcaster and journalist)

Case study 17
Crude morning

The Rude Awakening, a morning show on 94.7 Highveld Stereo, and its host Jeremy Mansfield built a reputation as just that: crude, crass and vulgar. It was a South African light version of the US phenomenon of the shock jock, who attracts audiences by being offensive.

On 30 October 1998 the show included a spoof quiz show in which the contestant had 20 questions to guess an object which had been disclosed to the audience. In this case, the contestant was identified as Carike Keuzenkamp, a well-known Afrikaans singer and actress. The quizmaster was identified as Les Franken, who had played the role in several real television quiz shows. Both were being played by actors.[28]

The audience was told that the mystery object that had to be guessed was ''n swart man se piel' (a black man's cock). 'Keuzenkamp' asked her first question: Could the object be eaten? After some hesitation 'Franken' said, Yes, it could. She immediately guessed: 'Isn't it perhaps a black man's cock?'

The complaints came fast and furious, and the BCCSA considered the matter in terms of the provision that prohibits material that is 'indecent or obscene or harmful or offensive to public morals'. The station's programme manager, Malcolm Fried, argued that the show was, at worst, vulgar or in poor taste, but not indecent or obscene. The intended audience was adult and open-minded, and the show was intended as a parody of the absurdities of the apartheid-era ban on sex between white and black.

The panel, chaired by the BCCSA's chairperson, Kobus van Rooyen, found the show 'in poor taste, vulgar and crude'. The judgment said: 'All the members of the panel conceded that after having read the papers before this hearing, they had felt that the broadcast on Highveld Stereo had probably gone too far.' But the show was aimed at an adult, broad-minded audience, and various legal precedents were cited to show the difficulty in defining indecency. The show had not broken the code's provisions, the BCCSA found in its judgement.

Soon after, the station rebroadcast the segment. This time, Keuzenkamp herself complained on the grounds that it impaired her dignity and invaded her privacy. The BCCSA again considered the matter, this time with a different panel chaired by Ratha Mokgoatlheng. Keuzenkamp's lawyers said she had been portrayed 'as embracing sexual depravity, promiscuity and permissiveness' even though she in fact had a 'church orientated wholesome image'.[29]

For this hearing, Fried seems to have taken his defence of the show as seriously intentioned to quite astonishing lengths. He argued the parody intended to shock white South Africans by making fun of their historical prejudices about the alleged potency of black men. 'The language, the intonation, and the mimicking of prominent South African showbiz celebrities through the vehicle of the traditional broadcasting quiz game show, satirises the emblematic broadcasting norms in the apartheid era utilised by the then government as social control mechanisms to prevent inter-racial relationships and sexual intercourse between blacks and whites,' he said.

This time, Highveld Stereo lost. Paying scant attention to the station's elaborate (and in parts barely intelligible) defence, the panel found that there was 'no justification to broadcast the sequence using the impersonation of the complainant, or her persona'. The broadcast exposed her to humiliation by associating her publicly with 'the offending, vulgar, lewd and profane broadcast'. The station was ordered to broadcast an apology, and fined R30 000, R10 000 of which was suspended for a year.

Although the case does not come from the world of journalism, it does illustrate some issues around public sensitivities and their handling by the BCCSA. Van Rooyen's judgment in the first complaint scoured local and international legal precedent for the handling of offensive material. He found judgments from the South African Constitutional Court and elsewhere that terms like 'indecent' and 'obscene' were so vague as to be almost impossible to apply. In any event, freedom of expression meant that even undesirable material needed to be tolerated, he ruled: 'ultimately one has to live with matters which are utterly offensive to one's sense of propriety, so as to ensure one's own freedom of choice and freedom of expression.'

The judgment makes little attempt to explain what would be bad enough to fall foul of the provisions on obscenity. Elsewhere, Van Rooyen has said that offensive material only becomes actionable once it can be shown to cause actual harm.[30] The second finding seemed to find such harm in the damage to Keuzenkamp's reputation, and the invasion of her privacy. But if the clauses of the code dealing with indecency are to be interpreted so narrowly, then it would be better to remove them entirely.

The BCCSA sees itself as a quasi-legal tribunal, and takes a legal view of things. From that point of view, it is undoubtedly correct to be very cautious about any infringements of freedom of speech. But a distinction should again be made between law and ethics.

Ethically there do seem to be grounds for saying that the broadcast overstepped the mark. The panel members all felt the station had 'gone too far' and said that if polled, most listeners would probably have rejected the broadcast.

Ethics accepts that offensive material can be justified if there is public interest. Fried tried to paint the show as an attempt at serious social commentary, particularly for the second complaint. But the defence seems to be a post facto justification for an insert that was simply entertainment. It seemed a little thin.

The BCCSA's difficulty is that it has no instruments at its disposal to take an ethical view. Any adverse finding is regarded as a punishment, and therefore as potentially infringing a station's freedom of speech. And its code is in fact a hybrid document, presented as an ethical document but drafted and interpreted by lawyers.

Case study 18
A space to imagine the horror

Medical staff get used to seeing what human beings can do to each other. But when a little six-year-old girl was brought in to Johannesburg Hospital in September 2002, nurses and doctors wept. The little girl had been raped, and her body was terribly damaged.

Professor Peter Beale was the paediatric surgeon who treated the child, called Lerato in newspaper reports. He told *The Star*: 'I'm tired of doing surgery in such cases. I spent 20 hours in theatre this weekend on numerous [rape] cases when I could be focusing on transplants.'[31] Among the cases he also dealt with that weekend was another small child: a three-year-old the media later called Nkanyezi.

Beale challenged the newspaper to publish pictures of the injuries suffered by the two little girls to shock South Africans into 'realising what we are doing to our society'. Society was in denial and not acknowledging rape as a social problem, and not doing anything was like treason against the people. He said: 'This is happening too often – the scourge, the shame of rape.'

But the newspaper judged the pictures too graphic to use. Instead, it published a large, prominent white space on its front page, with a thick black border and the headline 'Child-rape picture too horrific to publish'. The accompanying words left little to the imagination, however. The caption said the picture showed the child's 'intestines ballooning out of the hole where her perineum – the skin between her rectum and vagina – should be.' And the story itself refers to her colon hanging out 'like a grotesque red cauliflower'.

The Star received 'a flood of calls' from people demanding that the picture be published, it reported the next day.[32] But one person who was not impressed was the police commissioner, Jackie Selebi. The newspaper sent a team off to Pretoria to show him the pictures, but he was unmoved and instead showed them his own material: a video of a man raping a baby, and a picture of a woman being penetrated by a dog.[33]

Selebi accused Beale and *The Star* of distributing child pornography. The pictures should not have been taken, and Beale might face prosecution if they found their way into the public domain. Selebi said the police did not need to be shocked into taking action. 'We live with these things daily – we see them every day,' he said. It was an extraordinarily defensive reaction, which drew much criticism.

The newspaper's editor, Moegsien Williams, describes the ethical dilemma of Beale's challenge: 'When we looked at the picture we just thought no, there's no way we're going to publish this, it was just too horrific. Part of the ethical issue was just protecting the sensibilities of our readers.'[34] He describes the publication of white space as a device to attract readers' attention without offending them.

'We had to come with a clever way to try and draw readers' attention to the horror of this without publishing pictures. It's one way of being gimmicky, but the idea was to achieve more or less the same thing with a different kind of device,' he says.

One should take the 'flood of calls' the paper said it got, calling for the picture to be published, with a pinch of salt. Had it run the picture, the chances are it would have received a 'flood of calls' from other readers who objected to it.

Nevertheless, the device was very effective. It was not the first time that blank space had been made to speak loudly. During apartheid's state of emergency in the late 1980s, gifted designers at the *Weekly Mail*, as it was then, turned front pages of the paper into posters of witty defiance against censorship, using text, blank spaces and demonstratively blacked-out words.

Did the unpublished picture of little Lerato put a stop to child rape? Such expectations would probably have been unrealistic. It would take more than a photograph to root out an evil of this kind. But it certainly created a stir, adding significant impetus to public awareness of the issue. That blank space left room for readers' own imaginations to fill in the horrible details. It probably had greater impact than the actual picture would have done.

The Star deserves credit for finding a creative solution to an ethical dilemma, and simultaneously contributing substantially to raising public awareness.

Case study 19
Rape on tape

The footage was graphic and intimate, a kind of pornographic home movie. It had been filmed secretly by one of the people featured. The woman involved did not know about the filming, and did not even know that the sex was taking place. The film clearly showed her as unresponsive, believed to have been knocked out by a 'date rape' drug. It involved things she would not have agreed to if she had been conscious.

Robyn Thompson had lived with Durban butcher Martin Kruger for many years when she discovered that he had been drugging and then raping her. When he threatened to distribute pornographic pictures of her which showed incidents she did not remember, she went to the police, who got the videotape from Kruger. Having to watch the video at the police station, Thompson felt 'physically ill', she later said.[35] Kruger was charged, and she approached *Carte Blanche* with her story. A report was aired in July 2001.

The executive producer of *Carte Blanche*, George Mazarakis, says the story raised many ethical questions.[36] The first was how to deal with the pornographic footage that was being made available to the programme. It was clear that this would certainly offend public sensitivities. But at the same time, the story really was about this tape. Mazarakis says: 'To what degree do we show? We had every single shot; we've got the tape. How much of it do we show? Do we show him enjoying himself?'

In the end, extensive use was made of the footage, woven around Thompson's narrative of what happened to her. 'We showed the moments, which were pretty graphic, but most of the time her legs were wide open so we had to cover and put smudges so that you couldn't see,' says Mazarakis. 'But you could see him moving around and you could see what his intentions were, it was very clear.'

In assessing *Carte Blanche*'s handling of the material, we should be mindful of the audience. The programme goes out at 7 p.m. on a Sunday evening, when children may well be watching. But the programme always issues warnings about material that might 'offend sensitive viewers'. Viewers have ample opportunity to avoid footage they don't feel comfortable with. In this case, warnings coupled with the use of smudges to take the pornographic edge off the footage were sufficient to deal with public sensitivities.

Another ethical issue arose. Filming the rapes constituted a clear invasion of Thompson's privacy, and broadcasting the images to a large audience would have worsened the injury if she had not given consent. That made all the difference. She not only agreed to their use, she approached *Carte Blanche* with a view to having them used. Mazarakis says the programme would 'not have considered' using the material if she had not agreed.

The final ethical issue that arose for Mazarakis and his team revolved around fairness. Kruger initially declined to respond to the allegations, and only supplied a very short snippet in which he claimed that Thompson had known about the tapes. After the programme was aired, he complained he had not been given enough opportunity to respond, and *Carte Blanche* conducted a separate interview with him.[37]

It is clear that the programme gave him the chance to respond, but that he did not take it up. The producers then went further by giving him another opportunity. *Carte Blanche* satisfied the requirements of fairness in the way it handled Kruger, who later pleaded guilty to criminal charges and was given a suspended sentence. As a whole, the 'Rape on tape' report remained a shocking and disturbing one, but it successfully navigated a series of difficult ethical challenges.

. . . .

NOTES

1   *The Star*, 29 March 2001.

2   *The Star*, 27 March 2001.

3   Interview, 30 January 2003.

4   Quoted in Louis Day, *Ethics in media communications: cases and controversies.* Belmont, CA: Wadsworth, 2000. 258.

5   Quoted in Johan Retief, *Media ethics: an introduction to responsible journalism.* Cape Town: OUP, 2002. 214.

6   Marjorie Heins, *Violence and the media: an exploration of cause, effect and the First Amendment.* Nashville: First Amendment Center, 2001. v.

7   *Sunday Times*, 21 February 1999.

8   Heins, *Violence and the media.* 2.

9   Cited in ibid. 3.

10 Ibid. 7.

11 Louis A Day, *Ethics in media communications: cases and controversies.* Belmont, CA: Wadsworth, 2000. 258.

12 John Corner, '"Influence": the contested core of media research' in James Curran and Michael Gurevitch (eds.), *Mass media and society.* London: Arnold, 2000.

13 Heins, *Violence and the media.* 1.

14 Ibid. 393.

15 Matthew Kieran, *Media ethics: a philosophical approach.* Westport, Conn: Praeger, 1997. 90.

16 Interview, 30 January 2003.

17 Interview, 30 January 2003.

18 Icasa Code of Conduct for Broadcasters.

19 *Rhodes Journalism Review* 14, May 1997. 17.

20 Kieran, *Media ethics.* 144.

21 Interview, 8 November 2002.

22 Interview, 2002.

23 Jay Black, Bob Steele and Ralph Barney, *Doing ethics in journalism: a handbook with case studies.* Needham Heights, MA: Allyn & Bacon, 1995. 157.

24 *The Star*, 17 April 2003.

25 BBC, *Producers' guidelines.* London: BBC, 1996. 63.

26 Quoted in Retief, *Media Ethics.* 180.

27 Interview, 18 October 2002.

28 BCCSA judgment in case 1999/01.

29 BCCSA judgment in case 1999/07.

30 Interview, 30 January 2003.

31 *The Star*, 10 September 2002.

32 *The Star*, 11 September 2002.

33 *The Star*, 12 September 2002.

34 Interview, 13 September 2002.

35 Summary of story posted at http://www.mnet.co.za/CarteBlanche/Display/Display. asp?Id=1774, accessed on 16 January 2004.

36 Interview, 11 September 2002.

37 'Rape on tape revisited', 11 August 2001. Transcript posted at http://www.mnet.co.za/ CarteBlanche/Display/Display.asp?id=1784, accessed on 16 January 2004.

Unnamed sources should be avoided unless there is absolutely no other way to handle the story and if the source is backed by others. No unnamed source should be used without the explicit agreement of the relevant department head or editor, who, under normal circumstances, will require the reporter to tell him or her the identity of the source, in the strictest confidence.
Mail&Guardian: Journalists' Guidelines

The journalist shall observe professional secrecy regarding the source of information obtained in confidence.
International Federation of Journalists: Declaration of Principles on the Conduct of Journalists

No payment shall be made for feature articles to persons engaged in crime or other notorious misbehaviour, or to convicted persons or their associates ... except where the material concerned ought to be published in the public interest and the payment is necessary for this to be done.
Press Code of Professional Practice

10

OF TRUST AND SCEPTICISM: RELATING TO THE SOURCE

Jonny Steinberg's book *Midlands*[1] unravels the story of the 1999 murder of a white farmer. In seeking explanations for a crime the police were not able to solve, he investigates local relationships and racial conflict in great detail, as well as the personalities involved. As a whole, the book throws a unique light on the phenomenon of farm murders in post-1994 South Africa.

Although the book is factual, Steinberg has changed the names of the people involved, and tried to disguise the locality. So many people spoke to him on condition of anonymity, he writes, that it was simpler to change every name. The father of the murdered man was one of them, and

Steinberg says he agreed on the basis of an 'ethical consideration ... which stems from my understanding that every journalist hurts the person about whom he writes ... Everybody who is written about has an image of what he will look like on the printed page. He is always disappointed.'[2]

Despite the care Steinberg took, his book was sharply attacked for harming the family. Mary de Haas, a violence monitor who has done extensive work in the region where the murder occurred, writes that Steinberg's attempts to hide the family's identity were unsuccessful. She accuses the author of misleading Arthur Mitchell, as he calls the father of the murder victim: 'Mr Mitchell is adamant that although Steinberg had told him he was writing a book, he had not told him it was about him specifically ... For his pains in assisting the author Mitchell has been rewarded with disparaging descriptions of himself, his wife, their relationship, and his home.'[3]

The controversy closely echoed an American case, in which a triple murderer sued the journalist who wrote a book about his case. The murderer accused the journalist of fraud and breach of contract, on the basis that the writer had pretended to be sympathetic to him – but then wrote a very critical account. The case is documented by Janet Malcolm in her book, *The journalist and the murderer*, which begins: 'Every journalist who is not too stupid or too full of himself to notice what is going on knows that what he does is morally indefensible. He is a kind of confidence man, preying on people's vanity, ignorance, or loneliness, gaining their trust and betraying them without remorse.'[4]

Writing a book requires very detailed research, and success often depends on the relationships that can be built with its subjects. By contrast, daily and weekly journalism is dominated by stories that are researched through a phone call or two. In that sense the *Midlands* case is not typical of journalism, but it does throw into sharp relief the question of how we should relate to our sources.

Few journalists would accept Malcolm's view that they are essentially confidence tricksters. But we should acknowledge how heavily we rely on our sources: they give us the raw material without which we would have very little to say. The relationship with sources is one of three important relationships journalists have, the others being with their audiences and their employers. What do we owe them in return, these people who trust us with their stories?

Firstly, we should deal with them *honestly*. We need to be open with them about who we are, and our intentions. Steinberg warned Mitchell: 'I can be completely truthful and still upset you,' and on another occasion: 'I have been in touch with your tenants, and they have a story to tell. I am going to tell it and you are not going to like it.'[5] Trickery can take many forms, and in Chapter 13 we will need to consider whether there are exceptional situations that justify misleading a source.

Secondly, we should show them *consideration*. As we have seen, a fundamental principle of journalism ethics is to avoid doing harm. The source and the subject of our report (and it's as well to remember that they are often not the same) are most directly at risk of harm. There can be damage to their reputation, to their relationships, even to their lives.

Consideration does not mean that the source's concerns override everything else. They can be trumped by the public interest. But they should be taken seriously. We should think about what's at stake for the source, and about the kinds of risks they take.

Finally, we should maintain a professional *distance*. There's nothing wrong with 'cultivating sources' – building a relationship of trust in order to encourage people to talk to us. But we should not allow a closeness to develop that undermines our professional judgment. We need to maintain a healthy scepticism, no matter how much we like the person we are dealing with. The *New York Times*'s code advises: 'Scrupulous practice requires that periodically we step back and take a hard look at whether we have drifted too close to sources we deal with regularly. The acid test of freedom from favouritism is the ability to maintain good working relationships with all parties to a dispute.'[6]

In order to signal the necessary professional distance, broadcasters generally address interviewees with their title and surname. The familiarity of first names is reserved for other journalists, artists and sportspeople.

702 presenter John Robbie: Manto, Manto …

The minister of health, Manto Tshabalala-Msimang: I am not Manto to you. Let me tell you I am not Manto to you.

Robbie: So, what must I address you as, Miss Minister or Ms Minister or Mrs Minister?

Tshabalala-Msimang: I don't know whatever you address me, but I am not a friend.[7]

From an acrimonious interview on Aids policy, broadcast in September 2000

Sources are not all created equal

Sources come in all shapes and sizes, and there is no sense in treating them all exactly the same. There are those people who appear often in the media: politicians, public relations people, celebrities and others who benefit in various ways from developing a relationship with reporters.

One could call them professional sources, and they are usually adept at 'playing the media game'. In dealing with them, the journalist's ethical duty is to avoid being manipulated.

Then there are others who get pushed into the limelight. Sometimes, they will find journalists on their doorsteps because they are beneficiaries of some government project. Many others will have to deal with the media because of suffering or tragedy. These are the relatives of people who die in a horrible bus accident or rape survivors or the parents of a teenager who commits suicide. People in this category deserve much more consideration than the first, simply because they are unused to the often strange ways of the journalist. Chapter 11 will deal fully with issues around covering various forms of trauma.

There is another reason for thinking very carefully about who the source is: it helps us evaluate what they are telling us. Judging the value of evidence according to its source should be basic journalism. Unfortunately, it is an underdeveloped skill in the South African media. One finds reports that quote 'impeccable sources' as predicting the outcome of an internal party election quite confidently. Nobody seems to have asked the basic question: how would they know? And nor has anybody factored in the fact that party hacks are adept at planting stories of this kind as part of the campaign for their candidate.

Some basic questions should always be asked:[8]

- *How does the source know this?*

Very often, people will pass on things they have heard, or what they believe happened. Clearly this is not nearly as reliable as a first-hand account.

- *Can the information be corroborated?*

Other sources or documentary evidence should always be sought, particularly if the claim is controversial.

- *What is the source's past reliability?*

Has he or she proved reliable in the past?

- *What motive does the source have?*

It is important to know what the source is getting out of passing on the

> In August 2003, the Democratic Alliance MP Nigel Bruce grabbed the headlines when he confronted the auditor-general, Shauket Fakie, with a letter apparently showing that one of the bidders in the controversial arms deal had been allowed to change a quote after the tender's closing date. It was widely seen as smoking gun evidence of long-suspected irregularities in the deal. It soon turned out that the letter was real enough, but Bruce had misread the closing date of the tender. In fact, the letter had been written before the closing date, and Bruce and those who reported him were left with egg on their faces.[9]

information. But having an axe to grind does not mean the information is unreliable. It simply means the need to find corroborating evidence is stronger. Some of the best stories have seen the light of day thanks to a source with a grievance.

- *How representative is this person?*

Too often, we see reports that feature one or two people as representing an entire community or sector. We hear the phrase 'economists say', and find only one or two have been canvassed. The small word 'some' would make all the difference.

The voice of authority

Say the words 'official sources'. Feel their weight on your tongue, notice the taste of ink and slightly dusty documents that seems to cling to them. Imagine the person behind them: a man with many chins and an air of grave authority.

When the person in charge speaks to us, we usually accept the validity of their information. After all, the authorities must know what's going on; it's an assumption we work with every day, and yet it can prove dangerously wrong.

In March 2001 a police spokesperson told journalists that a hijacking was under way at Wonderboom airport in Pretoria. Local and foreign media sent the story out into the world, and dispatched teams to the scene to cover the action. But it turned out to be a false alarm. It was merely a police exercise, and the spokesperson had got it wrong. Journalists were furious at the waste of time and money, and the embarrassment of having filed stories that proved incorrect. But Jackie Selebi, the police commissioner, thought it was very funny.

The head of TV news at SABC, Jimi Matthews, commented afterwards: 'The problem with his reaction was that when you start doubting official comment and announcements, that's when the possibility of getting important stories wrong is multiplied, because reporters will stop checking with the relevant officials.'[10]

It is impossible to cross-check everything official sources tell us. But at the same time, it is worth remembering that they can and do get it wrong. Scepticism is just as appropriate in our dealings with them as with other types of sources.

Wheeling and dealing

Sources may try to bargain with the journalist. Often, but not always, this is about payment. South Africa's main codes are clear that criminals should not be paid for their stories (see the quotes on p. 173). The argument is that this would be tantamount to allowing them to benefit from their crime. However, many journalists would go further, and 'chequebook journalism' is widely frowned upon even if the person involved is not a criminal. The academic, Nigel Harris, writes: 'There is something rather distasteful about such sources gaining financially from disclosing the personal secrets of others. There is also a risk that those who are paid in this manner will resort to exaggeration in order to reap the highest rewards.'[11]

The magazines *You* and *Huisgenoot* are well known for buying people's stories, but otherwise the practice is comparatively rare in South African journalism. Tim du Plessis, editor of *Rapport*, says he occasionally buys exclusivity in a human-interest story. The situation arose when a Cape Town woman, Nadia Abrahams, accused the manager of the British football club Manchester United, Sir Alex Ferguson, of sexual harassment in October 2002. Du Plessis says she demanded payment, but he was completely outbid by British papers, who were later reported to have paid up to £100 000 for the story.[13] Du Plessis says: 'I was prepared to pay, but not an exorbitant amount.'[14]

Sources may bargain for other things besides money. The TV journalist Jacques Pauw describes how Craig Williamson, the former police spy, would agree to an interview only if it took place in his lawyer's office, rather than with the black backdrop that the crew wanted to use for all interviews. 'It was either get him on these terms or not: this was the only way we could get him,' says Pauw.[15]

Deals can be justified as long as they don't undermine the basic integrity of the journalism. If they threaten the basic truthfulness of the report, they are not acceptable.

> "Time and time again, those who have no bargaining power other than their HIV-status ask the 'gatekeepers': 'What is in it for me if I co-operate with journalists?' ... To salve our consciences, some journalists offer groceries or money in exchange for stories ... While some may reject this 'paying' for stories as an odious tabloid press habit, at least it offers benefits to both sides. The journalist gets the story, and the family can eat for another month."[12]
> *Kerry Cullinan, Health-e News Service*

Naming names

Attribution is one of the distinguishing features of journalism. Our reports indicate where information comes from, allowing our audiences to judge its reliability for themselves. The technique has another advantage for journalists: it allows us to distance ourselves from the claims made. We can say: 'I'm not vouching for this information, I'm just the messenger.' This is reasonable up to a point, but it can become a cheap cop-out. Journalists have the responsibility to check the reliability of information we put into the public domain.

> "It's like a bullet that comes out of the woods and hits somebody in the back and you have no idea who shot it or why."
>
> "If I don't know who said it, how do I know if it's true?"[16]
>
> *Comments gathered in discussions with members of the public by Bob Haiman of the Poynter Institute*

Most people regard anonymous accusations as unfair (see box alongside). In a survey by the American Society of Newspaper Editors, 77 per cent of respondents said they were 'somewhat' or 'very' concerned about the credibility of a story that contained unidentified sources.[17]

And yet there are occasions when sources will speak only on condition of anonymity. Some of the most important and explosive stories would never have been told without an unnamed source. Anton Harber, professor of journalism and media studies at the University of the Witwatersrand, writes: 'The scandals of Watergate, Muldergate and Inkathagate would never have burst into the open, bringing down presidents and ministers, if it wasn't for a lonely, hidden Deep Throat.'[18]

Anonymous sources often have 'nefarious, self-serving purposes', he writes, and 'many a tax dodger has been brought down by a disgruntled former employee.' Referring to the politically charged controversy on corruption allegations that raged around Deputy President Jacob Zuma in 2003, he writes: 'Leaks are inevitable, even desirable, to ensure that the process is dragged out of the dark corridors of power into the open. Our democracy looks stronger and more vigorous for it.'

Most editors say that unnamed sources should be used only if there is no other choice. But there are big differences in how strictly the approach is applied. *USA Today* has a very rigorous approach, allowing anonymous sources under only three conditions:[19]

- if the story is of great significance and absolutely unavailable otherwise;
- if the story has been published elsewhere and is in general circulation, in which case the other news organisation is credited;
- if an experienced reporter has developed the story on the basis of a

highly trusted source, and then only if he or she can convince the editor.

Reporters have often been sent back to their sources to push them to go on the record – and often they succeeded. John C Quinn, a former *USA Today* editor, says: 'We figured that if we refused to let unnamed people lie in the news columns there would be a lot less lying in print.'[20]

Mondli Makhanya, editor of the *Sunday Times*, says he tends to disbelieve stories if he sees the word 'source'. He says: 'I think the word "source" in print has been severely discredited because it is used by lazy journalists who don't want to push their sources to speak on the record.'[21] If it's not possible to name somebody, journalists should still be as specific as possible by referring to 'a senior departmental official', 'an official in the Presidency' or the like.

Martin Welz, the editor of the investigative magazine *Noseweek*, has a radically different approach: he has dispensed with attribution altogether. He checks claims carefully, he says, and once he's satisfied himself that they are valid, he expects his readers to accept them on his say-so. 'We follow a policy on my publication that we don't quote sources. I stand in for everything in my publication, I don't shift the blame.'[22]

> "For the edification of those who may be unaware of the etymology, the family tree, so to speak, of the wellsprings of news, it goes something like this: Walter and Ann Source (née Rumour) had four daughters (Highly Placed, Authoritative, Unimpeachable, and Well-Informed). The first married a diplomat named Reliable Informant. (The Informant brothers are widely known and quoted here; among the best known are White House, State Department, and Congressional.) Walter Speculation's brother-in-law, Ian Rumour, married Alexandra Conjecture, from which there were two sons, It Was Understood and It Was Learned. It Was Learned just went to work in the Justice Department, where he will be gainfully employed for four long years."[23]
> *Washington Post, 12 February 1969*

Off the record

Probably thanks to Hollywood films on journalism, the phrase 'off the record' has become deeply embedded in popular consciousness. Real journalists are confronted with it in the most unlikely places: people with no previous exposure to the media use it with surprising ease. The problem is that it has several meanings. Among other variants, it can mean:

- that the information being offered is not to be used in any way – even if it can be confirmed through other means;
- that it should not be published but can be followed up;
- that it can be used as long as the source is not identifiable; or
- that it can be used with unspecific sourcing, like 'according to a senior official', 'an informed source said', or similar phrase.

These nuances are used quite precisely in politics and some other areas, and reporters need to be very clear what exactly the source has in mind. Sometimes, the expectation is implicit, and it's important to make sure if there is any doubt.

It is perfectly reasonable to negotiate the terms. A source may be quite happy with a lesser variant of the 'off the record' arrangement. For the journalist, the more precise the sourcing is, the better. These arrangements must be sorted out before the start of an interview. Sometimes, sources will realise they said something unfortunate and then afterwards try to change the deal, to put some elements 'off the record'. Such attempts should be resisted.

Even unpublishable information can be useful background, helping journalists understand and judge developments, and helps inform their reporting. At the same time, it is often used by public relations people to spin stories in particular directions. It can even be used by a source in order to keep information out of the public domain. Reporters are sometimes better off not knowing something, if it means they will be bound not to do anything about it. For this reason, too, it is important to think carefully before agreeing to any arrangement.

Promising confidentiality

Once a journalist has accepted an off-the-record arrangement of whatever kind, it must be strictly observed since honouring confidentiality is a cornerstone of journalism ethics. It has become a touchstone of the relationship of trust that needs to exist between a journalist and a source, and of our claim of independence. In some countries, it is recognised in law, much like the confidentiality that exists between priest and confessor, doctor and patient, or lawyer and client.

That's not the case in South Africa. We have already discussed Section 205 of the Criminal Procedures Act, which can be used to force anybody – including journalists – to provide information to the police and justice system (Chapter 6). Judge Arthur Chaskalson, the president of the Constitutional Court, has said that journalists cannot claim absolute privilege to information. Press freedom is not an absolute right. 'It has an impact on

> "The confidentiality of sources [ensures] that a newspaper is able to perform its role of a public watchdog uncovering wrong-doing, maladministration, corruption and other crimes especially in the public service. It is that promise not to reveal the identity of the source that enables informants to come forward and a newspaper to gather the information that leads to the exposure of these evils."[24]
> *Raymond Louw, former Rand Daily Mail editor*

other rights and interests and has to be balanced against them,' he told a 1996 conference of the Commonwealth Press Union in Cape Town.[25] It 'does not entitle a journalist to trample upon the dignity and privacy of others, a constraint that some journalists and newspapers are reluctant to acknowledge,' Chaskalson said.

Despite these sentiments, the legal situation has not been fully clarified. Although the authorities have not often tried to force journalists to disclose information, the threat remains in place. This means that a promise to protect somebody's identity can have serious consequences. It can bring the journalist into conflict with the law, and so it should not be lightly offered.

If a source asks to remain anonymous, we should consider whether the information is reliable, and whether it is worth putting ourselves at risk for. It is a good idea to consider carefully what likely scenarios might develop, and how we would feel about them. As *USA Today* found, it is often possible to persuade a source to go on the record. Sometimes, a request for anonymity is quite unreasonable, when there is no possible risk to the source. At the same time, it would be unethical to pressure a source who really is at risk. It is certainly worth exploring various options with the source. Sometimes people want complete invisibility, where nothing can be traced back to them; sometimes they are happy with something less. The BBC suggests the possibility of agreeing to protect an identity 'unless and until ordered by a court'.[26] Whatever arrangement is made, it must be clear to both sides.

The next question is: Does a promise of confidentiality extend to the journalist's editor? In a news organisation that takes itself seriously, the editor would want to satisfy him- or herself that the information is reliable, and that the story is worth it. Also, if there is a possibility of legal complications, it is in reporters' interests to ensure that the organisation will back them. The *Mail&Guardian* says an unnamed source may be used only with the agreement of an editor, who will usually need to be told the identity of the source (see the extract on p. 173). Makhanya says: 'The trust between the editor and the staff must be such that they can tell him who the source is.'[27] There may be exceptions, but they are rare.

Once an undertaking has been given, care must be taken to protect the source. This includes being careful with notes and similar material: the BBC points out that no document, computer file or other record that could identify the source should be kept; and that notes on the confidential source should be made separately from other notes.[28]

Ultimately, we have to honour a promise to protect a source. Even if it means going to jail.

. . . .

Relating to sources:
a test of five questions

Journalists should ask these questions:
1. Do you have sufficient grounds to believe the source?
2. What are the source's motives for talking to you?
3. What risks is the source taking?
4. Can you accept the terms around confidentiality the source expects, taking into account the need to attribute as clearly as possible?
5. Are you sure you can keep your word?

. . . .

TALKING POINT

Sources are like a garden
Mzilikazi wa Afrika

For any journalist, a reliable source of information is a treasure to cherish and guard with his or her life. Many journalists are arrested or sent to jail for refusing to divulge the names and identity of their sources, and I have no doubt many others will follow.

One may ask what makes a source of information so important to journalists that they will take such risks. To me, reliable sources of information are like your bank pin numbers. They should be kept as secrets and should not be revealed to anybody – not even a high court judge.

A friend of mine, also a journalist, once said that a reliable source of information is like having an affair outside your marriage – you don't want anybody to know about it.

Writing a letter to the editor of *The Guardian* newspaper, Tim Crook, a senior lecturer in media and ethics at Goldsmiths College, University of London, noted: 'Protecting a source is without qualification. It should never be given up – not to the editor or proprietor, not even after death. Journalists should never identify confidential sources on any traceable record, without the knowledge and permission of their informant.' Journalists therefore have a duty to protect their sources and make sure that they remain anonymous.

As they say, every man can make a baby but not every man can be a father. The same applies to sources: anybody can be a source but not everybody can be a reliable source. A source should not be just a faceless person giving you a scoop or exclusive information but an honest individual without malice or interest in the information he or she is sharing with you; somebody who, without prejudice, believes that the public has a right to know the real truth.

Journalists must investigate their sources to find out whether they are indeed credible and honest individuals with no criminal convictions or bad reputation. Sources with tainted backgrounds are neither credible nor reliable.

I do not think that the public would want to know that you got your information from a drug pusher who has just come out of jail for rape or other crimes. Nobody is perfect, of course, but you can't believe anything you hear from a chronic liar, somebody who was sent to jail for perjury. It does not matter whether such person is an eyewitness or not; it is his or her history that talks volumes and gives credibility to your story.

I always warn my sources beforehand that if they lie to me, I will without a doubt expose them because they are not honest and truthful. The 'marriage' between a journalist and his source is not of convenience but is based on trust, honesty and credibility.

I always tell my friends that sources are like a garden, you choose which flowers you want and where you want them – when you have all your favourite flowers, you must water them from time to time to keep them well and alive.

It is every journalist's dream to have a busload of reliable and credible sources but we have to be careful that our sources do not influence the way we present our stories.

As journalists, we do not work for our sources but for our publications.

Sources only supply us with information and we do not push their agendas. At the end of the day, we have to present a fair and well-balanced story to our readers. Regardless of how powerful or powerless your sources are, your independence must remain unquestionable.

If sources play fair with us, we should look after them.

(Mzilikazi wa Afrika is an investigative journalist
on the Sunday Times)

Case study 20
The word of a killer

Captain Dirk Coetzee was the kind of source to set all kinds of alarm bells ringing. In the mid-1980s, he was telling two investigative journalists, Martin Welz and Jacques Pauw, all kinds of wild stories about a police death squad he claimed to have commanded. The claims were extraordinary and explosive. Coetzee talked about having been involved in kidnappings, parcel bombs, the killing of anti-apartheid figures both in South Africa and abroad, and much else, all undertaken on the official order of the police's most senior generals. He said the unit was based on a farm near Pretoria, known as Vlakplaas.[29]

Coetzee's motives were less than pure. Once a rising star in the police, he had been given a series of hardship postings after embarrassing the police through a botched kidnapping in Swaziland, disrespect to superiors and other misbehaviour. He was ultimately retired in disgrace on a minuscule pension in 1986. Coetzee was deeply embittered by the way the police had treated him.

And yet there were several things that gave credibility to his stories. Welz says weeks and weeks of informal interviews gave him the opportunity to evaluate Coetzee's character. 'I discovered he'd tell stories over and over again without changing them, he's highly intelligent, and he distinguished between hearsay (and first-hand information). He'd distinguish between good rumour and bad rumour.'[30] In other words, his way of telling his tales lent them some credibility.

Welz also talks about Coetzee's motives: 'It became clear to me why he was telling me the information; it was pride, sometimes anxiety and discomfort. Suddenly in the depth of his conscience some questions were beginning to arise which were obviously beginning to nag him. Which would make him laugh nervously about some of the anecdotes.'

Welz says he believed the stories, 'but there was no way I could verify [them]'. Some of the incidents Coetzee described, like the murder of the Durban lawyer Griffiths Mxenge, had been reported, and that provided some corroboration.

But substantial verification came from an unexpected source: a prisoner on death row, Almond Nofemela, told human rights attorneys that he had been part of the Vlakplaas unit under Coetzee, and had participated in several assassination missions, including that of Mxenge. His claims were made in a last-minute appeal for clemency just days before his scheduled execution, and were reported prominently in the *Weekly Mail* of 20 October 1989.

The media landscape had changed dramatically by then. A new generation of alternative newspapers had developed, brash and ready to take risks. One of them was *Vrye Weekblad*, which Pauw had helped found. He writes: 'The story was at the heart of apartheid's most evil face and struck to the core of government ethics and morality ... This was our kind of story.'[31]

He says the fact that Nofemela was making these claims from death row reduced their credibility. 'But for [*Vrye Weekblad* editor] Max du Preez and me, the confessions provided much-needed corroboration. Coetzee had mentioned Almond Nofemela as one of his death squad operatives, and their accounts converged in nearly all aspects.'[32]

There remained the question of Coetzee's own safety – no small matter, as it turned out later when his former colleagues made attempts to kill him. With the support of the still-banned ANC, Coetzee was spirited to safety abroad, and in late November 1989 *Vrye Weekblad* published Coetzee's story. It was an immediate sensation around the world.

The story of Dirk Coetzee and the hit squad revelations went on for years, leading to court cases, a commission of inquiry, the closure of *Vrye Weekblad* and at least one assassination. But we will stop here, since we need to focus on the way in which an important but controversial source was handled. The journalists involved took account of his motives, and invested considerable time and energy in the verification of his claims. Once the decision had been taken that they were credible enough to be published, extraordinary measures were taken to secure Coetzee's interests.

It was an exceptional story of great public interest, which took years to find its way into print and had a huge impact. As Pauw writes: 'It was a hell of a newspaper story, the kind of exposé that every journalist and editor dreams about.'[33]

Case study 21
Who used whom?

A charismatic church leader, an adulterous inter-racial affair and the apartheid security police provided the ingredients for a sensational story that had the country agog in early 1985. The episode still provides an excellent example of some of the complexities around journalists' relationships with sources.

The cleric involved was Dr Allan Boesak, then president of the World Alliance of Reformed Churches and a respected anti-apartheid leader. A typed pamphlet made its appearance in various newsrooms, claiming that the married Boesak was having an affair with Di Scott, an official of the South African Council of Churches. The pamphlet was accompanied by specific details of their encounters in various hotels, as well as a trip to Tiger Bay in Zimbabwe: dates, times, flight and room numbers. There was also a tape recording of the two together in one of the hotel rooms.

Most journalists believed that the security police were behind the pamphlet and tape in order to discredit an important anti-apartheid leader. A reporter on *The Star*, Chris Steyn, wrote in an affidavit later: 'When I read the pamphlet it seemed to me that a sophisticated surveillance operation had tracked the movements of Dr Boesak and Miss Scott for several months in 1984.'[34] Most news organisations would not touch the story. The head of news at e.tv, Joe Thloloe, later recalled having been at the *Sowetan* at the time: 'We got the package at the *Sowetan*. We listened to the tape, looked at the documents and we concluded this was from the security police and we decided we were not going to use it.'[35]

But *The Star* told Steyn to investigate the matter. She was able to verify many of the details in the pamphlet, approached Boesak and Scott for comment (they declined) and then managed to get the security police to admit their involvement.

On 11 January 1985, the story ran under the banner headline 'Police spies expose Boesak's love affair'. The story confirmed the affair, but focused on the police's role in exposing it. A front-page editorial said: 'The nation lives with the fear that "dirty tricks" … are neither controlled nor punished.' *The Star*'s decision to run the story was panned by other news-papers including the *Cape Times*, who called it an 'almost unprecedented departure from the South African practice of treating people's private lives as their own business.'[36] In a later comment it said *The Star* had 'with the highest intentions, played into the hands of agencies who would destroy the influence of a formidable opponent of the Botha administration'.[37]

But *The Star*'s editor, Harvey Tyson, defended the decision vehemently. In a response to the *Cape Times* he wrote: 'What *The Star* did was to inves-tigate the matter … – bring the facts out in the open – and put the spot-light where it belonged: on the alleged "dirty tricks" of security police.'[38] In his memoirs Tyson argued later that the story was significant, since it provided 'the first palpable evidence' of police dirty tricks.[39] In any event, an illicit affair by a church leader was of public interest, Tyson argued: 'Regrettably, in Dr Boesak's case, his private affairs were relevant to his public stance.'[40]

Even though the Media Council later backed Tyson's decision to pub-lish, the story remains as controversial today as it was then. Expressing a widely held view, Thloloe says: 'They didn't just damage the security police by publishing that story, they damaged Boesak's reputation very badly and they were in fact instruments of the security police.'[41]

Sources rarely pass on information without some motive, as we have seen, and journalists don't as a rule discount information on those grounds alone. In this case, it was well known that the source was the security police, and their motive was clear. Why, then, did most journal-ists not want to use it?

There was something particularly despicable about an agency of state behaving in this way. And it involved not just any state, but a thoroughly discredited one, and not just any of its agencies, but one that was known as brutal and repressive. The motives here were so nasty that few wanted to be associated with them.

The Star tried valiantly to turn the story onto its originators by focusing on the police's dirty tricks. But the attempt was not persuasive. The detailed investigation of the affair itself, and the way the story was played, persuaded many that the newspaper was at least as interested in the scan-dal around Boesak as in the security police's role. There was some embar-rassment to the police, but the damage to the cleric's good name was substantial. (Of course Boesak later found himself in the news for other controversies, but that is another matter.)

The smear had succeeded. Many years later, the apartheid spy Craig Williamson claimed the episode as a success when he testified before the TRC's media hearing.[42]

Case study 22
Taking the pain

One of the mechanisms the apartheid state used to protect itself from opposition was the banning order. Hard to imagine from a post-apartheid perspective, this meant that people considered a threat to the state were served orders that restricted them, usually for five years. They were not allowed to travel outside their magisterial district, could not attend a gathering of more than two other people, could not be quoted, and much else.

One day, banned Catholic priest Cosmas Desmond broke his order by having lunch at a restaurant with three other people. Six security policemen swooped on this subversive event and took everybody's names with a view to prosecuting Desmond. One of the lunch guests was Peter Wellman, at the time a senior journalist on the *Rand Daily Mail*.

Wellman was issued with a subpoena under Section 205 of the Criminal Procedures Act, compelling him to give evidence against Desmond under threat of a jail sentence. The priest could have stopped this by telling the state he would not challenge the police evidence against him, Wellman wrote later: 'But I told him it was politically necessary for someone to set an example against a rash of prosecutions of people for breaking their restriction orders, which were unjust in the first place. It simply happened to be me.'[43]

And so in 1974 Wellman became the first journalist to be sentenced to a jail term under the recently toughened provisions of the act. He served six months in prison, and describes the experience with wry humour in a contribution to Harvey Tyson's book *Editors under fire*. He was released – and promptly served with another subpoena. He was ready for the maximum sentence of a year in jail. 'If [security police commander Brigadier Johan] Coetzee wanted to push this thing I was ready for him, and I would not have cared how heavy the sentence was.'[44] In the event, Desmond conceded the case and so the second subpoena fell away.

The apartheid police made extensive use of Section 205 subpoenas against journalists. During a single fortnight in 1984, Tyson writes, three

Cape Town editors and nine reporters from newspapers in the then Transvaal were issued orders to give evidence. Journalists and editors developed various techniques to avoid both giving evidence and going to prison. Sometimes editors would insist that the subpoena be issued to them personally, in which case they could tell the court honestly that they did not know the sources their reporters had spoken to.[45] Another reporter, Gary van Staden, played for time by using every legal avenue possible, and finally supplied a list of names of activists who were already dead.[46]

The protection of sources is a basic tenet of journalistic ethics. In pre-1994 South Africa, the rule became even weightier. The broader political situation made the moral line crystal clear: it was unthinkable to assist the apartheid state's repressive tactics. Co-operating with the police, even under the threat of jail, would have wrecked a journalist's credibility and ability to do his or her work. Nobody would have spoken to them again. Peter Wellman's brave stand during a difficult time set an example to many other journalists.

....

NOTES

1   Jonny Steinberg, *Midlands*. Johannesburg: Jonathan Ball, 2002.

2   Ibid. x.

3   Mary de Haas, 'Book on Midlands murder puts journalistic ethics in the dock', *Natal Witness*, 4 November 2002. Posted at http://www.witness.co.za/showcontent. asp?id=10771&action=full, accessed on 20 January 2004.

4   Janet Malcolm, *The journalist and the murderer*. London: Papermac, 1998. 3.

5   Quoted in Charlotte Bauer, 'A love affair doomed in the printing', *Sunday Times*, 17 November 2002.

6   *The New York Times*, 'Ethical journalism: code of conduct for the news and editorial departments'. New York: *The New York Times*, 2003. 9.

7   *Sunday Independent*, 9 September 2000.

8   Based on Bob Steele and Al Tompkins, 'Who said that? Guidelines for evaluating sources', 1 August 1999. Posted at http://www.poynter.org/content/content_view. asp?id=4634, accessed on 23 March 2004.

9   See *Business Day*, 21 and 22 August 2003.

10 Interview, 27 November 2002.

11   Nigel GE Harris, 'Codes of conduct for journalists' in Andrew Belsey and Ruth Chadwick (eds.), *Ethical issues in journalism and the media*. London: Routledge, 1992.

12   *The Star*, 12 July 2000.

13   *MediaGuardian*, 16 October 2002.

14   Interview, 15 October 2002.

15   *Rhodes Journalism Review* 14, May 1997. 8.

16   Robert J Haiman, 'Best practices for newspaper journalists', Freedom Forum, Washington, undated. Posted at http://www.freedomforum.org/publications/ diversity/bestpractices/bestpractices.pdf, accessed on 19 March 2004. 22.

17   Quoted in Robert J Haiman, 'Best practices for newspaper journalists', Freedom Forum, Washington, undated. Posted at http://www.freedomforum.org/publications/ diversity/bestpractices/bestpractices.pdf, accessed on 19 March 2004. 17.

18   Anton Harber, 'Sources light up dark corridors of power', *Business Day*, 8 August 2003.

19   Haiman, 'Best practices'. 19.

20   Quoted in ibid. 19.

21   Interview, 9 December 2002.

22   Interview, 8 November 2002.

23   Quoted in Johan Retief, *Media ethics: an introduction to responsible journalism*. Cape Town: OUP, 2002. 118.

24   Raymond Louw, 'Journalists and press freedom: setting the record straight', FXI, undated. Posted at http://fxi.org.za/archives/update/chaskal.htm, accessed on 23 March 2004.

25   Quoted in Sapa report of 15 October 1996, and in Johan Retief, *Media ethics: an introduction to responsible journalism*. Cape Town: OUP, 2002. 119.

26   BBC, *Producers' guidelines*. London: BBC, 1996. 122.

27   Interview, 9 December 2002.

28   BBC, *Producers' guidelines*. 122–3.

29   The following account is based largely on the account in Jacques Pauw, *Into the heart of darkness*. Johannesburg: Jonathan Ball, 1997. Ch 11.

30   Interview, 8 November 2002.

31   Pauw, *Into the heart*. 161.

32   Ibid. 162–3.

33   Ibid. 161.

34   Statement for Media Council of South Africa hearing, 25 January 1985.

35   Interview, 2 September 2002.

36   *Cape Times*, 16 January 1985

37   Quoted in Harvey Tyson, *Editors under fire*. Sandton, Johannesburg: Random House, 1993. 208.

38   Quoted in ibid. 209.

39   Ibid. 203.

40   *The Star*, 12 January 1985.

41   Interview, 2 September 2002.

42   Evidence by Craig Williamson to TRC media hearing, 15–17 September 1997. Transcript posted at http://www.doj.gov.za/trc/trc_frameset.htm, accessed 21 January 2004.

43   Tyson, *Editors under fire*. 280.

44   Ibid. 282.

45   Ibid. 284.

46   Ibid. 288–91.

The Star respects the individual's right to privacy, except where it conflicts clearly with the public interest.
The Star: Code of Ethics

Insofar as both news and comment are concerned, broadcasting licensees shall exercise exceptional care and consideration in matters involving the private lives and private concerns of individuals, bearing in mind that the right to privacy may be overridden by legitimate public interest.
Icasa: Code of Conduct for Broadcasters

A journalist should avoid violation of individual privacy unless such violation is done for a provable public interest.
Media Council of Tanzania: Code of Conduct

11

MY HOME IS (NOT ALWAYS) MY CASTLE: PRIVACY

In March 1996 the long-awaited divorce case of *Mandela* v *Mandela* came to court. Nelson Mandela, then the president, was suing for divorce from Winnie Madikizela-Mandela after almost forty years of marriage. The public was agog as the most intimate details of the couple's life together were laid bare in court.

The media could not get enough of the story. Reportage was extensive – and largely illegal. The Divorce Act allows the reporting only of the fact of a divorce action, the names of the couple, and the judgment. The law is designed to protect the privacy of the people involved. Dennis Davis, a constitutional law expert, said it was 'unbelievable' that the law was being so brazenly breached.

'Being president gives you a reduced right to privacy, but it can't possibly destroy your privacy completely. He might be the most famous person in the world, but he is not public property,' said Davis.[1] Mandela's legal team took a more sanguine view. One of his lawyers said: 'I don't know what our client's attitude is. We did not discuss it and no one from our legal side expressed any objection. The publicity did not do him any harm. It would have done him more harm if the trial was held in secret.'[2]

The Divorce Act is one of several laws that recognise the individual's right to privacy. Section 14 of South Africa's Bill of Rights guarantees it. But why do we feel so strongly about our right to privacy?

The British philosopher Matthew Kieran writes: 'Revelations about ourselves are a matter within our gift: not just anyone has a right to know anything about us.'[3] It is a mark of our autonomy as an individual, and people may suffer real damage if that right is overridden. Kieran cites the example of a doctor who without his consent is revealed to be gay, and who as a result finds it hard to work with patients because of their irrational prejudices. Kieran adds: 'Privacy is … required to protect us from the irrelevant and slanderous judgments of others that may prevent us from pursuing and attaining public goods.'[4]

However, Kieran also points out that the right cannot be absolute. It must be weighed against questions of public interest and freedom of expression. In an editorial on the reporting of the Mandela divorce, the *Mail&Guardian* said the two rights required careful balance. 'But the Mandela divorce case demonstrates precisely why, in the case of public figures – and, in particular, politicians – the balance needs [to] be weighted heavily in favour of freedom of information.' The case was 'a test of the character of two public representatives', wrote the newspaper.[5]

Journalism very often takes us into the private spheres of the people we write about. Sometimes this desire for privacy is not legitimate, as when people try to hide corrupt behaviour. In other cases it is entirely reasonable, as when a grieving family asks to be left alone after the suicide of a teenage son. Deciding when an invasion of privacy is permissible is not easy, and requires careful consideration. It is the area in which the journalistic duty of truth-telling most often runs up against the duty to avoid doing harm (see Chapter 1). As in so many areas of journalism ethics, we use the notion of public interest to resolve particular dilemmas – as reflected in most codes (see the extracts on p. 193).

South Africa's Constitution says the right to privacy includes the right not to have one's person, home or property searched, one's possessions seized, or the privacy of one's communications infringed. For our purposes, the constitutional definition is of limited value. But the law recognises four ways in which privacy can be invaded, and these are more relevant to journalists.[6]

(1) Intrusion

When journalists intrude on the private space of a person they are reporting on, that's an invasion of privacy. It arises during reporting, rather than writing or publication. Most famously, the treatment meted out to their royal family by elements of the British media falls into this category. Photographers with impossibly long lenses will lurk in the shrubbery like some sort of B-movie detective, in the hopes of catching inappropriate royal behaviour. In this world, a picture of a duchess sucking the toes of a man who is not her husband is the pinnacle of achievement. It's a sorry excuse for journalism.

In 1996 Earl Charles Spencer, the brother of Britain's Princess Diana, went to court to protect himself and his family – then living in Cape Town – against the attentions of Fanie Jason, possibly South Africa's only paparazzo.[7] Countess Spencer said: 'He made an emotional wreck of me. It seems as if he knows all my movements and has targeted me. His conduct interfered with my right to privacy and this is traumatic for my children.' The court confirmed an agreement by which Jason bound himself, among other things, to stay more than a certain distance from the family, and to photograph them only in public places.

> "The paparazzi merely do out loud what everyone thinks about, and the press is the physical representation of what goes on in our minds … Di has a lover: Oooooh! So does Winnie: Aaaaah! So be faithful, be boring, be conservative and the paparazzi will leave you alone. They are in fact the allies of the very moral majority that shrieks its outrage at their excesses. The truth is that the ratpack thrive because they feed off a ratbag society."[8]
>
> *Yves Vanderhaeghen, assistant editor of the Natal Witness, commenting on the role of paparazzi photographers after Britain's Princess Diana died in a car crash while fleeing from them*

The case illustrates various forms of invasion of privacy, including intrusion. Jason was accused of trespassing on the countess's property. Trespass is a criminal matter, and the threat of a trespass charge has been used by many farmers, for instance, to ward off unwelcome inquiries. Jason was also accused of intruding through the use of long lenses, which allow photographers to put themselves – and the public – in the heart of a family gathering or other private moment.

Things that happen in the privacy of somebody's home are, in general, private, while things that take place in a public place are not. The BBC points out: 'People in a public place cannot expect the same degree of privacy as in their own homes. They can be seen by anyone, and that means they may be spotted by cameras or recorded by microphones.'[9] On this basis, the organisation allows some surreptitious recording in public places. 'Although we cannot guarantee that the broadcasting of recordings made in public will not cause individuals embarrassment, we should not intend this unless they are engaged in clearly anti-social activity,' the BBC says.

(2) Private facts

People are entitled to keep details of their private lives to themselves. The publication of embarrassing facts can be an invasion of privacy. But this is one area where people are not treated equally. Ordinary people have significant rights to privacy, but celebrities, politicians and others who live their lives in the public eye forfeit a large part of these rights. The public has the right to know what their elected representatives and other officials are doing. Where private behaviour touches on their suitability for public office, then that justification is very clear. Film stars and other celebrities aren't accountable in the same way, but they benefit in many ways from being in the public eye, and have to take the rough with the smooth. That kind of prominence is hardly ever achieved without the willing, often eager participation of the person involved. Kieran writes: 'We should think in terms of a sliding scale that seeks to weigh up news figures' political, economic and public power and influence, their celebrity status, or their rights as ordinary citizens against whatever public interest and considerations of harm might speak in favour of intruding into their privacy.'[11]

> "I get so tired of these celebrities complaining. You know, they spend most of their life trying to get into this business and then when they get in, they come up with all this bullshit attitude … The public and the photographs have made the celebrities, and all of a sudden they run and hide and act like immature three-year-olds."[10]
>
> *Phil Ramey, celebrity photographer*

Still, even prominent people retain some rights. The editor of *The Star*, Moegsien Williams, says: 'The rule of thumb for me is if Minister So-and-so is drunk over the weekend in his lounge at home, it is his business. If Minister So-and-so is drunk on a Wednesday in the office, it's my business. So yes, there are certain privacy rights … that public figures have.'[12]

But what about the family members of prominent people? In the Spencer case, much legal argument revolved around whether or not members of his family were public figures.[13] Jason's lawyer argued they were, while the family's representative said the earl was not necessarily one, but his wife and children were certainly not. People sometimes become the subjects of media attention merely because of their relationship with somebody who is legitimately in the public domain, even though they themselves have not sought publicity. Sometimes an argument can be made that their behaviour reflects on the relative. If the son of the minister of education is expelled from school for misbehaviour, for instance, one can argue that an inability to instil good values at home reflects on his or her ability to run an important area of government.

But the family members of prominent people sometimes find themselves in the media spotlight without that kind of public interest argument having any strength. We should be careful about the harm that can be caused to people who have not sought public attention, simply because of some connection to a big name. Journalists can easily cause collateral damage to quite innocent people.

Death is an area of great privacy, where intrusion and the disclosure of private facts can be particularly hurtful. It deserves careful consideration, and will be fully discussed in Chapter 12.

(3) False light

A third type of invasion of privacy, according to the US ethicist Louis Day, is the publication of information that creates or supports a wrong public impression about somebody.[14] Situations that might fall under this category are more commonly treated as possible defamation.

(4) Misappropriation

Taking somebody else's name or picture without their consent is also regarded as an invasion of privacy. In 2003 the story of Happy Sindane gripped the public imagination. He was a light-skinned, Ndebele-speaking teenager who walked into the Bronkhorstspruit police station saying he believed he had been kidnapped from his Afrikaans parents and brought up in a black home. He now wanted to find his parents. As DNA tests were done to help a court determine his parentage, the paint company Dulux used his photograph in their advertising campaign, with the payoff line 'Any colour you can think of'. It was a classic case of misappropriation, and the company was forced to apologise and paid Sindane an undisclosed amount in compensation.[15]

This kind of invasion of privacy is mostly relevant to the commercial exploitation of an image. In general, the use of photographs for normal reporting purposes would be regarded as legitimate.

Before court

People have been ruined by being put on trial for offences they did not commit. Even an acquittal is not always enough to clear their name. The fact of being arrested and charged is enough to suggest guilt in the minds of many people. An impression is created which is very difficult to shake. Some legal systems deal with the problem by not allowing the publication of the names of accused people. They may only be named after they have been convicted.

In other countries, including South Africa, trials are almost always a public process. Justice must be seen to be done, as the saying goes. This principle is seen as more important than any damage that can be caused to individual reputations. Accordingly, the law allows the media to name the accused in a trial, unless they are children.

> "There is a price tag attached to widespread dissemination of information, especially when journalists are naming individuals accused of wrongdoing. We, in essence, put a Scarlet Letter on someone's forehead."[16]
> *Bob Steele, ethicist*

However, it should be noted that the trial only begins properly when the accused person enters a plea. The accused's identity is supposed to be protected until that point. A plea of guilty or not guilty gives an accused at least that small chance to state his or her side of the story in the court of public opinion, even before they mount a full defence before the judge. Before charges are formally brought, the media can be at risk of a defamation suit if they identify somebody facing trial.

In the South African media, people are routinely identified as soon as they have been arrested. It's become common practice because people affected rarely take the media on. But in 2003 a Cape Town businessman, Waleed Suleiman, won damages of R100 000 from the *Cape Times* after it published a photograph of him being arrested at Cape Town International Airport. In an accompanying report, he was linked to the 1997 bomb blast at the Planet Hollywood restaurant on the city's Waterfront. It later turned out that he was being held for a passport irregularity.[17]

Another case illustrates the ethical pitfalls of naming people before they have been charged, even where they do not sue. In late October 2001 six Upington men were arrested for the gang rape of a nine-month-old baby who came to be known as Baby Tshepang. There was an outpouring of revulsion at people who could commit such an appalling deed, and the identities and even photographs of the six were published far and wide. Even though nobody explicitly declared them guilty, the prominent publication of their photographs was just like the medieval practice of pillorying the guilty. Look at these monsters, the pictures seemed to say. It soon turned out that they weren't. Early in 2002, DNA tests showed the men could not have committed the crime and all charges had to be dropped.[18]

Mistakes happen. At least the case of Baby Tshepang had achieved such notoriety that the collapse of the case against the six men received a fair amount of coverage. But in many other cases the arrest of a person gets far more prominence than an eventual acquittal, leaving the initial stigma much harder to eradicate. As journalists, we should remember that an arrest is very far from a conviction. We should take care to project an arrest as just that, avoiding the implication that it indicates guilt. Also, it's important to record an acquittal if we've covered the initial charge.

Child abuse is a particularly emotional subject. Andrew Bolton, the news editor of *Cape Talk*, remembers a story about the arrest of a man for abusing children at his wife's nursery school in Bellville. Because the man had not been charged he could not be named, but Bolton says he decided to run the name of the school even though that indirectly identified the man and his alleged victims. 'The people that live in that area need to know that their children might be at risk,' he says.[19]

Let's talk about sex

What people get up to in the privacy of their own bedrooms is their own business. At the same time, it is a matter of immense interest to others. Let's face it: there's nothing as fascinating as a juicy bit of gossip. For the media, the principle that sex sells has long been understood. Tabloid newspapers trade on the public appetite for sex and scandal with relentless determination; but even media that think of themselves as highbrow are happy to play the sex card if it presents itself.

> "When the public interest demands it, then one loses the right to privacy."[20]
> *Robin Comley, pictures editor at The Star*

What are the ethical considerations in covering people's sexual peccadilloes, which always amount to invasion of a very private sphere? The question illustrates neatly some of the difficulties in balancing the public interest against the individual's right to privacy.

To address the question, we need to work out what the public interest in these matters can be. Some cases are very clear: it is fully justified, for instance, to report that an anti-porn campaigner has a huge collection of pornographic videos in his cellar (assuming, of course, that the evidence is solid). Such a report would uncover blatant hypocrisy and stop a kind of ongoing fraud being perpetrated on the public. Similarly, adulterous politicians who preach family values or church figures who abuse children are fair game. Where somebody's private behaviour contradicts their public stance, the invasion is fully justified. 'Vicious hypocrisy,' Kieran calls it – 'where public figures cynically use their publicly declared aspirations as camouflage for actions that do not even truly aim at their professed goal'.[21]

The issue is less clear-cut where public figures offend against social norms without having particularly set themselves up as paragons of virtue. A married businessman visits a brothel – is that of any public concern? Some would argue that everyone in a prominent position has leadership responsibilities and should behave properly. Also, if the man's wife can't trust him, why should his customers? Others would say it's a matter between him and his family only, and the media should leave him alone.

Our decisions on matters like this depend heavily on our own set of morals. People with very strict ideas on how people should behave are more likely to see the public interest in private lapses of morality. Others with more tolerant attitudes will be more likely to dismiss their value as stories. Attitudes in society as a whole also play an important role. The former French president François Mitterand conducted a long-running extramarital affair and even had a son with his mistress. If this had been England, he would have been forced from office. But in France nobody cared, and the media there paid little or no attention to the fact.

● ●

Privacy:
a test of five questions

Journalists should ask these questions to check their reporting:
1. What exactly is the public interest in this story?
2. How important is it?
3. How will the people involved be affected by the invasion of their privacy?
4. How much protection do they deserve?
5. Are there alternative approaches that might reduce any risk or harm to them?

● ●

How do you knock
when there's no door?
Ferial Haffajee

The debate on the limits of the right to privacy inevitably deals with the private lives of the powerful – corporate titans, government officials, and politicians. How far can we go in crossing into the sphere and when is it justifiable? Is it going too far to follow a philandering politician? What about checking the property and company records of a director-general – does he or she have more assets than their salary allows? And what of the share dealings of executives?

These are the limits of privacy that we interrogate most often, yet a trip to a land occupation at Bredell on the East Rand some years ago showed up the ways in which we recklessly abandon the privacy rights of the powerless.

The city council's Red Ants were out in full force, there to tear up the shacks put up by the migrants who had overnight declared this plot of unused peri-urban land their own.

They invaded; we followed, right into and through what were very clearly people's homes; we picked about the god-forsaken remains, poking our noses in here, digging around there, shoving microphones (or notepads) into the middle of the trauma of those being 'removed'. A shard of zinc on a pink cot; washing being torn off lines; a forlorn woman looked up at God. A journalist asked her how she felt. I'd have told the reporter to fuck off.

How do you knock when there is no door? How do you not intrude but still try to capture a story that is not only that of the official who is briefing a line: 'This government will not allow illegal land invasions.'

If we are to do our jobs well, it will mean locating ourselves in the transient, poverty-stricken communities like Bredell; to tell their stories of policy failure and of delivery's slow coming. That will entail true location for weeks and if not months on end – a model far removed from the parachuting in and out that passes as development journalism.

The parachuting model necessarily entails the privacy invasion of a Bredell, where the poor become only backdrop or 'wall-paper' (in the lingo of the broadcasters) to the inevitable dramas and dilemmas that development entails. Without the paraphernalia of the powerful – the gatekeepers and spin-doctors; the officialese and the threat of legal cen-sure – it is up to us to ensure privacy rights of the poor. For me, this means asking for permission to take photographs every time. It means setting up interviews with local community leaders who will introduce you to people in the community. You would not arrive at Anglo American unan-nounced or just walk into the Reserve Bank governor Tito Mboweni's office. The same rules should apply in grassroots reporting.

For colleagues in newspaper and television, it's often unnecessary to explain your craft – usually those with bucks and those without want to be on TV and most South Africans listen to the radio, but newspapers are a different story. The *Sowetan* and now the *Daily Sun* are probably known brands, but for the rest, warm-up interviews may be necessary to explain where you're from and why you're interested. While we at the *Mail&Guardian* like to think we represent the poor and the disadvan-taged, my wake-up call long ago came from people I've tried to interview: 'The Mail what? What's that?'

(Ferial Haffajee is editor of the Mail&Guardian)

Case study 23
The politician
and the rent-boy

In May 1998 the *Mail&Guardian* reported claims by a convicted thief, John David Hermanus, that the leader of the National Party (as it then was), Marthinus van Schalkwyk, had paid him R20 for sex. The politician strongly denied the claims. Allegations to this effect had been swirling around for some time, but journalists from vari-ous news organisation could find no corroboration. The *Mail&Guardian* finally decided to run the story when Hermanus laid a charge, and a senior sex-crimes investigator in the Western Cape took the case on.

The paper still made it clear that it doubted the truth of the claims. Its front page said: 'Smear fears: A convict has laid sodomy charges against National Party leader Marthinus van Schalkwyk. But is it part of a dirty tricks campaign aimed at crippling the NP?' The story described problems with Hermanus's story, but also focused on the police investigation. The paper suggested the claims might be a smear related to the upcoming general election.[22]

The decision to publish attracted much criticism. The parliamentary editor of Independent Newspapers, Zubeida Jaffer, wrote that the story had been motivated by a desire to seek political advantage. 'The opposition leader does not stand to be the only loser. Another will be the South African news media, battling to restore its reputation as truth-teller in the country – a reputation besmirched by how this story has been reported.'[23]

The National Party lodged a complaint with the press ombud, essentially on the grounds that the report smeared Van Schalkwyk. It had been presented in a way intended to lend authenticity to the allegations, the NP argued. The ombud dismissed the complaint, but criticised the *Mail&Guardian* for failing to mention an important fact.[24] The Western Cape premier, the NP's Gerald Morkel, had asked the police to investigate the matter urgently and at high level, to clear the party leader and ensure there could be no claims of a cover-up. This was reported only in the following week's edition, and threw a very different light on the police probe.

The party took the matter on appeal, but lost again. In fact the appeal panel also overruled the finding about Morkel's role on the grounds that his involvement had been unknown at the time of the first report.[25]

The case is, in the first instance, about an invasion of privacy. Sex clearly belongs in the private sphere, and journalists need to demonstrate public interest if they want to enter this terrain. Where's the public interest here? Let's first dispense with the theme of homosexuality, which the married Van Schalkwyk found particularly damaging. Many conservative South Africans will have found the notion of a gay party leader very shocking, and the allegation that he used a 'rent-boy' deeply disturbing. But there is really no public interest here. People's sexuality is their own business.

Where prominent people commit crimes – particularly when they are involved in electoral politics – the public interest is clear. But although sodomy was then still formally on the statute books, it was hardly ever prosecuted since it was probably rendered ultra vires by the new Constitution.

The claim itself did not stand up, and the paper always made it clear that it did not believe Hermanus's story. But sometimes rumours and falsehoods have an impact in the real world, and deserve to be reported on that basis.

The story had two additional layers, and the *Mail&Guardian* referred to these in arguing the public interest. The first was the possibility that this was an orchestrated smear, the second was that the police were seriously investigating the story. It wrote: 'It is difficult to imagine a matter of more relevance to the public interest than an attempt to smear and/or blackmail the leader of the second-largest political party in the country.'[26] Elsewhere, it said: 'What the police, as public servants, do with public money is public business, particularly if it is pursuing a charge like sodomy, which is no longer deemed to be an offence.'[27]

The paper was completely right in identifying the public interest in these layers of the story. The problem is that a smear is given credence by merely mentioning it. Once the claims about Van Schalkwyk were in the public domain, some people will have found them credible, no matter how dismissively they were reported. 'No smoke without fire' is an empty but seductive and very popular saying.

Is that enough to trump the public interest the *Mail&Guardian* identified? No, but it does highlight the importance of thinking carefully about how such a story should be handled. Here, the paper could have been criticised. Although the emphasis provided by the headline and other elements was on the possibility of a smear, the story dwelt on the details of Hermanus's story. The paper said it presented these in order to demonstrate the holes in the story. But besides asserting the possibility of a smear, there was little evidence of an investigation in this direction. Just because a story doing the rounds is implausible doesn't mean it is a smear. The story would have benefited from some consideration of who might have been involved in the smear, how it was being perpetrated, what Hermanus stood to gain, and so on. If the emphasis had been different, the story might not have made a lead, but it would have attracted less criticism.

Case study 24
The hidden minister

Rape is an appalling crime, gang rape even worse. When four young men in a residence of the University of Pretoria allegedly raped a young woman, it was no wonder that the story ran prominently in the media. In September 2003 the university announced the incident. The matric student had allegedly been taken to the Maroela residence late one night and raped. There were suggestions that a date rape drug had been used. Three of the young men were university students, and were suspended. All four were quickly arrested and appeared in court.

Despite the obvious seriousness of the incident, coverage seemed extravagant. There was one element in the story that drew journalists like bees to honey, and yet it was something that could not easily be spelt out. Two of the four young men were the grandsons of Pik Botha, who had been minister of foreign affairs in the apartheid government and also served in the government of national unity.

But the law is quite clear. The accused in a crime like rape cannot be identified until the trial begins. They cannot be named, nor can any information be published which can lead to their being identified. The complainant is also legally protected, but her identity was not an issue in this case.

For some time the media tiptoed around the issue. Some reports said two of the accused were 'the grandsons of a former prominent politician'. The SABC spoke to Botha, who confirmed his connection to the two. However, the report did not identify him by name.[28] Others, including *The Citizen*, named him directly. *Rapport* took the approach to its logical conclusion, identifying the accused as 'Pik's grandsons', naming them directly and quoting their father and the former minister at length. The paper also carried their account of the incident: one of the accused admitted having had sex with the complainant but claimed she had agreed, another said he'd had oral sex with her consent, and the two others said they had done nothing wrong at all.[29]

The editor, Tim du Plessis, defended himself a week later against the charges that he had prejudged the case and mounted a trial by media. He said selective leaks by the state and the university had put the accuser's version of the story into the public domain without allowing the young men to defend themselves. 'While there was no complaint when the dailies played around with one side of the case, there was condemnation when *Rapport* presented both sides.'[30] Referring to other incidents in which sensational cases had been reported without regard to legal restrictions, he added: 'We just say there are rules that need revision.'

Early in 2004 chargers against the men were dropped due to insufficient evidence – apparently lending weight to Du Plessis's argument.[31] He was right to point out that in prominent cases the rules are freely ignored. But we should remind ourselves what these particular rules are designed to achieve: they protect the people involved – accusers and accused – against the terrible stigma that attaches to crimes like rape. Can we honestly say that people are less fully entitled to that protection because they are related to a former politician?

The link to Botha made the story more prominent than it would otherwise have been. The public is greatly interested in a scandal in a prominent family, even if there is little public interest in the strict sense. Journalists should not be embarrassed to admit that they cover stories that people *want* to know about even when there's no great *need* to know. Sometimes we construct tortuous 'public interest' justifications when we should simply admit that we're appealing to people's curiosity about prominent people.

However, the price must be worth paying. In this case the damage to the reputations of those involved was too great to justify breaking both legal and ethical guidelines – even if it was done in other cases.

Case study 25
Will you be my ex?

A Valentine's Day broadcast on Highveld Stereo in 2001 illustrated the perils of live broadcasting. The host, Jeremy Mansfield, offered a slot on his programme for callers to send messages to their loved ones. A caller by the name of Brad called in, and his girlfriend was contacted and put on air with him. Her expectation, and that of the station, was that he was going to propose marriage to her on air.

Instead, he told her that he had not been entirely honest with her. After some embarrassed hesitation he came out with the truth: he was gay. The young woman broke down in tears, and then her mother picked up the telephone, according to Kobus van Rooyen, the BCCSA chairperson who heard a complaint on the matter.

'And then the mother came and she said, "So what's going on here? I've got a crying girl here. What has he been doing, he has been going out with my daughter for two years." '[32] Van Rooyen said it later appeared that 'Brad' had promised his friend that he would come out, and do it live on air. Mansfield immediately apologised to the girl and her mother: the revelation had caught him by surprise as well.

Highveld Stereo was discussing the incident in its later programmes on the same day, and played the episode again in order to inform the discussion. The BCCSA heard a complaint about this rebroadcast.

In its ruling the BCCSA said that 'Brad's' message to his girlfriend was 'to say the least, cruel'.[33] However, the station had not known that he intended to end his relationship during a live Valentine's Day broadcast, and so could not be held responsible.

However, the rebroadcast was a different matter. By this time the content was obviously known, and this made the station 'an associate in the humiliation'. The rebroadcast amounted to a 'double invasion' of her privacy, the BCCSA ruled: 'Listeners were informed of exactly how the young lady had been humiliated and the intensity of her grief, which clearly emerged, was replayed.'

The station had argued that the rebroadcast was necessary to inform listeners of the incident. The BCCSA said this was a mitigating factor, but the host could simply have recounted what had happened. The commission reprimanded Highveld for the rebroadcast, saying it had been not malicious but negligent.

Talk radio is always exposed to some risk that a caller might say something inappropriate. Some radio stations used to have a slight time-lag between a call being received and its broadcast, just enough to allow something regarded as unsuitable to be stopped. Nowadays, those techniques are no longer used. Most shows simply rely on a producer, who chats briefly to callers before putting them through, to do some filtering. But live radio can't be sanitised, and so there remains an element of risk.

The BCCSA judged the case fairly: the original humiliation could not be foreseen, but it did not need to be repeated.

. . . .

NOTES

1   Quoted in Philippa Garson, 'Mandela versus Mandela', *Mail&Guardian*, 22–28 March 1996.

2   Ibid.

3   Matthew Kieran, *Media ethics: a philosophical approach*. Westport, Conn: Praeger, 1997. 74.

4   Ibid. 76.

5   *Mail&Guardian*, 22–28 March 1996.

6   Louis A Day, *Ethics in media communications: cases and controversies*. Belmont, CA: Wadsworth, 1991. 99–100.

7   The case is described in Johan Retief, *Media ethics: an introduction to responsible journalism.* Cape Town: OUP, 2002. 163–4.

8   Yves Vanderhaeghen, *Rhodes Journalism Review* 15, November 1997.

9   BBC, *Producers' guidelines.* London: BBC, 1996. 35–6.

10 Ramey: Quoted by Vanderhaeghen, ibid.

11 Kieran, *Media ethics.* 83.

12 Interview, 13 September 2002.

13 Retief, *Media ethics.* 163.

14 Day, *Ethics in media communications.* 125.

15 *Saturday Star*, 20 June 2003. In the end, he was found not to have been born into an Afrikaans family after all.

16 Bob Steele, 'In pursuit of ethical standards: getting past conventional wisdom on crime stories'. Posted at http://www.poynter.org/content/content_view.asp?id=3539, accessed on 23 March 2004.

17 Sapa report. Posted at http://www.iol.co.za/index.php?set_id=1&click_id=13&art _id=qw1037203201475B263, accessed on 24 January 2004.

18 *Saturday Star*, 18 January 2002.

19 Interview, 8 November 2002.

20 Interview, 2002.

21 Kieran, *Media ethics.* 78.

22 *Mail&Guardian*, 1–7 May 1998.

23 *The Star*, 11 May 1998.

24 Press Ombudsman of South Africa adjudication, 14 August 1998.

25 Press Ombudsman of South Africa (appeal panel) judgment, 6 December 1998.

26 *Mail&Guardian*, 8–14 May 1998

27 *Cape Argus*, 15 May 1998.

28 SABC, 'Tukkies rape suspects related to ex-minister', 12 September 2003. Posted at http://www.sabcnews.com/south_africa/crime1justice/0,2172,65657,00.html, accessed on 27 January 2004.

29 *Rapport*, 14 September 2003.

30 *Rapport*, 21 September 2003, own translation.

31 Sapa, 'Pik glad "trial by media is over,"' 17 February 2004. Posted at http://www. news24.com/News24/South_Africa/News/0,,2-7-1442_1485077,00.html, accessed on 22 September 2004.

32 Interview, 30 January 2003.

33 BCCSA ruling in case no 2001/15.

We respect an individual's right to privacy, except where this clearly conflicts with the public interest, and we discourage any actions which entail unjustifiable intrusion into private grief and distress.
Independent Newspapers: Code of Conduct

Always show the greatest possible consideration for victims of crime and accidents.
Code of Ethics for Press, Radio and Television, Sweden

The identity of rape victims and other victims of sexual violence shall not be published without the consent of the victim.
Press Code of Professional Practice

12

THE DARK SIDE: REPORTING DEATH, AIDS AND TRAUMA

The veteran British foreign correspondent Edward Behr describes how thousands of Belgian civilians, mostly women and children, were packed into aircraft hangars waiting to be airlifted out of the newly independent Congo. There had been some excesses by Congolese soldiers and rebels, and Belgians were fleeing in their numbers.

'Into the middle of this crowd strode an unmistakably British TV reporter,' he writes, 'leading his cameraman and sundry technicians like a platoon commander through hostile territory. At intervals he paused and shouted, in a stentorian but genteel BBC voice: "Anyone here been raped and speaks English?"'[1]

The unnamed reporter's call provided Behr with a title for his book of memoirs, and has become emblematic of the callousness of many reporters. We deal with a lot of death and trauma in our jobs. The issue raises important ethical questions, which need to be considered from two perspectives.

The impact on subjects and sources: As discussed in Chapter 10, the people we report about may be powerfully affected both by our interaction with them and by how their story is told. Writing about people's pain and suffering invades their privacy, and therefore needs thought and sensitivity.

The impact on audiences: Sometimes the reporting of horrifying events can be profoundly disturbing to audiences. This applies very strongly to the use of images, as discussed in Chapter 9.

The two perspectives may intermingle: audiences are sometimes offended by reporting they consider infringes the dignity of victims. (On occasion, people in the news may not be unhappy with coverage, but audiences may be offended on their behalf.) In considering the ethics involved it is as well to remember that, although the two perspectives may not be neatly separable, they are distinct. We will touch on both in the following discussion.

The compassionate reporter

We cannot avoid stories about tragedy and suffering, and we will often have to approach those directly affected in order to tell them properly. Bob Steele, an ethicist at the Poynter Institute, writes: 'There is little doubt that it is intrusive and invasive to approach someone at one of the worst moments of their life. At the same time it is often necessary to do just that to carry out the legitimate professional role that a journalist plays in a community.'[2]

The first requirement in dealing with these situations, says Steele, is excellent reporting. Getting things wrong can be very hurtful, so reporters must take extra care. Secondly, reporters should be compassionate. Dr Martin Cohen, a psychologist, says: 'To approach someone [who is suffering] is difficult but important. But you must show an increased level of sensitivity. If you are going to

> "Our lives became a nightmare. Our yard, our street and our neighbourhood were suddenly covered with reporters and cameras at all hours for several days. A neighbour told us she had seen a writer actually putting our trash bag in his car and speeding away. They put our family finances in the paper, which was totally irrelevant in the murder of our daughter."[3]
> *A woman whose daughter was murdered on her nineteenth birthday*

make use of this family's plight, you have a responsibility to do it as a *mensch*, a really good person, to not treat people as an object.'[4]

A lot will depend on the initial approach. It is easy and humane to acknowledge grief and apologise for intruding. The BBC says: 'People in a state of distress must not be put under any pressure to provide interviews against their wishes.'[5] As Johan Retief, a media ethics lecturer at Stellenbosch University, points out, 'Victims feel (and often are) vulnerable. Journalists should therefore grant the victim a sense of power or control.'[6] As difficult as it is, we should respect a person's decision not to talk to us.

Often there are ways of getting a story while still remaining respectful of a family's wishes. Jimi Matthews, the head of television news at the SABC, tells the story of a camera team that was sent out to report on a soldier who had killed his wife and then himself. Relatives asked them not to film, and they returned empty-handed. He says he was very angry. 'If there were objections to photographing the house I would have filmed the street. I would have found one or two of the neighbours to find out what kind of person this was.'[7]

One should not make the mistake of believing that everybody will object to speaking to the media. In many cases, people find the opportunity to tell their story helpful and cathartic.

The interview itself should also be conducted sensitively. This means explaining your intentions clearly and honestly. Remember that people often don't have experience of the media, and it would be unfair to take advantage of that. While journalists generally don't like to give their sources any say over the end-product, the rules can be bent a little when dealing with people who have been traumatised. They may want to see a particular family photograph used, for instance, and there's no harm in negotiating this or other aspects of usage.

Where you do make promises, it's essential to keep them. Kerry Cullinan, of Health-e News Service, tells the story of how US reporters interviewed sex workers in Carletonville about the use of condoms. The women did not hide their identities on the strict understanding that the story would be published overseas only. A few months later, they were devastated when the story appeared in the local press and they were revealed as prostitutes.[8] Clearly, promises must be kept.

Being compassionate can mean taking a bit more time to gain the trust of an interviewee. But that extra investment of time often improves the final product. Bill Lord, a US news director, says reporters may have to talk informally for an hour or so before the interview begins. 'They gain trust and they sympathize … they really get a feeling on how to convey that person's experience to the audience, which is pretty profound,' says Lord.[9]

However, compassion does not mean that a reporter should suspend all disbelief. Sometimes the person may initially seem like a victim, only to be revealed as the villain later. And more often than we like to believe, people are a bit of both. Bob Haiman, of the Poynter Institute, says: 'Reporters must always retain their professional scepticism. The challenge is not to let scepticism become cynicism, which can translate into a lack of compassion and concern.'[10]

Culture, race and death

Although all cultures practise respect for the dead and bereaved, this respect takes different forms. Journalists should develop an awareness of the ways in which various groups pay their respects to the dead. It costs little to take cultural practices into account. Matthews says: 'If we sent a female reporter [to cover a Muslim funeral, I would insist] that she wore a scarf and preferably pants, and that if we sent a male and he went into the mosque that he would remove his shoes.'[11]

In African cultures it is not usual for the immediate bereaved family to talk publicly, says John Dludlu, former editor of the *Sowetan*.[12] In practical terms, this means that an approach for an interview might best be made via a relative. Sometimes the family will agree to speak directly; on other occasions they will speak through a spokesperson.

> "The poor, the sick and the dying of Africa have found that their suffering is newsworthy as journalists flock to the continent to document the spread of the modern Bubonic Plague. Forget renaissance. It is deaths of Africans that is big news."[13]
> *Kerry Cullinan, Health-e News Service*

Cultural differences become more difficult to pin down when it comes to determining the limits of what may be said or seen. Reporting on death and grief is always an invasion of privacy. But where does legitimate public interest become unacceptable voyeurism? And is that line drawn differently in different cultures?

Joe Thloloe, the head of news at e.tv, feels differences between African and Western cultures are overstated. During the days of political violence 'you would wake up and find bodies lying on the streets in the townships. The old ways of dealing with death, of respecting the dead, died around that time. There is very little difference between what the West believes and what the African tradition believes is correct.'[14] He says accusations of cultural insensitivities are sometimes simply expedient: 'The difficulty I have is if you don't like something, then you say: according to our tradition it's not done.'

For many others, the whiff of racism still hangs over the handling of death in the media, as we saw in Chapter 7. White victims still matter more, the dignity of black people deserves less consideration. Dludlu asks whether the people who died in the bombing in Bali in October 2002 would have got as much coverage if they had been black.[15]

In an insightful article, Libby Brook considers the value given to different kinds of death, contrasting the saturation coverage the British media gave to the seven astronauts who died in the space shuttle *Columbia* with the virtual silence about seven children who died in an avalanche in Canada.[16] She quotes Dominic Lawson, the editor of the London *Sunday Telegraph*, saying: 'News value is equivalent to surprise. It's not a comparative exercise in the value of human life.' She also cites Roy Greenslade, *The Guardian*'s media commentator, who says: 'There is a hierarchy of death and if you fit a certain role then you are going to get more exposure.'

A hierarchy of that kind is distasteful, and doubly so when it is racially defined. Journalists have to be careful not to signal that some lives are more valuable than others. Some deaths will always command more attention, and it would be naïve to pretend otherwise. But decisions of that sort should always be carefully made, and journalists should be prepared to defend them publicly. And particular care should be taken to ensure that race plays no role in them.

The power of naming

When white right-wingers bombed a Soweto mosque and several railway lines in October 2002, one woman was killed. In initial reports, she hovered in anonymity as just a 'victim'. But the media soon gave her a name: she was Claudina Mokone, a Lesotho national hit by debris in her home. For Zubeida Jaffer, the former parliamentary editor of Independent Newspapers, when the media named her they also restored her dignity.[17] No longer faceless, she became a real person.

One sometimes hears the criticism that victims of disasters far away are reduced to faceless numbers (see box on p. 214). When the numbers are large and the people far away, it is clearly impossible to give details of each individual. But too often, victims remain anonymous even when the excuse doesn't apply. It is never a wealthy white businessman hijacked in his BMW who remains faceless, but often the family wiped out in a shack fire, or the boy who falls victim to gang violence in the townships. It is easier to find the businessman, but that is not enough to explain away the class and racial bias that shows up in who gets named and who doesn't.

Claudina Mokone could very easily have remained anonymous. With a bit of effort, journalists were able to give her the dignity of a name.

> "'500 killed in bombing raids in the DRC' (Kfm, 5/08/1999) … The accumulative effect of this depersonalisation of black deaths is the perception that blacks die in numbers … This consequently strips black people's dignity away from them."[18]
> *Media Monitoring Project*

Speaking ill of the dead

Death is a great leveller of reputations. Countless eulogies are written about 'devoted family men, caring husbands and fathers', when the reality may have been quite different. There's a very human desire to remember people in positive terms; we find it distasteful when others tarnish their memories.

As understandable as the habit is, it poses problems for journalists. What do you do when an important apartheid leader dies and you're called upon to write an obituary? Do you just forget the bad parts? When the former Transkei leader Kaiser Matanzima died in 2003, even politicians from the ANC paid tribute to the man. He had done much for the development of his people, they said, despite the grinding poverty that still marks the Transkei region. His role in accepting apartheid-style 'independence', thereby legitimising the policy, was reduced to 'political differences'. Many of those tributes were simply driven by political expediency.

There is no need to set out purposely to slander the dead. But if there are issues raised by a person's life, they should be explored. That can be done with due sensitivity to family, but it should nevertheless be done honestly. In the case of prominent people, the journalistic imperative to tell the truth trumps the human desire not to speak ill of the dead.

Bearers of bad tidings

It is a well-established principle that victims should not be named until the next of kin have been informed. People should not have to hear bad news about a loved one through the media. The BBC says: 'Concern for next of kin calls for special care over reports that people have been killed or injured or are missing.'[19] However, the organisation recognises some exceptions for prominent people 'or because of some other special circumstances'. The media often rely heavily on the police, who will ensure that next of kin are informed, and only then release names.

News of a disaster can cause anxiety for people who have relatives or friends in the area, for instance. That is not entirely avoidable. But the damage can be lessened if reports are as precise as possible, particularly in 'narrowing the area of concern [by including] details such as airline, flight number, place of departure, and destination as early as possible', the BBC says.[20]

Occasionally a disaster unfolds live on television – as it did during a stampede of spectators at the Ellis Park stadium in April 2001. It can't be expected of television to withdraw its cameras and walk away from the event. A disaster of this kind is too big to ignore. But coverage should be sensitive to the fact that relatives of people at the stadium might be watching. Close-up shots should be avoided: one can easily imagine the trauma of watching a loved one suffering, or even dying, live on national television.

Pictures of death

Images of dead bodies can be shocking to audiences, but we have already seen how journalists sometimes feel it necessary to cause offence in order to show the full truth of an unpalatable reality (Chapter 9). Some newspapers steer far away from images of dead bodies. The editor of *Rapport*, Tim du Plessis, says he sees little need for them. 'Freshly mangled bodies, what purpose do they serve? People say it shows you the horrible world, [but] people know it's horrible.'[21] He points out that there were hardly any pictures of bodies during coverage of the 9/11 attack on the Twin Towers in New York.

Others recognise the difference made by placement. Some pictures may be too gory to run on the front page but may be acceptable inside. The difference is that pictures on the front page may be seen casually, by children or by people who happen to be passing a newsstand.

"It was important to show the face, to show people this was Hani that died, to show people it really happened. Otherwise they would not have believed, that's how much they loved him."[22]

Alf Khumalo of The Star, on photographing the body of the assassinated Communist Party leader, Chris Hani

Using the same kind of logic, television news will sometimes warn viewers that an upsetting or offensive image is about to be shown – as suggested in the news section of the Icasa code. 'More sensitive viewers' can then turn off, or simply close their eyes.

The editor of *City Press*, Mathatha Tsedu, says it's important for cameras to respect the privacy of the dead or grieving by keeping their distance. He says television has become more circumspect in its use of graphic detail. 'If there are visuals of bodies, there will be long shots of people being carried away. All that says is that there are bodies. There isn't this zooming onto a pool of blood, and all those kinds of things.'[23]

On occasion, public interest will trump the need for respect. Tsedu says that when Jonas Savimbi was killed, the media were justified in showing graphic images of the body of the dead Angolan rebel leader who had evaded his enemies for so many decades. 'Nobody would believe that Savimbi is dead until they see the flies,' he says.

What can be very disturbing is the repeated use of graphic images. It is not necessary to use the same bit of footage of people trampling each other every time the Ellis Park stampede is back in the news for some or other reason. 'Avoid needless or repeated use of traumatic library material, especially if it features identifiable people. It should not be used as "wallpaper" or to illustrate a general theme,' says the BBC.[24]

The trauma of reporting trauma

Dealing with profound tragedy can be very stressful for the reporter. In their book, *The bang-bang club*, the photographers Greg Marinovich and Joao Silva describe how they covered the violence of the early 1990s. 'The stress from what we were seeing and the at times callous act of taking pictures was making an impact on all of us. Ken [Carter, another photographer] was waking up in the middle of the night sweating and screaming about things he had seen. Joao had become quiet and withdrawn, and I [Marinovich] sank into a deep depression that I only clawed my way out of years later.'[26]

> "Victims and rescue workers are likely to receive counselling for the stress they suffer, most journalists are not."[25]
> *Bob Haiman, Poynter Institute*

Admitting the stress caused by covering gruesome death and violence is not a sign of weakness. Media houses should consider making counselling available to reporters dealing with stress of this kind, as Bob Haiman suggests.[27]

REPORTING AIDS

HIV and Aids are such important themes in South Africa that they deserve special consideration. Although there are no different ethical principles that apply in this area, they do play themselves out in particular ways that are worth discussing.

The problem of stigma

On World Aids Day in 1998, Gugu Dlamini publicly disclosed her HIV-positive status.[28] Soon after, a mob attacked her outside a shebeen in KwaMashu, near Durban, beating and stoning her to death. They accused her of bringing shame to their community. The stigma still attached to HIV and Aids is very real, and identifying people living with Aids can carry a heavy price.

Another story of disclosure is recounted in the American handbook *Doing ethics in journalism*.[29] In 1982 a reporter phoned the former tennis star Arthur Ashe and asked if he had Aids. Ashe would not confirm or deny the story, but the paper said it would continue seeking confirmation despite his wishes. The next day Ashe held a press conference to confirm that he had Aids. 'I am angry that I was put in the position of having to lie if I wanted to protect my privacy,' he said.

The stigma attached to HIV and Aids represents a real dilemma for journalists. On the one hand, it will only be broken down when people begin to deal with the issue openly. In Ashe's case, disclosure arguably had some benefits for the fight against the disease. The fact that he had been infected through a blood transfusion helped break down stereotypes of the disease as being just about sex and drugs. But it is doubtful that this gives a journalist the right to force somebody into the open. Is it right to 'out' somebody living with Aids?

"To name a rape victim is to guarantee that whenever somebody hears her name, that somebody will picture her in the act of being sexually tortured. To expose a rape victim to this without her consent is nothing short of punitive."[30]
Helen Benedict, journalist and author

In considering the issue, we can draw on the older discussion about how to deal with rape and the stigma attached to it. The press code is quite clear that survivors of rape or other sexual violence may be identified only with their consent.

A code on Aids reporting from the Journ-Aids website follows this pattern, adding the important qualification that consent should be informed, in other words the person needs to understand clearly what is at stake.[31]

This includes requirements that journalists should clearly identify themselves, that the purpose and use of the material be discussed, and that the possible ramifications be set out.

Another provision in this code requires journalists to make sure the person has disclosed their status to their family. That seems to give the reporter too much responsibility. It's one thing to insist that reporters satisfy themselves that the person knows fully what is at stake. It is quite another to take decisions on their behalf as to how they want to deal with their situation. It is, of course, preferable for someone infected with HIV to disclose their status to their family. But it is their business, not the reporter's.

Significantly, the code allows for exceptions to the right to privacy. Where there is a threat to an identifiable person, for instance, or where hypocrisies and falsehoods need to be exposed, a person's status can be revealed against their will.

Of course, it is important to remember that none of this would have changed Gugu Dlamini's fate. Nobody forced or tricked her into it; she herself decided to disclose her status.

Getting it right

The science around the disease is complex and has generated much controversy. It is essential for reporters to understand the subject in detail, and to report accurately. 'Inaccurate reporting fuels the epidemic,' says a booklet published by Soul City.[32] Stories about advances, or setbacks, in the search for treatments will be taken very seriously by readers, listeners or viewers who are themselves infected. Getting it wrong is very unfair to them.

For many, journalists' truth-telling role in this context means they should refute the many myths and fallacies that surround the disease. The Soul City booklet says that if an interviewee repeats a myth, you should find an expert to contradict it.

Of course, these debates have become very political, and powerful interests will try to influence reporters. It is important to remain sceptical of all groups and to be careful of all sources.

Diversity

The South African media mostly present Aids as a black disease, according to Tsedu,[33] and this is of course inaccurate. It is important to present the diversity of the disease. 'Care should be taken to present the full spectrum of people affected and infected with HIV, and not to simply focus on stereotypes of gay, white men, or to create the impression that Aids is a problem among "black people" only,' according to a series of workshops on Aids and the media.[34]

Personal responsibility

Reporters who are themselves ill may infect a person with Aids. What could be a relatively minor illness for the healthy reporter could become life-threatening for the other. Under such circumstances, an interview should be cancelled or postponed.

Language

The language we use in reporting Aids needs to be considered carefully. A range of common words and expressions around HIV and Aids are held to further the stigma surrounding the disease. Examples include 'sufferers', 'scourge', 'suspected of having HIV' and others. The preferred term is 'people living with Aids', or slightly more elegantly, 'people with Aids'.

Reporting death, Aids and trauma: a test of five questions

Journalists should ask these questions to check their reporting:

1. Have you dealt compassionately with the people affected?
2. Have you taken cultural sensitivities into account?
3. How will your report affect those you are reporting about?
4. Have you struck the right balance between the public interest and the private concerns of those affected?
5. Is there a different approach that would give the individuals more protection while still allowing you to tell the story effectively?

A place for respect
Jacob Ntshangase

Media consumers have to deal with a lot of death and trauma, including issues of HIV and Aids. Television and newspapers sometimes worsen the pain the public is going through because of the manner in which images of dead people are used.

Sowetan once used a front-page colour picture of the grossly disfigured body of a man who had been dragged behind a bakkie by a farmer in the Free State. The story was important: it challenged the nation to tackle deep-rooted racial tensions and human rights abuse on farms. However, I wonder whether the story wouldn't have had the same impact if the picture had been used inside.

Isolezwe, a Zulu newspaper, once ran a story about a girl whose rotting body was buried after it had started decomposing in the mortuary. The story was aimed at challenging undertakers to take better care of bodies in their care. Fine and well, but I had serious problems with the image of the girl's body used with the story. It surely must have been traumatic to her parents and those close to her, and it was actually not necessary. Ironically *Isolezwe* targets a Zulu audience, which is very respectful about issues of death.

Both these stories are of public interest but I find a lack of sensitivity in the manner the graphic images in both stories were used.

When Fana 'Khabzela' Khaba, the YFM DJ, died of an Aids-related disease, the media went to visit the family to get a story – even though the family reportedly requested to be left alone to grieve. Granted, Khabzela built himself into a public figure and, as such, what happens to him is of public interest. But the media should respect the bereaved family and give them space to mourn.

I note with interest the point in this chapter that 'on occasion, people in the news may not be unhappy with coverage, but audiences may be offended on their behalf.' I don't think it's a question of being 'not unhappy', but the media makes it difficult to avoid coverage. Journalists have the misconception that a bereaved family will find the idea of being in the media limelight so appealing that it will somehow make up for the loss of a loved one. That couldn't be further from the truth.

To me it's enough that the media covers the news of the death of a public figure, including explaining the cause of death to the public. The problem starts when the bereaved family is further traumatised in times of grief – as was the case with Khabzela's family.

I agree that 'there's no need to set out purposely to slander the dead', but the media must not mislead the public about the character and contribution of a prominent public figure. The traditional practice that it's not acceptable to speak ill of the dead should be challenged.

In dealing with suffering, trauma and death the media should take account of cultural differences. This might be a bit difficult for mainstream media because of their diverse audience – what could be taboo to some may not be problematical for others.

Community media are in a different position in this regard because their audience generally have a uniform set of values. The community media's mandate is to reflect the norms and values, lifestyles and practices of their particular community. For instance, in some rural communities children are not allowed near any situation where there's a dead person. This is difficult nowadays because children are exposed to even gruesome images of dead bodies by the media.

Journalists should just remember that they are human beings, too, and respect cultural values and family sensitivities.

(Jacob Ntshangase is director of the Institute for the Advancement of Journalism)

Case study 26
Politics, Aids and reputation

Parks Mankahlana was the voice of two presidents. He was the spokesperson of Nelson Mandela as well as his successor, Thabo Mbeki, whose often controversial views on Aids he had to defend and articulate. In one incident, he declared that the Durban Declaration – a document signed by thousands of scientists from around the world, asserting that HIV causes Aids – belonged in the dustbin. On another occasion he was reported as saying the government was hesitant to provide drugs to pregnant women to reduce mother-to-child transmission of HIV because of the orphans it would then have to care for.

On 26 October 2000 Mankahlana died at the age of 36. He had been ill for some time, and speculation was rife that he died of an Aids-related illness. The presidency skirted the issue, saying it was up to the family to disclose the cause of death. His widow, Nthabiseng, said he had suffered from chronic anaemia, which had ultimately led to heart failure. She denied there was any link to Aids.

But the explanation was simply not believed, and many media organisations looked for ways of reporting the rumour. *Business Day* said 'colleagues believed' he had died of an Aids-related illness, while the *Mail&Guardian* and e.tv both quoted 'ANC sources' as confirming an Aids-related illness as the cause of death.

For several news organisations, Mankahlana's death provided an opportunity to call for greater openness about the disease. The journalist Mark Gevisser wrote in the *Sunday Times*: 'Parks Mankahlana was a victim of Aids. How can I make so bald a statement when I have no knowledge at all as to whether he had HIV or not? I make it because, whether or not he had the virus, he was the victim of the stigma and silence and denial that surrounds this syndrome.'[35]

The story provoked a furious controversy that divided journalists largely on racial lines. At a debate on the subject held by Sanef, Jim Jones, at the time editor of *Business Day*, said Mankahlana had been 'promiscuous, no icon and no saint', and that made it acceptable to report the cause of death.[36] The journalist Drew Forrest wrote in *Business Day* that calls not to publish were 'asking the media to collude in a conspiracy of silence based on irrational fear and prejudice. These are the same emotions that drive rural people to kill Aids sufferers, and which evidently made it so hard for Mankahlana and his family to unburden themselves. How can they be overcome if South Africa's leaders and media pander to them?'[37]

But many black journalists were outraged. Lizeka Mda, at the time executive editor of *The Star*, said at the Sanef debate that the 'gumboot dance' on Mankahlana's grave was motivated by 'spoiled brats' who wanted Mbeki to toe their own line on debates on Aids. She said none of the newspapers that alleged he had died of Aids had any evidence.[38]

John Dludlu, then with *Business Day*, accepted that it would be a good thing if prominent people with Aids said so publicly, in order to fight the stigma attached to the disease. However, this had to be done voluntarily, and the media had no right to take that choice away from Mankahlana. 'It is not clear how public interest was served by "outing" him. Instead, the media may have set the cause of the fight against Aids back. Who will dare come out under these circumstances?' Dludlu said the handling of the story betrayed a desire to get at Mbeki over his stand on Aids.[39]

A complaint against e.tv was lodged with the BCCSA, but dismissed. The commission accepted that there was sufficient public interest in the matter, and pointed out that common law does not protect the dignity and privacy of a dead person.[40]

What should we make of this row? We should, perhaps, begin by acknowledging the stigma attached to Aids, which makes it quite different from any other disease. The ANC said the revelations were designed to rob Mankahlana of his revolutionary legacy – it is unthinkable that they would have said the same if the cause of death had been alleged to be cancer. Every time a prominent person comes out openly as HIV-positive, the stigma is pushed back a little. In that sense, it was clearly desirable for the cause of death to be acknowledged openly.

But as Dludlu pointed out, that should be voluntary. It isn't fair people are 'outed' against their or their family's will, unless there is a pressing public interest. There was of course public interest in Mankahlana's death, particularly in the light of his role in the Aids debate. But I doubt that it was quite pressing enough to justify overriding his family's clear wishes.

Finally, we need to consider the demands of accuracy. The belief he had died of Aids was very widespread, but hard evidence was scarce. Reports quoted 'ANC sources' as confirming the story – but that didn't amount to very solid evidence. It could simply reflect the fact that many people in the ANC believed it to be so. In the light of all the other issues swirling around the story, better evidence should have been sought.

Case study 27
The death of a dissident

Peter Mokaba, a prominent ANC leader, was among the speakers at a memorial service for Parks Mankahlana, the presidential spokesperson. Mokaba took the opportunity to attack the media for having reported that Mankahlana had died of an Aids-related illness. 'The media has disappointed us and I do not know how they are going to repair the damage,' he said. 'A comrade passes away ... a comrade who served them [the media] well ... and they want us to bury him with a diminished status.'[41]

About 18 months later, Mokaba was also dead, amid similar controversies. Where Mankahlana had articulated President Thabo Mbeki's controversial views on Aids, Mokaba had emerged as a key voice arguing the cause of Aids dissidents in his own right. He helped draft a party discussion document, 'HIV-Aids and the struggle for the humanisation of the African', which argued that the causal link between HIV and Aids had not been established, that anti-retroviral drugs were toxic, and that the Aids lobby was driven by a racist agenda.

Like Mankahlana, Mokaba had been rumoured to be living with HIV himself. In early 2000 an unidentified illness drove him from public view for some time, leading to reports that his death was then imminent. He later told the Helen Suzman Foundation's Patrick Laurence that his mysterious illness had been a lung infection.[42] In the interview, published around the time of his death in June 2002, he also said that Mankahlana did not have Aids, but was killed by anti-retroviral drugs after being persuaded that he did.

When Mokaba died at the age of 44, the ANC gave the cause of death as acute pneumonia linked to a respiratory problem,[43] but speculation continued that his pneumonia had been Aids-related. The media, however, were much more restrained in dealing with these rumours than they had been in the Mankahlana case. 'The cabinet has refused to speculate on Peter Mokaba's HIV status,' wrote *The Star*, after the government spokesperson Joel Netshitenzhe brushed the question of his status aside.[44] Other media contented themselves with oblique hints, or references to earlier reports on his illness.

The difference from the coverage of Mankahlana's death was marked, and one can only speculate on the reasons. The furious row over the earlier death (discussed in Case Study 26) had probably caused media organisations to be much more cautious in their treatment of the second. Other factors probably included the considerable shift in the debate around Aids. The row about the media's coverage of Mankahlana's death was in some ways a fight by proxy about the legitimacy of the dissident position. But by June 2002 the orthodox view had gained considerable ground, as shown most clearly in the cabinet statement of 17 April of that year, which accepted the value of anti-retroviral drugs.

While the privacy debate did not emerge as strongly around Mokaba's death, other ethical issues did. The ANC sharply criticised the media for reporting the event before the family had been properly informed. His daughter had first heard the news on the radio, the party said.

It was unfortunate for the news to have reached her in this way. But one has to ask whose responsibility it is for next of kin to be informed. It surely cannot be the media's. Those closest to him – his party and his family – needed to make sure that the news was broken to his daughter and others quickly and properly. Mokaba was a very prominent figure, and news of his death was not going to remain under wraps for long.

Yet another issue arose. Days after his death, the *Mail&Guardian* published an extensive account of persistent claims that Mokaba had been an apartheid spy. In an editorial justifying the decision, the paper wrote: 'We do not wish to worsen the grief of the family and friends of any dead public figure. But let us tell the truth about the dead, just as we seek to do so about the living.'[45]

The story provoked a strong reaction from the ANC, with some leaders calling for the paper to be boycotted. Some journalists were also critical. In a letter to the *Mail&Guardian*'s editor, the former parliamentary editor of Independent Newspapers, Zubeida Jaffer, said the paper was guilty of double standards. Other public figures had not had dubious aspects of their past highlighted immediately after their death. 'What I would like to see … is that you be uniformly indecent. Let Peter Mokaba's family not be the only family to be reminded that their son, daughter, mother or father was not a paragon of virtue. Be consistent in exposing the dead just before their funeral or just afterwards, whatever will cause similar or uniform hurt and create the greatest sensation.'[46]

Dealing with the reputations of people on their death is a difficult issue. As I have argued above, people have a natural dislike for speaking ill of the dead. But the journalist's truth-telling duty means that attempts to sanitise people's lives should be resisted. Setting out to cause offence is a different matter, but it should be possible to give a balanced account of somebody's life without being needlessly hurtful.

Jaffer is right to call for people to be treated equally, however. She points to the way the national cricket captain Hansie Cronje was eulogised without reference to the corruption scandal that caused his fall from grace. Journalists would have much to answer for if they let political or personal agendas, or racism, influence the treatment of people after their death.

Case study 28
The death of a
right-wing dream

Just over a month before South Africa's founding democratic election, Lucas Mangope was still insisting that his Bophuthatswana homeland was independent and would not take part. But his people had other ideas. Unrest flared, and a right-wing force led by the Afrikaner Weerstandsbeweging's Eugene Terre'Blanche mobilised in support of Mangope. But the homeland's troops were no longer on Mangope's side, and they quickly routed the white right-wingers.

During a day of violence in March 1994, three AWB members were shot dead in front of several journalists. The photographer Greg Marinovich describes how colleagues came across an ageing Mercedes and the three AWB members surrounded by about a dozen soldiers.[47] One of the white men was already dead; another was wounded and asking for an ambulance. 'Kevin [Carter, a colleague] recognised how important this scene was and tried to capture it all: the swastika-like emblem; the blood; the fear of their victorious black enemies etched on the right-wingers' faces. The worm had well and truly turned.'

Several journalists were questioning the wounded man, Alwyn Wolfaardt. 'The cameras and tape recorders worked on. Without warning, one of the Bop soldiers walked swiftly up to the two surviving right-wingers and executed them with rapid single shots from his assault rifle.'[48]

The historical significance of the failed right-wing intervention and the brutal execution of the AWB men was immediately apparent. It had been the white right's last stand for apartheid, and there was now no prospect of democracy being derailed. Marinovich continues: 'It was over in a heartbeat. The death of white supremacy.'

Photographs and TV footage of the white right crushed so mercilessly by black soldiers were widely used, and marked a highly visible turning point in the media, too, writes Guy Berger, professor of journalism at Rhodes University. 'Henceforth, the picture seemed to signal, whites had had their day, and the newsmakers were black South Africans.'[49]

There was criticism of the journalists for interviewing and photographing the wounded men rather than helping them. But according to an account by Andriette Stofberg, a reporter from *Beeld*, she did ask the police for help and was told that an ambulance had already been summoned.[50]

The actual execution of the two wounded men came unexpectedly, according to Marinovich's description. He says journalists there felt 'the peak of danger' had passed, and the fact that the incident was captured on film was simply because a CBS cameraperson was keeping his camera rolling. There are times when journalists should put their professional duties aside in the interests of saving lives. But in this case it seems there was nothing that could reasonably be done.

Should the footage have been shown? It caused severe distress to the families of the men. Amelia Uys, the wife of the other executed man, later told a commission of inquiry that she and her children had learnt of the death of her husband, Fanie, when it was reported on television. Her children later needed medical and psychiatric help to deal with the trauma.[51]

There is no doubt that it must have been terrible for the families, and one has to have great sympathy for them. But the significance of the incident was such as to make it unthinkable to withhold the footage. The hapless AWB men were caught up in a historic moment, and their tragedy was no longer private.

. . . .

NOTES

1   Edward Behr, *Anyone here been raped and speaks English?* London: New English Library, 1985. 136.

2   Bob Steele, 'The bummer beat'. Posted at http://www.poynter.org/content/content_view.asp?id=5540 on 1 May 1996, accessed on 28 January 2004.

3   Quoted in Robert J Haiman, 'Best practices for newspaper journalists', Freedom Forum, Washington, undated. Posted at http://www.freedom forum.org/publications/diversity/bestpractices/bestpractices.pdf, accessed on 19 March 2004. 30.

4   Quoted in Bob Steele, 'The bummer beat'.

5   BBC, *Producers' guidelines*. London: BBC, 1996. 44.

6   Johan Retief, *Media ethics: an introduction to responsible journalism*. Cape Town: OUP, 2002.

7   Interview, 27 November 2002.

8   *The Star*, 12 July 2000.

9   Quoted in Steele, 'The Bummer beat'.

10 Robert J Haiman, 'Best practices for newspaper journalists', Freedom Forum, Washington, undated. Posted at http://www.freedomforum.org/publications/ diversity/bestpractices/bestpractices.pdf, accessed on 19 March 2004. 35.

11 Interview, 27 November 2002.

12 Interview, 18 October 2002.

13 *The Star*, 12 July 2000.

14 Interview, 2 September 2002.

15 Interview, 18 October 2002.

16 *Mail&Guardian*, 7–13 February 2003.

17 Interview, 7 November 2002.

18 Media Monitoring Project (MMP), 'The news in black and white: an investigation into racial stereotyping in the media'. Johannesburg: MMP, 1999. 24.

19 BBC, *Producers' guidelines*. 45.

20 Ibid.

21 Interview, 15 October 2002.

22 Quoted in Catherine O'Dowd, 'Truth or taste: the depiction of the Hani murder', *Rhodes Journalism Review* 11, December 1995.

23 Interview, 11 December 2002.

24 BBC, *Producers' guidelines*. 45.

25 Robert J Haiman, 'Best practices'. 35.

26 Greg Marinovich and Joao Silva: *The bang-bang club*. London: Arrow Books, 2001. 69.

27 Haiman, 'Best practices'. 35.

28 *Daily Dispatch*, 12 January 2001.

29 Jay Black, Bob Steele and Ralph Barney, *Doing ethics in journalism*. Needham Heights, MA: Allyn & Bacon, 1995. 183.

30 Quoted in Bob Steele, 'Naming rape victims', 8 August 2002. Posted at http://www. poynter.org/column.asp?id=36&aid=4010, accessed on 23 March 2004.

31 Journ-Aids, 'Reporting on HIV/Aids: ethical guidelines for South African media', June 2003. Posted at http://www.journ-aids.org/Guidelines%20Change.htm, accessed on 28 January 2004.

32 Health-e and Soul City, 'HIV/Aids: a resource for journalists'. Johannesburg: Soul City, undated. 23.

33 Interview, 11 December 2002.

34 Sanef, Soul City and Health-E News: 'Issues emerging from "Aids and the Media" workshop series'. Unpublished mimeograph.

35 *Sunday Times*, 5 November 2000.

36 *Business Day*, 10 November 2000.

37 *Business Day*, 9 November 2000.

38 *Business Day*, 10 November 2000.

39 *Business Day*, 2 November 2000.

40 BCCSA, *Biannual report* 1999–2001.

41 Agence France Presse (AFP), 'AFP report', 3 November 2000. Posted at www.mg.co.za, accessed on 22 September 2004.

42   'Patrick Laurence interviews Peter Mokaba: a dissonant view on Aids', in the Helen
     Suzman Foundation publication *Focus* 26, June 2002. Posted at
     http://www.hsf.org.za/focus26/focus26interviewaids.html, accessed on 28 January
     2004.

43   Sapa, 'Mokaba had acute pneumonia – ANC', 10 June 2002. Posted at http://www.
     iol.co.za/index.php?set_id=1&click_id=13&art_id=qw1023683041567B234, accessed
     on 22 September 2004.

44   *The Star*, 12 June 2002.

45   *Mail&Guardian*, 14–20 June 2002.

46   Personal communication.

47   Marinovich and Silva, *The bang-bang club*. 178 ff.

48   Ibid. 180.

49   Guy Berger, 'Deracialisation, democracy and development: transformation of the
     South African media 1994–2000'. Posted at http://journ.ru.ac.za/staff/guy/index.html,
     accessed on 23 April 2003.

50   Quoted in Retief, *Media Ethics*. 185.

51   Ibid. 186.

As a matter of policy, the SABC does not use hidden cameras and microphones to gather news. In exceptional circumstances – such as illegal, antisocial or fraudulent activity, or clear and significant abuse of public trust, and where alternative means of newsgathering are impossible – the use of such equipment might be in the public interest.
SABC: Editorial Policies

Staff members should disclose their identity to people they cover … though they need not always announce their status as journalists when seeking information normally available to the public.
The New York Times: Code of Ethics

[Journalists] do not practice dishonest means in obtaining information, pictures or documents.
Swiss Federation of Journalists: Code of Conduct

13

FLYING A FALSE FLAG: DECEPTION

Professor Kewitz, a German toxicologist, receives a phone call from Dr Strathmann, of the ministry of defence in Bonn. The official wants Kewitz to attend a meeting about a possible research contract.[1]

But Kewitz is not keen: 'Do you know what's going on here in Berlin about research contracts from the ministry of defence?' He's referring to reports about German research into biological and chemical weapons. He's constantly in the media, he says. Strathmann says these programmes can't be stopped just because of some fuss in the media. He tells the scientist it's an important matter: the synthetic development of blood toxins, and Kewitz has the best expertise in the field.

The professor doesn't protest at the suggestion that he's an expert in biological weapons. But he claims to be too busy to take on additional work. Strathmann promises him an additional assistant, and they agree to talk again when things are quieter.

Strathmann phones several other academics and invites them to similar meetings, to discuss research into various chemical and biological weapon technologies. All show an interest: the invitations are no surprise, the idea of doing this kind of work is not strange.

At the time of these phone calls – late 1969 – Strathmann is the senior defence official responsible for commissioning this kind of research, but he's not the person on the phone. His identity has been 'borrowed' by Günter Wallraff, a prominent German investigative journalist. Wallraff publishes accounts of his conversations in the magazine *konkret*, disproving official denials that Germany is researching chemical and biological weapon technologies.

Wallraff built a reputation for unconventional, often personally risky techniques of this kind. He altered his appearance and adopted a broken accent in order to pass for a Turkish migrant worker. After two years of research he wrote a damning account of racism and the exploitation of illegal workers. On other occasions he posed as a would-be police spy to test official attitudes to right- and left-wing opposition groups, and as a homeless man to investigate conditions in shelters. He played the roles of alcoholic, manufacturer of napalm, worker – even journalist.

Wallraff wrote about his decision to pose as Dr Strathmann: 'It was decided to pose as somebody in the know, in the position of a commissioning authority, to penetrate the tissue of lies presented by official denials. I believe that this unusual method is justified by the appalling intentions of those who have included biological and chemical weapons in their military planning.'[2] His technique has been described as 'misleading, in order not to be misled'.[3]

Wallraff's systematic use of impersonation was undoubtedly effective, even though deception of this kind is usually frowned on. Most codes that make reference to the issue say journalists should be honest about their identity and their intentions (see extracts on p. 230). But most also leave the door open just a crack. Sometimes the public interest weighs so heavily that exceptions can be made. This approach shines through in Wallraff's own words: he acknowledged that the method was unusual, but justified it on the basis of the story's importance.

Liar, liar, pants on fire

Before we consider the exceptions, let's be clear about why lying is a problem in the first place.

Societies depend on a level of trust, according to the US handbook *Doing ethics in journalism*. People need to believe that others 'will exchange and share information that is true. Without such trust, interaction among people will be stifled, and the functioning of society will be thwarted.'[5] In reality, of course, there's plenty of lying and deception going on, but that's no reason to jettison the value.

> "The issue of deception is a significant ethical matter, for it deals with truth, and seeking truth is what journalism is all about."[4]
> *Doing ethics*

As journalists, our business is truth-telling, and truthfulness is a standard we apply to the rest of society. When we expose the lying politician, the double-dealing businessman or the dishonest official, we make our most important contribution to society. We affirm the importance of truth by exposing dishonesty and deceit.

What implications are there for our own behaviour? We should live by the standards we set others, it's as simple as that. For deontologists, for whom ethics is a matter of doing one's duty, that's where the argument can end. Deception is simply wrong; it's our duty to play the game by the rules.

For others, who need more than a simple assertion of duty, the argument can be taken further. If we don't live by the morals we expect of others, we lay ourselves open to a charge of double standards. And that undermines credibility, just as people lose trust in a priest or a judge or anybody else who breaks their own code. As we've seen, credibility is essential for a journalist. If our audience stops believing our reporting, we might as well run a tuckshop instead.

> "At this third lie his nose grew to such an extraordinary extent that poor Pinocchio could not move in any direction. If he turned to one side he struck his nose against the bed or the window-panes, if he turned to the other he struck it against the walls or the door, if he raised his head a little he ran the risk of sticking it into one of the Fairy's eyes."
> *C Collodi, Pinocchio*

Deception is also unfair. In any exchange, it places one party at a disadvantage. A situation from outside journalism makes the argument very clear: a used-car dealer who does not tell a potential client about a fatal problem in the engine is obviously being dishonest and unfair. Deliberately misleading people involves using the power of knowledge to gain an advantage over them. In journalism, the unjust advantage we gain is access to information the source might not otherwise part with.

In purely practical terms, deception can throw up other problems for journalists. It can detract attention from the validity of the report. Certainly it's a card often played by people exposed in this way. In a celebrated US case, a producer for ABC's *Primetime Live* got a job in the meat-packing department of a well-known supermarket chain, Food Lion. Using a hidden camera, she collected damning footage of rotten meat being washed and rewrapped for sale. The report was aired in November 1992.[6]

Food Lion fought back hard (grocers, too, need people's trust), and ultimately won a fraud and trespass case against ABC. As the Poynter Institute's Bob Steele points out, their legal strategy 'sidestepped questions about the truth' of the investigation.[7] The methods used by ABC came to overshadow the reality of problems at the company.

Breaking the rules

Some journalists recognise no exceptions to the rules about deception. Ben Bradlee, executive editor of the *Washington Post*, said: 'You can't break the law and you can't tell a lie … And you can't pass yourself off as someone you aren't.'[8]

However, most will allow exceptions when the story is of sufficient public importance. Many ethical codes take this position (see extracts on p. 230), and we've seen that kind of argument from Wallraff. But it raises another, more difficult, question: What makes a story important enough to warrant some level of dishonesty? How high should the bar be set?

Steele puts it very high. 'To justify deception we must be pursuing exceptionally important information. It must be of vital public interest, such as preventing profound harm to individuals or revealing great system failure,' he writes.[9]

Ultimately, judging a story's weight remains a subjective matter. Newsrooms don't have importance-o-meters to use. In the heat of the moment it's easy to overstate the case to oneself. *Doing ethics in journalism* suggests a number of criteria that should be applied, in addition to the core test of importance:[10]

- All other possibilities to get the same information must have been exhausted. In other words, deception needs to be a measure of last resort.
- The journalists must be willing to disclose the methods they used and

their reasons. If we are unwilling to discuss our methods publicly, that is a good indication they are probably not justifiable.

- The journalists and their organisation must 'apply excellence, through outstanding craftmanship as well as the commitment to pursue the story fully'. Deception is unlikely to be condoned if our reporting is generally sloppy.
- The reporting must prevent harm greater than that caused by the deception. This is really another way of weighing a story's importance against the use of otherwise dubious methods.
- The journalists must make the decision in a 'meaningful, collaborative and deliberative' way. Careful and thorough discussion will prevent the thrill of the chase carrying us in directions we may later regret. Generally, news organisations insist that the use of deception is only allowed after consultation with a senior editor. It is not a decision junior reporters should take on their own.

The book also identifies reasons that are not good enough to justify the use of deception. They include winning a prize; beating the competition; getting the story with less cost and trouble; because others have already done it; and the subjects of the story are themselves unethical.[11] The last condition may be arguable: techniques of this kind mostly come into consideration when journalists are trying to expose wrongdoing in some form. However, we can accept that the fact of wrongdoing is probably not enough to justify deception; we need to satisfy other criteria too.

The bottom line is that a decision to use deception should not be taken lightly. It is a serious step, and we devalue our craft if we take it lightly. 'Telling the truth never needs any moral justification; lying and deception do,' says the US academic Louis Day.[12]

Degrees of deception

Public acceptance of a particular tactic is likely to depend not only on the importance of the story, but also on what kind of deception was practised.

Silence: The most basic form of deception is not identifying one's identity as a journalist, leaving sources in the mistaken belief they are dealing with an ordinary member of the public. The *New York Times* says reporters 'need not always announce their status as journalists when seeking information normally available to the public'.[13] In some areas of journalism, this mild kind of deception is virtually obligatory. Restaurant critics would almost certainly get special treatment if they declared themselves as such, which would make the exercise pointless.

The argument here is that anybody can get access to this kind of information. Martin Welz, editor of *Noseweek*, says sometimes people will withhold information normally available to the public if they are dealing with a journalist: 'I know that even [with] ordinary information that ordinary citizens do get, when you announce yourself as the media, an anxiety creeps in.'[14]

Disguise and misrepresentation: We go a step further if we pretend we are something other than a journalist. Failing to admit to being a journalist is a kind of passive deception in that we simply allow an incorrect impression to stand. But as soon as we disguise ourselves as something we are not, we are actively misleading people. The bar for using this method should be set higher, but there are occasions when it can be justified. Wallraff's tactics, described above, fall squarely into this category, as does the Food Lion case from the US.

Hidden cameras and microphones: Television is a thirsty medium, thirsty for pictures. Viewers have high expectations of being taken to the event being reported on. Older styles of TV journalism relied heavily on talking heads telling the audience about an event. That is no longer seen as good enough: people want to see the flooded river or the dramatic rescue.

When it comes to exposing misconduct, this creates particular difficulties for the TV journalist. Corrupt officials don't generally like performing for the camera, and hidden cameras are the obvious answer.

> "Seeing is believing, that's why television has higher credibility with the public than print."[15]
> NBC field producer, Bob Windrem

In the US, programmes like ABC's *Primetime Live* make extensive use of the technique. The freelance writer Russ W Baker says that the programme makes more use of hidden cameras than any other US news magazine. 'We've watched from the inside of a refrigerator as dishonest repairmen did nothing for a lot of money, witnessed televangelists faking miracle cures, watched day-care workers slap their charges and crooked doctors line up to buy and sell fraudulent workers' compensation claimants.'[16]

In South Africa, M-Net's *Carte Blanche* probably makes more use of the technique than anybody else. Some of the better-known reports have uncovered the abuse of abortion patients at an Mpumalanga hospital, bribery at drivers' licence testing centres, and theft at the post office.

Baker writes that a thin line divides substantive footage from voyeurism.[17] 'Watching someone do virtually anything without their knowing can be titillating. Daydreaming on the job, licking an envelope while looking around nervously – innocent acts can seem dubious, even nefarious.'

Hidden cameras can also mislead, and sometimes footage can seem to support a case when in fact it doesn't. In the Food Lion case, one sequence showed a worker saying she didn't know how to clean the meat saw – with the implication that the saw did not get cleaned. The report omitted another clip in which she added that it was not her job to clean it.[18]

Baker also points to the tendency to focus on the immediate perpetrators when the problem is systemic. In many cases the real villains are not the people who are rewrapping bad meat or mistreating abortion patients, but people higher up in the chain of command who design policies that allow these practices or push for profits that demand them. But it's harder to film them 'in the act'.

George Mazarakis, the executive producer of *Carte Blanche*, says hidden cameras are used as a last resort: 'On television you've got to capture the moment, you have to be physically in the event.'[19] Thorough discussion takes place whenever cases of this sort arise, says Mazarakis, but the final decision rests with him.

Hidden cameras and microphones are an important part of the investigative journalist's armoury. But if they are used carelessly, credibility can suffer.

Testing the system: A reporter at *The Star* presented herself to a number of police stations to make an affidavit in support of an application for a child support grant. She found police very helpful – quite happy to suggest the inclusion of false details to improve her chances of getting the grant. Of course she did not say she was a journalist. It was a classic case of using deception to 'test the system'.

The technique is a time-honoured one, but it is not without its risks. It may seem like a good idea to check airport security systems by trying to smuggle a gun through a checkpoint, but officials don't take such things lightly. There's even a law against making jokes about hijackings and the like. As Steele points out, such techniques could cause panic or distract officials from their important work, creating risks for ordinary passengers.[20]

Entrapment: When a situation is created which could lead suspects to behave in ways they would not normally, it is called entrapment. The courts don't accept evidence obtained in this way, and journalists should also stay away from it. The subject of entrapment can legitimately argue that the story was 'created' by the journalist, and that it therefore does not reflect reality. Journalists should observe the behaviour being reported on, not create it.

Deception:
a test of five questions

Journalists should ask these questions to check their reporting:
1. How important, really, is this story?
2. What kind of deception are you contemplating?
3. Have all other options been exhausted?
4. How will those deceived, and your credibility, be affected?
5. Are you willing to justify the techniques contemplated in public?

TALKING POINT

Truth in hidden places
Max du Preez

Proper investigative journalism, like any form of detective work, could not exist without some form of deception by the journalist – which, ethically speaking, makes it a particularly risky form of journalism.

At the most innocent level, a journalist would pretend to be sympathetic to an interviewee, or pretend to agree with an interviewee's point of view. You don't announce your own credo of non-racialism and non-sexism when you try to get inside information from a member of the white right wing, for instance. Before you go to the interview, you brush up on your knowledge of rugby and perhaps of the latest gossip about your interviewee's political opponents, and you take a few tablets that would compensate for the amounts of alcohol you would have to take. Well, do you want the story or not?

But, to stick to the same example, it would be a breach of ethics if you made racist remarks yourself to butter up your interviewee. There's a fine line between not volunteering information and lying, but there is such a line and one shouldn't cross it unless the circumstances are extreme.

A much more difficult decision is whether it would be acceptable to pretend that you're not a journalist when you try to get information from someone. If you're sitting in a bar and someone voluntarily divulges information you want to use, I think it is fine to then not volunteer that you're a journalist. To hide your notebook, camera or tape recorder when you're in a group or crowd around a news event, is also fine.

To pretend actively that you're someone or something else, or to use a disguise or false identity and therefore lie about your intentions, is mostly problematic. Still, a female colleague of mine painted her face black and put on a wig in order to be safer while covering the June 1976 Soweto uprising. She did not hurt anyone, she only got a better story and didn't get attacked.

Of course the use of a disguise or false identity would be acceptable if it was an investigation of overwhelming public importance and interest. Few reporters would ever work on a story like that. The same goes for the use of listening devices, phone taps and computer hacking.

Journalists have to respect the laws of the country and the constitution, like any other citizen. It is illegal to bug someone or to hack into someone's computer. As citizens we are against the invasion of our privacy, so we have to be very careful when a news story demands the invasion of the privacy of other citizens.

But sometimes the use of some of these methods is acceptable. If you want to test the security of an airport, I would have no problems if you dressed like a member of the airline staff and walked into sensitive areas with something that could have been a bomb. In your eventual story you would own up and state that you had pretended to be an airport official.

I once had good reason to suspect that a gathering of five men in a hotel room were discussing a political assassination. I had no hesitation in using a sophisticated directional microphone from a room nearby to pick up their conversation. Ideally one should in the eventual story on such an event admit that such a device was used. And one should be reluctant to ascribe direct quotes to individuals based on such a recording.

Bugging someone's telephone or planting a bug in someone's home or office means one also gets to hear private conversations, such as between a husband and wife or parent and child, which have nothing to do with the investigation itself. This is a blatant invasion of privacy and can clearly only be permissible in very extreme cases. I have never used these methods myself.

I have, on several occasions, used or sanctioned the use of a tiny video camera and/or microphone concealed on the person of a reporter. There can't be much of a debate about the ethics of this method of recording evidence if the person carrying the devices identified him/herself as a reporter but was not allowed a camera or microphone. It is a more problematic practice if the carrier of the equipment pretends to be someone other than a reporter.

A useful guide to these ethical questions is whether the reading/viewing/listening public will find your methods acceptable when you divulge them in your eventual report. Then again, sometimes that is impossible: some of your methods might have been illegal or close to it, and yet you were convinced they were absolutely essential and ethical under the circumstances.

The acceptability of using deceptive or covert methods of gathering or recording information increases with the level of public interest attached to the story. If the story is, for instance, a pending terrorist attack or assassination, I would not hesitate to break the law or use almost any form of deception to get the story out.

But in all cases I would consult and inform one or two trusted senior colleagues beforehand – and preferably the editor or news executive of your organisation, if you respect him/her as a journalist.

(Max du Preez is a columnist, journalist and author)

Case study 29
Resculpting a story

In 1998 the *Mail&Guardian* was running a regular column by Angella Johnson under the title 'View from a Broad'. It was a very personal kind of journalism. Johnson would expose herself to various experiences and then write about them. In November, Johnson consulted a plastic surgeon, Dr Siegmund Johannes, about a possible facelift.[21] She did not at the time tell him she was a journalist, but later in the day phoned his practice to say she intended to write about it, and meant to use his name.

He was unavailable, and she made several more attempts to reach him, leaving a message every time. The paper ultimately decided to go ahead with the column in that week's edition, after she established with the medical authorities that the report would not place Dr Johannes in conflict with their rules.

The story appeared under the headline 'An about face on plastic surgery'.[22] She described her consultation, and her decision, in the end, to leave her body alone. 'Later that night I stood naked in front of the bathroom mirror and concluded there was no way in hell I would let anyone put knife, chisel or suction hose to my bod. Let gravity take its course. I'll fight fat, but not mother nature and the march of time,' she wrote.

Johannes lodged a complaint against the article on three grounds. He complained that Johnson had behaved unfairly by not disclosing that she was researching a story; that the story contained factual inaccuracies and took things out of context, thereby damaging his reputation; and that she had put him in possible breach of professional regulations by using his name without his permission.

In support of his first complaints, Johannes said he had not returned Johnson's calls because he had been in surgery whenever she would have been at the *Mail&Guardian* offices. He disputed that the quotes attributed to him could possibly be accurate, since she had made only sketchy notes. He objected, particularly, to a paragraph in which she wrote: 'He kept talking about lifting my bust as an analogy of how facelifts work. (Was that a hint or something?) One more mention of breasts drooping and he'd have his nose re-sculpted by my fist.' The doctor said he had made no reference to her breasts, just that the sutures used in a facelift supported the face like a bra.

In his judgment the ombud, Ed Linington, accepted the paper's defence of the deception. 'The method used is legitimate and any other view would stifle personalised journalism such as Ms Johnson practises,' he wrote.

Linington said the question of accuracy was difficult to resolve. But in dealing with technical issues such as those involved in plastic surgery, it would have been 'wise and proper' to check technical facts with Johannes before publication. He also accepted the doctor's strenuous denial that he had made any unprofessional references to her breasts, and upheld the complaint in this respect.

On the question of using his name, Linington said it was difficult to accept that Johannes had been too busy to phone Johnson back. But the paper should not have taken his silence to mean consent, and could in any event have run the report without using his name.

The ombud's ruling seems to have been fair and well reasoned. It provides a useful illustration of how a complex issue can be dissected in order to come up with a sensible view of the whole. It also shows that there are instances when ethics do allow for a measure of deception. In this case, it was correct of the *Mail&Guardian* to at least attempt to inform the doctor of its real intentions as soon as possible after the interview. It was just unfortunate that he did not return his calls.

Case study 30
A bug in the wall

Colonel 'Staal' Burger was one of the hard men of apartheid. He was a former policeman who headed the Civil Co-operation Bureau, a secretive unit that played a central role in the government's dirty-tricks campaign against the anti-apartheid movement. He was later named as an accomplice in the assassination of the Swapo activist Anton Lubowski, and the Truth Commission refused him amnesty for two other attempted assassinations. But in 1992 none of this was publicly known.

At the time, he had offices at a hotel in Hillbrow, Johannesburg. One day he found a small hole in the skirting board of his office. He called police, and when they kicked open the door of the room next door, they found a private investigator and three other men who had set up a bugging operation.[23]

It turned out that they were acting on instructions of the *Weekly Mail*, as it was then. Burger quickly obtained a court interdict against the newspaper, which was also charged with *crimen injuria*. During the trial, evidence was led about the paper's ongoing investigation into the causes of violence then sweeping the country. It was widely believed that a 'Third Force' from inside the security forces was fomenting the violence to disrupt the negotiations then under way between the government and the ANC.

Eddie Koch, a senior reporter, testified that he headed a team investigating the matter, and had received information that Burger was involved in meetings at the hotel with people involved in covert activities.[24] He also said that all other ways of investigating the matter had been exhausted. The case dragged on for years, but in April 1996 the paper was found guilty and fined R3000. Its co-editor, Anton Harber, was fined another R1000. In an editorial comment that week, the paper continued to justify its decision.

Bugging was tolerated in civilised societies, but generally only allowed by state agencies because of the potential for abuse, the paper wrote. 'But what of a society in which the "responsible" state agencies were made up of men like Burger; in which ministers had shown themselves to be parties to murderous conspiracy? If ever there was a criminal activity which warranted electronic surveillance it is treason. But who is to take these measures when those charged with defence of the nation are seemingly involved in the treason? We stepped into the vacuum.'[25]

However, it added that with the advent of democracy, that vacuum no longer existed. 'It is with relief that we say our days as buggers are over.'

Bugging Burger's office was clearly illegal. But the *Weekly Mail* argued that the public interest in the case was so overwhelming as to justify the decision. Lives could have been saved if the covert activities it believed were being planned in the hotel could be disrupted.

It's a persuasive argument. No journalist should lightly decide to break the law. But the credibility of the state itself was badly tarnished. In those years, the media played a crucial role in exposing the terrible crimes that the state security organs had been committing, and arguably helped in moving the country towards democracy. Those were extraordinary times, and extraordinary measures were justified.

Case study 31
Sweets from strangers

The camera hidden in the front of the car watched impassively as the three men talked. The driver was giving the two others a lift so they could buy supplies for their business, selling sweets outside schools. As they drove, he listened to their stories. 'For 35 to 40 nauseating minutes they described to him what they did to children,' says George Mazarakis, the executive producer of *Carte Blanche*.[26]

The programme had begun investigating after the driver, named only as Nick, came forward with a disturbing tale of paedophilia. The two other men, named as Hannes and Jan, had asked him 'whether he wanted a young boy'.[27] Mazarakis says the programme's producers had to be very careful. They needed to make sure that Nick was not involved himself, and also that he was telling the truth. 'Initially we didn't believe him, but eventually he convinced us that it was very solid. We checked and double-checked and everything panned out – he wasn't a storyteller.'

The decision was taken to install a camera in his car in order to get the men's own account on tape. According to a story summary on the *Carte Blanche* website, 'our hidden car camera recorded some of the sordid stories about what goes on at Hannes's flat and Jan's house. Hannes and Jan claim to have had repeated sexual encounters with young boys – many involving payment. This appeared to have been going on for several years.'

But was it just talk? Producers equipped Nick with another hidden camera, and he went to the flat of one of the other men, ostensibly in order to meet a 15-year-old boy for sex. He had been carefully briefed beforehand that things could not be allowed to get out of hand. The boy was about to take off his clothes and accept money – 'this was about a few bob, or a Coke and a hamburger,' says Mazarakis – when Nick left. 'We got that moment on tape. We were comfortable that we hadn't actually provoked the act.'

The footage was damning, and made for disturbing viewing. The report was aired in February 2001 under the title 'Sweets from strangers'. *Carte Blanche* then also facilitated a meeting between Nick and the police. Mazarakis says: 'He wanted the police to get involved but he was scared of going to the police himself because he felt that the police would betray him. So he felt that by coming to us and our going to the police, these guys would get caught and he would be safe. This is very important; we could never have spoken to the police about the source unless the source wanted us to.'

After getting his written permission, the programme also made its footage available to the police. Later in the same year, Hannes was sentenced to 23 years in jail, while Jan was given a suspended three-year sentence, house arrest, and banned from getting closer than 500 metres to a school.[28]

Several ethical issues arise from this case. For one thing, the use of a hidden camera is a form of deception that breaks journalistic norms. To justify the use of such techniques, journalists need to establish that the story is exceptionally important and that there is no other way to gather the necessary evidence. In this case, those conditions were met. Detailed inquiries were made before the step to secret filming was taken. Of course, television needs pictures, which would have been hard to come by otherwise. Also, paedophilia is a particularly repulsive crime, about which society is very deeply concerned.

Carte Blanche took a risk in sending Nick into the flat to get direct evidence of an encounter. If something had actually happened to the boy, the programme would have had to take responsibility. But the producers made sure the situation was stopped in time, protecting both the boy and the ethics of their report. There was also a risk that the situation might become entrapment. Nick could not be allowed to do anything that might later seem to be pushing the other man towards attacking the boy. The report's credibility would have suffered if he had been seen to be a player in the situation, rather than an observer. Again, the producers successfully navigated this difficulty.

Finally, the decision to assist the police was unusual and, to some, controversial. Journalistic independence usually means that the media steer clear of direct co-operation with the police. Presented with a similar but hypothetical scenario, Joe Thloloe, e.tv's head of news, said he would report fully on a ring of paedophiles 'and I will give all the information I can in my piece. And it is up to the police to then go and do their investigations rather than try and use me as a journalist.'[29]

But this case has some unusual aspects. Again, the particular nature of paedophilia plays a role. Children were being harmed, and might have gone on being harmed if the two men had been allowed to go on operating. The possibility of preventing real and serious harm must weigh heavily in any ethical discussion.

Then, Nick himself wanted the police to act, and apparently approached *Carte Blanche* with the express purpose of enlisting their help in securing police involvement. This was a crucial aspect, as Mazarakis himself points out. The source's wishes had to be taken into account.

The principle of independence should not be lightly bent. But if there is a case where there is an argument for some flexibility, this is it.

....

NOTES

1 Günter Wallraff, '13 unerwünschte reportagen'. Hamburg: Rowohlt Taschenbuch Verlag, 1982. 177–84.

2 Ibid. 177, own translation.

3 Ibid, cover notes, own translation.

4 Jay Black, Bob Steele and Ralph Barney, *Doing ethics in journalism: a handbook with case studies*. Needham Heights, MA: Allyn & Bacon, 1995. 119.

5 Ibid. 119.

6 Russ W Baker, 'Truth, lies and videotape', *Columbia Journalism Review*, July/August 1993.

7 Bob Steele, 'A message about reporting methods: make no mistake' in Radio-Television News Directors Foundation (RTNDF), 'Hidden cameras, hidden microphones'. Posted at http://rtnda.org/resources/hiddencamera/contents.html, accessed on 29 January 2004.

8 Quoted in Johan Retief, *Media ethics: an introduction to responsible journalism*. Cape Town: OUP, 2002. 70.

9 Bob Steele, 'High standards for hidden cameras', August 1999. Posted at http://www.poynter.org/content/content_view.asp?id=5543, accessed in August 2003.

10 The basic list comes from Black, Steele and Barney, *Doing ethics*. 124. The notes in between are the author's.

11 Ibid. 125.

12 Louis A Day, *Ethics in media communications: cases and controversies*. Belmont, CA: Wadsworth, 1991. 70.

13 *The New York Times*, 'Ethical journalism'. New York: *The New York Times*, 2003. 8.

14 Interview, 8 November 2002.

15 Quoted in Russ W Baker, 'Truth, lies and videotape', *Columbia Journalism Review*, July/August 1993.

16 Ibid.

17 Ibid.

18 Ibid.

19 Interview, 8 November 2002.

20 Bob Steele, 'Beware the dangers of 'testing the system', 3 October, 2001. Posted at http://www.poynter.org/column.asp?id=36&aid=860, accessed 23 March 2004.

21 The following account is based largely on the Press Ombudsman of South Africa adjudication, Dr S Johannes v *Mail&Guardian*, 28 April – 4 May 1999.

22 *Mail&Guardian*, 20–26 November 1998.

23 Sapa report of 8 June 1993. Posted at http://www.anc.org.za/anc/newsbrief/1993/news9306.09, accessed on 30 January 2004.

24 *Weekly Mail*, 27 January 1995.

25 *Mail&Guardian*, 4–10 April 1996.

26 Interview, 8 November 2002.

27 Posted at http://www.mnet.co.za/CarteBlanche/Display/Display.asp?Id=1572, accessed on 30 January 2004.

28 'Paedophile gets 23 years'. Posted at http://www.mnet.co.za/CarteBlanche/Display/Display.asp?id=1232, accessed on 30 January 2004.

29 Interview, 8 November 2002.

AN ETHICS ROADMAP

THREE STEPS TO RESOLVING A DILEMMA

Note: This roadmap can be used to work through a particular issue. It is based on a formula developed by the US ethicist Louis Day and approaches used in the Ethics Tool of the American Society of Newspaper Editors and Poynter Institute, as well as other sources. The roadmap should be used after reading the discussion on practical decision-making in Chapter 3. Remember particularly that discussion with colleagues will improve your decisions, particularly if those colleagues have different backgrounds to your own.

Step 1: Define the issue

What are the facts of the case?

. . . .
. . . .
. . . .
. . . .
. . . .
. . . .
. . . .
. . . .
. . . .

What is the question?

. . . .
. . . .
. . . .
. . . .
. . . .
. . . .

Step 2: Think through the issue

Why am I doing this story? What is the public interest?

. . . .
. . . .
. . . .
. . . .
. . . .
. . . .

Who is affected and how? What would they want? Are those desires legitimate? (Possible stakeholders include sources, the subject of the story, their families, the news organisation.)

. . . .
. . . .
. . . .
. . . .
. . . .
. . . .
. . . .

Which principles are involved? Which of them clash? (Tick the relevant ones, adding your own if necessary, and explain below.)

- ☐ Accuracy
- ☐ Fairness
- ☐ Independence
- ☐ Duty to inform the public
- ☐ Minimising harm
- ☐ Avoiding unnecessary offence
- ☐ Respecting privacy
- ☐ Honesty in relating to the source
- ☐ Honouring a promise
- ☐ Avoiding deception

. . . .
. . . .
. . . .
. . . .
. . . .

Is race or gender a factor? How?

....
....
....
....
....

Which guidelines and precedents are relevant?

....
....
....
....
....
....
....
....
....
....

What are the alternative courses of action? Are there ways I can handle the situation that satisfy various conflicting interests or principles? What advantages and disadvantages are there in each case? (Add more if necessary.)

Option 1: ....
....
....
....
....

Option 2: ....
....
....
....
....

Option 3: ....
....
....
....
....

Step 3: Decide

The best option is:

....
....
....
....
....

How will I defend my decision to colleagues, the different stakeholders and to my audience?

....
....
....
....
....

DISCUSSIONS AND EXERCISES

FOR USE IN THE CLASSROOM

Talking points and case studies
The talking points and case studies accompanying each chapter can be used as the basis for discussion. Many of the box quotes could also be used in this way.

Questions and scenarios
The following questions and fictional scenarios can also be used for discussion.

Chapter 1: Introduction
a) 'Journalists in South Africa should stop following Western ethics and develop their own values.' Discuss.
b) Can you think of situations in which African values would change the way journalists behave?
c) Is 'public interest' just a figleaf that the media use to justify sensationalism?

Chapter 2: The South African media landscape
a) Should journalists serve the national interest or the public interest?
b) Are the South African media racist? How?
c) Should the media give their audiences what they want, or what they need?

Chapter 3: Accountability and practical decision-making
a) Should journalists be registered like doctors and lawyers?
b) Discuss the way in which a newsroom you know deals with ethical issues. Does the system work well?
c) Choose any one of the case studies in this book, and use the Ethics roadmap in Appendix 1 to work through it.

Chapter 4: Getting it right: accuracy

a) Find somebody who has had an experience of being in the news, and ask him or her whether the reporting was accurate.

b) You visit a hospital and you find it dirty, with rats running around everywhere. However, the superintendent simply denies there is a problem with cleanliness. How do you write the story in a way that is fair to the superintendent without misleading your audience about the true state of affairs?

c) A senior official in the department of health declares publicly that the best way to treat HIV and Aids is to eat plenty of cabbage, potato and onion. Many scientists say this is nonsense. In reporting this statement, is it important to include the comment of scientists who disagree?

Chapter 5: Getting all sides: fairness

a) You broadcast a report by a highly respected investigative journalist to the effect that the leader of a major political party owns five slum buildings where drug dealing and prostitution are rife. In other words, he's a slumlord. The report is well researched, and has substantial evidence. But despite extensive efforts by the reporter, he hasn't been able to get comment from the politician himself. You decide to run it anyway since you fear it may break on a rival station if you don't. As you are on air, a party spokesman phones and demands to be put on air to reply to the allegation. The party leader himself is abroad and uncontactable. Do you let him? Why?

b) On World Aids Day, your radio station broadcasts a one-hour special phone-in programme on the issue, with prominent scientists taking calls. After the broadcast, a well-known Aids dissident phones to demand that you schedule another one-hour programme on the issue. But for the sake of balance, he says, you should use him and a colleague who shares his views, since the Aids Day special had only orthodox scientists. How do you respond?

c) Have a look at a couple of newspapers, and look for instances where you feel they are being unfair. Discuss what makes these reports unfair

Chapter 6: Keeping your distance: independence

a) Your newspaper has evidence that the arms manufacturer Denel has sold arms to rebels in the Great Lakes region, in defiance of government policy and UN sanctions. When you ask government for comment, they ask you to hold back the story until they've investigated, on the grounds that the revelation may scuttle delicate peace processes in the region. Do you comply?

b) The municipal reporter on your paper marries a woman who is her party's candidate for mayor in the upcoming local government elections. You are the editor. How do you deal with the situation?

c) Write a policy on freebies – gifts, free travel, etc. – for a newsroom you know.

Chapter 7: Writing race

a) Can you think of other words that carry racist baggage? (See page 119.)

b) The police raid a hotel in Hillbrow and arrest 15 alleged drug dealers. They say 12 of them are Nigerians. Does your report mention the nationality of the people held?

c) '27 British tourists die in a bus accident in Mpumalanga.' '42 commuters die in a taxi pile-up outside Pretoria.' Which is the bigger story? Why?

Chapter 8: The next frontier: gender

a) 'This call to use non-sexist language in the media is just a lot of politically correct nonsense.' Discuss.

b) A local official of the department of labour says that the unemployment problem would be greatly reduced if women stayed at home. How would you report this story?

c) Think of new approaches to reporting the national budget, taking gender into account.

Chapter 9: Stepping on toes: public sensitivities

a) An obscure musician records a song in which he swears at the former president Nelson Mandela. In reporting the ensuing outcry, should you quote the words he uses?

b)   A radio DJ introduces a regular slot for jokes about various groups –
     Greeks, Jews, blacks. Should the programme manager stop him, or
     allow him to continue?
c)   Which should we be more careful about, pictures of sex or of violence?

Chapter 10: Of trust and scepticism: relating to the source

a)   Sipho Williams works for a political party, and feeds reporter Dave
     Xundu information showing that the leader of another party stole
     money from the school where he was principal. Williams makes
     Xundu promise to protect his name. The information checks out, but
     the editor says the fact that one party is smearing the other in this way
     is a bigger story than the allegation itself. He wants to use Williams's
     name on the grounds he was trying to use the newspaper to fight a
     political battle. Xundu says he can't break his promise. Who is right?
b)   You get a phone call at your TV station, offering you a video showing
     abuse of elderly patients in a church old-age home. The caller wants
     to be paid R5000 for the tape. Do you buy it?
c)   The mayor invites you to a private background briefing about a
     planned casino development in your town. You agree to respect con-
     fidentiality, but during the briefing she lets slip that the town council
     agreed to the development after the developer made big donations to
     her political party. Do you keep to your promise, or do you report
     what you heard?

Chapter 11: My home is (not always) my castle: privacy

a)   An unmarked envelope arrives with a video recording of a top busi-
     nessman arriving at a brothel and later disappearing into the back
     with a prostitute. He's a happily married family man. You suspect that
     the video was sent to you by a business rival. How do you deal with
     the story?
b)   Peter Tshabalala, a senior advocate, is being considered for appoint-
     ment to the bench. You find out that he often used to act for the
     apartheid security police. Is this a story? How would you handle it?
c)   Residents of Acorn Street are angry because their new neighbour is a
     man who was jailed for child abuse. Even though he has done his time
     and swears to have turned over a new leaf, they fear that their children
     are at risk. Should you name the man in reporting the issue for your
     community newspaper?

Chapter 12: The dark side: reporting death, Aids and trauma

a) Yet another mining disaster claims six lives. Your photographer comes back with powerful close-up images of the grieving wife of one victim, weeping over the mangled body of her husband. Do you run the pictures? What questions might you need to ask the photographer in deciding whether to use the images?

b) *Reporter A*: 'The public must see pictures of the terrible results of terror attacks, so that such atrocities can be stopped.'
    Reporter B: 'People don't want to see awful pictures of bloody bodies at their breakfast table, and people aren't going to stop terrorism just because they see an unpleasant picture, anyway.' Who's right?

c) A prominent musician dies after a long illness at the age of 31. A close friend (who does not want to be named) tells you he died of Aids, but his family says it was pneumonia. Do you report what you heard from the friend?

Chapter 13: Flying a false flag: deception

a) Would you use illegal means, like phone tapping, to catch a corrupt official?

b) A building contractor tells you that his company paid bribes to get a contract for a big housing project. Your editor wants you to tape-record your interview with him in case there is legal action later. But the builder won't talk to you on tape, so your editor asks you to tape him secretly. Should you do that?

c) There have been several deaths of young men at circumcision schools in your area. You suspect that terrible beatings have been the cause, but you know that the men involved in the schools won't talk to you, a woman journalist. Should you dress up as a man to do the story, or should you accept the cultural taboo?

ICASA CODE OF CONDUCT FOR BROADCASTERS

· ·

Foreword

1. Section 2 of the Independent Broadcasting Authority Act No. 153 of 1993 ('the Act') enjoins the Independent Broadcasting Authority ('the Authority') to ensure that broadcasting licensees adhere to a Code of Conduct acceptable to the Authority.

2. In terms of Section 56(1) of the Act, 'all broadcasting licensees shall adhere to the Code of Conduct for Broadcasting Services as set out in Schedule 1.' The provisions of that subsection do not, however, apply to any broadcasting licensee 'if he or she is a member of a body which has proved to the satisfaction of the Authority that its members subscribe and adhere to a Code of Conduct enforced by that body by means of its own disciplinary mechanism, and provided that such Code of Conduct and disciplinary mechanisms are acceptable to the Authority'.

3. Definitions
   'audience' as referred to in this Code means a visual and an aural audience i.e. both television and radio audiences. 'broadcasts intended for adult audiences' as referred to in this Code means broadcasts depicting excessive violence and explicit sexual conduct and shall exclude broadcasts intended for children. 'children' as referred to in this Code means those persons below 16 years. 'watershed period' as referred to in this Code means the period between 21h00 and 05h00. Such restriction applies only to television services.

Preamble

4. Freedom of expression lies at the foundation of a democratic South Africa and is one of the basic prerequisites for this country's progress and the development in liberty of every person. Freedom of expression is a condition indispensable to the attainment of all other free-

doms. The premium our Constitution attaches to freedom of expression is not novel; it is an article of faith in the democracies of the kind we are venturing to create.

5. Constitutional protection is afforded to freedom of expression in Section 16 of the Constitution which provides:

   1) Everyone has the right to freedom of expression, which includes –
      a) Freedom of the press and other media;
      b) Freedom to receive or impart information or ideas;
      c) Freedom of artistic creativity; and
      d) Academic freedom and freedom of scientific research.
   2) The right in Sub-section (1) does not extend to –
      a) Propaganda for war;
      b) Incitement of imminent violence; or
      c) Advocacy of hatred that is based on race, ethnicity, gender or religion, and that constitutes incitement to cause harm.

6. Whilst in most democratic societies freedom of expression is recognised as being absolutely central to democracy, in no country is freedom of expression absolute. Like all rights, freedom of expression is subject to limitation under Section 36 of the Constitution.

7. The outcome of disputes turning on the guarantee of freedom of expression will depend upon the value the courts are prepared to place on that freedom and the extent to which they will be inclined to subordinate other rights and interests to free expression. Rights of free expression will have to be weighed up against many other rights, including the right to equality, dignity, privacy, political campaigning, fair trial, economic activity, workplace democracy, property and most significantly the rights of children and women.

8. In the period prior to the transition to democracy, governmental processes neither required nor welcomed the adjuncts of free expression and critical discussion and our country did not treasure at its core a democratic ideal. The right to freedom of expression was regularly violated with impunity by the legislature and the executive. Therefore the protection of this right is of paramount importance now that South Africa is grappling with the process of purging itself of those laws and practices from our past which do not accord with the values which underpin the Constitution.

Application of the Code

9. All licensees are required to ensure that all broadcasts comply with this Code and are further required to satisfy the Authority that they have adequate procedures to fulfil this requirement. All licensees should ensure that relevant employees and programme-makers, including those from whom they commission programmes, understand the Code's contents and significance. All licensees should also have in place procedures for ensuring that programme-makers can seek guidance on the Code within the licensee's organisation at a senior level.

10. While the Authority is responsible for drafting this Code of Conduct and for monitoring compliance therewith, independent producers or others supplying programme material should seek guidance on specific proposals from the relevant licensee.

11. Under the Act, the Authority has the power to impose sanctions, including fines, on licensees who do not comply with this Code of Conduct.

12. This Code does not attempt to cover the full range of programme matters with which the Authority and licensees are concerned. This is not because such matters are insignificant, but because they have not given rise to the need for Authority guidance. The Code is therefore not a complete guide to good practice in every situation. Nor is it necessarily the last word on the matters to which it refers. Views and attitudes change, and any prescription for what is required of those who make and provide programmes may be incomplete and may sooner or later become outdated. The Code is subject to interpretation in the light of changing circumstances, and in some matters it may be necessary, from time to time, to introduce fresh requirements.

13. In drawing up this Code the Authority has taken into account the objectives of the Act and the urgent need in South Africa for the fundamental values which underlie our legal system to accommodate to the norms and principles which are embraced by our Constitution.

Violence

14. Licensees shall not broadcast any material which judged within context –
   i)   contains gratuitous violence in any form i.e. violence which does not play an integral role in developing the plot, character or theme of the material as a whole;
   ii) sanctions, promotes or glamorises violence.

15. Violence against women
    Broadcasters shall –
    i)   not broadcast material which, judged within context, sanctions, promotes or glamorises any aspect of violence against women;
    ii)   ensure that women are not depicted as victims of violence unless the violence is integral to the story being told;
    iii) be particularly sensitive not to perpetuate the link between women in a sexual context and women as victims of violence.

16. Violence against specific groups
    16.1 Licensees shall not broadcast material which, judged within context sanctions, promotes or glamorises violence based on race, national or ethnic origin, colour, religion, gender, sexual orientation, age, or mental or physical disability.
    16.2 Licensees are reminded generally of the possible dangers of some people imitating violence details of which they see, hear or read about.

17. The above-mentioned prohibitions shall not apply to –
    i)   a bona fide scientific, documentary, dramatic, artistic, or religious broadcast which, judged within context, is of such nature;
    ii)   broadcasts which amount to discussion, argument or opinion on a matter pertaining to religion, belief or conscience; or
    iii) broadcasts which amount to a bona fide discussion, argument or opinion on a matter of public interest.

Children

18. Broadcasters are reminded that children as defined in paragraph 3 above embraces a wide range of maturity and sophistication, and in interpreting this Code it is legitimate for licensees to distinguish, if appropriate, those approaching adulthood from a much younger, pre-teenage audience.
    18.1 Broadcasters shall not broadcast material unsuitable for children at times when large numbers of children may be expected to be part of the audience.
    18.2 Broadcasters shall exercise particular caution, as provided below, in the depiction of violence in children's programming.
    18.3 In children's programming portrayed by real-life characters, violence shall, whether physical, verbal or emotional, only be portrayed when it is essential to the development of a character and plot.

18.4 Animated programming for children, while accepted as a stylised form of story-telling which can contain non-realistic violence, shall not have violence as its central theme, and shall not invite dangerous imitation.

18.5 Programming for children shall with due care deal with themes which could threaten their sense of security, when portraying, for example, domestic conflict, death, crime or the use of drugs.

18.6 Programming for children shall with due care deal with themes which could invite children to imitate acts which they see on screen or hear about, such as the use of plastic bags as toys, use of matches, the use of dangerous household products as play-things, or other dangerous physical acts.

18.7 Programming for children shall not contain realistic scenes of violence which create the impression that violence is the pre-ferred or only method to resolve conflict between individuals.

18.8 Programming for children shall not contain realistic scenes of violence which minimise or gloss over the effect of violent acts. Any realistic depictions of violence shall portray, in human terms, the consequences of that violence to its victims and its perpetrators.

18.9 Programming for children shall not contain frightening or oth-erwise excessive special effects not required by the story line.

Watershed Period

19. Programming on television which contains scenes of violence, sexu-ally explicit conduct and/or offensive language intended for adult audiences shall not be broadcast before the watershed period.

20. On the basis that there is a likelihood of older children forming part of the audience during the watershed period, licensees shall adhere to the provisions of Article 32 below (audience advisories) enabling par-ents to make an informed decision as to the suitability of the pro-gramming for their family members.

21. Promotional material and music videos which contain scenes of violence, sexually explicit conduct and/or offensive language intend-ed for adult audiences shall not be broadcast before the watershed period.

22. Some programmes broadcast outside the watershed period will not be suitable for very young children. Licensees should provide suffi-

cient information, in terms of regular scheduling patterns or on-air advice, to assist parents to make appropriate viewing choices.

23. Licensees shall be aware that with the advance of the watershed period progressively less suitable (i.e. more adult) material may be shown and it may be that a programme will be acceptable for example at 23h00 that would not be suitable at 21h00.

24. Broadcasters must be particularly sensitive to the likelihood that programmes which start during the watershed period and which run beyond it may then be viewed by children.

25. Subscription services

25.1 Where a programme service is only available to viewers on subscription and offers a parental control mechanism, its availability to children may be more restricted and the watershed period may begin at 20h00.

Language

26. Offensive language, including profanity, blasphemy and other religiously insensitive material, shall not be used in programmes specially designed for children.

27. No excessively and grossly offensive language should be used before the watershed period on television or at times when large numbers of children are likely to be part of the audience on television or radio. Its use during the periods referred to above should, where practicable, be approved in advance by the licensee's most senior programme executive or the designated alternate.

Sexual Conduct

28. Licensees shall not broadcast material which, judged within context, contains a scene or scenes, simulated or real, of any of the following:

i) A person who is, or is depicted as being under the age of 18 years, participating in, engaging in or assisting another person to engage in sexual conduct or a lewd display of nudity;

ii) Explicit violent sexual conduct;

iii) Bestiality;

iv) Explicit sexual conduct which degrades a person in the sense that it advocates a particular form of hatred based on gender and which constitutes incitement to cause harm;

29. The prohibition in 28.(i) to 28.(iv) shall not be applicable to bona fide scientific, documentary, dramatic material which, judged within context, is of such a nature. The prohibition in 28.(i), shall however be applicable to artistic material which, judged within context, is of such a nature.

30. Scenes depicting sexual conduct, as defined in the Films and Publications Act 65 of 1996, should be broadcast only during the watershed period. Exceptions to this may be allowed in programmes with a serious educational purpose or where the representation is non-explicit and should be approved in advance by the most senior programme executive or a delegated alternate.

31. Explicit portrayal of violent sexual behaviour is justifiable only exceptionally and the same approval process as referred to in 30 above must be followed.

Audience Advisories

32. To assist audiences in choosing programmes, licensees shall provide advisory assistance, which when applicable shall include guidelines as to age, at the beginning of broadcasts and wherever necessary, where such broadcasts contain violence, sexual conduct and/or offensive language.

33. Classification

   33.1 Where a Film and Publications Board classification exists in terms of the Films and Publications Act No. 65 of 1996 ('Films and Publications Act') for the version of a film or programme intended to be broadcast, such classification certification may be used as a guide for broadcasting.

   33.2 No version which has been refused a Film and Publications Board classification certification should be broadcast at any time.

   33.3 In all other instances, the provisions of this Code will apply.

34. News

   34.1 Licensees shall be obliged to report news truthfully, accurately and fairly.

   34.2 News shall be presented in the correct context and in a fair manner, without intentional or negligent departure from the facts, whether by –

      a) Distortion, exaggeration or misrepresentation;

b) Material omissions; or

c) Summarisation.

34.3 Only that which may reasonably be true, having due regard to the source of the news, may be presented as fact, and such fact shall be broadcast fairly with due regard to context and importance. Where a report is not based on fact or is founded on opinion, supposition, rumours or allegations, it shall be presented in such manner as to indicate clearly that such is the case.

34.4 Where there is reason to doubt the correctness of the report and it is practicable to verify the correctness thereof, it shall be verified. Where such verification is not practicable, that fact shall be mentioned in the report.

34.5 Where it subsequently appears that a broadcast report was incorrect in a material respect, it shall be rectified forthwith, without reservation or delay. The rectification shall be presented with such a degree of prominence and timing as in the circumstances may be adequate and fair so as to readily attract attention.

34.6 The identity of rape victims and other victims of sexual violence shall not be divulged in any broadcast without the prior consent of the victim concerned.

34.7 Licensees shall advise viewers in advance of scenes or reporting of extraordinary violence, or graphic reporting on delicate subject-matter such as sexual assault or court action related to sexual crimes, particularly during afternoon or early evening newscasts and updates when children would probably be in the audience.

34.8 Licensees shall employ discretion in the use of explicit or graphic language related to stories of destruction, accidents or sexual violence, which could disturb children and sensitive audiences.

35. Comment

35.1 Licensees shall be entitled to broadcast comment on and criticism of any actions or events of public importance.

35.2 Comment shall be an honest expression of opinion and shall be presented in such manner that it appears clearly to be comment, and shall be made on facts truly stated or fairly indicated and referred to.

36. Controversial issues of public importance

    36.1 In presenting a programme in which controversial issues of public importance are discussed, a licensee shall make reasonable efforts to fairly present opposing points of view either in the same programme or in a subsequent programme forming part of the same series of programmes presented within a reasonable period of time of the original broadcast and within substantially the same time slot.

    36.2 A person whose views are to be criticised in a broadcasting programme on a controversial issue of public importance shall be given a right to reply to such criticism on the same programme. If this is impracticable however, opportunity for response to the programme should be provided where appropriate, for example in a right to reply programme or in a pre-arranged discussion programme with the prior consent of the person concerned.

37. Elections

During any election period, the provisions of sections 58, 59, 60 and 61 of the Act shall apply, and all broadcasting services shall in terms of those sections be subject to the jurisdiction of the Authority.

38. Privacy

Insofar as both news and comment are concerned, broadcasting licensees shall exercise exceptional care and consideration in matters involving the private lives and private concerns of individuals, bearing in mind that the right to privacy may be overridden by a legitimate public interest.

39. Paying a criminal for information

    39.1 No payment shall be made to persons involved in crime or other notorious behaviour, or to persons who have been engaged in crime or other notorious behaviour, in order to obtain information concerning any such behaviour, unless compelling societal interests indicate the contrary.

Posted at http://www.icasa.org.za/default.aspx?page=1349

PRESS CODE OF PROFESSIONAL CONDUCT

PREAMBLE

The basic principle to be upheld is that the freedom of the press is indivisible from and subject to the same rights and duties as that of the individual and rests on the public's fundamental right to be informed and freely to receive and to disseminate opinions.

The primary purpose of gathering and distributing news and opinion is to serve society by informing citizens and enabling them to make informed judgments on the issues of the day.

The freedom of the press to bring an independent scrutiny to bear on the forces that shape society is a freedom exercised on behalf of the public.

The public interest is the only test that justifies departure from the highest standards of journalism and includes:

a) detecting or exposing crime or serious misdemeanour;

b) detecting or exposing serious anti-social conduct;

c) protecting public health and safety;

d) preventing the public from ebing misled by some statement or action of an individual or organisation;

e) detecting or exposing hypocrisy, falsehoods or double standards or behaviour on the part of public figures or institutions and in public institutions.

The code is not intended to be comprehensive or all embracing. No code can cover every contingency. The press will be judged by the code's spirit – accuracy, balance, fairness and decency – rather than its narrow letter, in the belief that vigilant self-regulation is the hallmark of a free and independent press.

In considering complaints the Press Ombudsman and Appeal Panel will be guided by the following:

1. Reporting of news

1.1 The press shall be obliged to report news truthfully, accurately and fairly.

1.2 News shall be presented in context and in a balanced manner, without an intentional or negligent departure from the facts whether by:

1.2.1 distortion, exaggeration or misrepresentation;

1.2.2 material omissions; or

1.2.3 summarisation

1.3 Only what may reasonably be true having regard to the sources of the news, may be presented as facts, and such facts shall be published fairly with due regard to context and importance. Where a report is not based on facts or is founded on opinions, allegation, rumour or supposition, it shall be presented in such manner as to indicate this clearly.

1.4 Where there is reason to doubt the accuracy of a report and it is practicable to verify the accuracy thereof, it shall be verified. Where it has not been practicable to verify the accuracy of a report, this shall be mentioned in such report.

1.5 A newspaper should usually seek the views of the subject of serious critical reportage in advance of publication; provided that this need not be done where the newspaper has reasonable grounds for believing that by doing so it would be prevented from publishing the report or where evidence might be destroyed or witnesses intimidated.

1.6 A publication should make amends for publishing information or comment that is found to be harmfully inaccurate by printing, promptly and with appropriate prominence, a retraction, correction or explanation.

1.7 Reports, photographs or sketches relative to matters involving indecency or obscenity shall be presented with due sensitivity towards the prevailing moral climate.

1.8 The identity of rape victims and other victims of sexual violence shall not be published without the consent of the victim.

1.9 News obtained by dishonest or unfair means, or the publication of which would involve a breach of confidence, should not be published unless there is an overriding public interest.

1.10 In both news and comment, the press shall exercise exceptional care and consideration in matters involving the private lives and concerns of individuals, bearing in mind that any right to privacy may be overridden by a legitimate public interest.

1.11 A newspaper has wide discretion in matters of taste but this does not justify lapses of taste so repugnant as to bring the freedom of the press into disrepute or be extremely offensive to the public.

2. Discrimination

2.1 The press should avoid discriminatory or denigratory references to people's race, colour, religion, sexual orientation or preference, physical or mental disability or illness, or age.

2.2 The press should not refer to a person's race, colour, religion, sexual orientation, or physical or mental illness in a prejudicial or pejorative context except where it is strictly relevant to the matter reported on or adds significantly to readers' understanding of that matter.

2.3 The press has the right and indeed the duty to report and comment on all matters of public interest. This right and duty must, however, be balanced against the obligation not to promote racial hatred or discord in such a way as to create the likelihood of imminent violence.

3. Advocacy

A newspaper is justified in strongly advocating its own views on controversial topics provided that it treats its readers fairly by

2.1 making fact and opinion clearly distinguishable;

2.2 not misrepresenting or suppressing relevant facts;

2.3 not distorting the facts in text or headlines.

4. Comment

3.1 The press shall be entitled to comment upon or criticise any actions or events of public importance provided such comments or criticisms are fairly and honestly made.

3.2 Comment by the press shall be presented in such manner that it appears clearly that it is comment, and shall be made on facts truly stated or fairly indicated and referred to.

3.3 Comment by the press shall be an honest expression of opinion, without malice or dishonest motives, and shall take fair account of all available facts which are material to the matter commented upon.

5.   Headlines, posters, pictures and captions

4.1   Headlines and captions to pictures shall give a reasonable reflection of the contents of the report or picture in question.

4.2   Posters shall not mislead the public and shall give a reasonable reflection of the contents of the reports in question.

4.3   Pictures shall not misrepresent or mislead nor be manipulated to do so.

6.   Confidential sources

A newspaper has an obligation to protect confidential sources of information.

7.   Payment for articles

No payment shall be made for feature articles to persons engaged in crime or other notorious misbehaviour, or to convicted persons or their associates, including family, friends, neighbours and colleagues, except where the material concerned ought to be published in the public interest and the payment is necessary for this to be done.

8.   Violence

Due care and responsibility shall be exercised by the press with regard to the presentation of brutality, violence and atrocities.

THE SUNDAY TIMES ACCURACY CHECK

(abbreviated version)

Stage one

- [ ] What is the story?
- [ ] Why are you doing the story?
- [ ] Is it because it is only of interest to you, or because it is of interest to our readers?
- [ ] Is it in the interests of the public to publish the story?
- [ ] Has all the background research on the story been done?
- [ ] Why has the source given you the story?

Stage two

Before writing the story, ask yourself:

- [ ] Have you got two or three sources on your story? (A source is not an anonymous caller or a single source who may be prejudiced)?
- [ ] Can I attribute everything I have in my story to at least two sources who have names and telephone numbers?
- [ ] Am I able to put my source/sources in court (should the need arise)?
- [ ] What proof do I have that my story is factually correct?
- [ ] Did you get documents or any other tangible evidence that can prove the facts?
- [ ] There are always at least two sides to every story – have you got both?
- [ ] Always be fair to those you are writing about.
- [ ] Read back quotes to your sources.
- [ ] Every reasonable effort must be taken to verify your facts and get comment.
- [ ] Speak to experts if you do not understand certain aspects of your story.
- [ ] Check the spelling of all names and places in your copy.
- [ ] Check every paragraph once the story is written and ask yourself:
- [ ] Can I stand these facts up in a court of law?
- [ ] Triple-check figures in your story.

- ☐ Do not lift quotes from library files or other newspapers without double-checking with the person concerned.
- ☐ You might find that the status of your story has changed or that the quotes you are lifting were wrong in the first place.
- ☐ Remember you are not above the law – you have the same rights as any other citizen.
- ☐ Did you break the law to get your story? If you did, reconsider.
- ☐ Did you obtain your information illegally?
- ☐ Was the case you are writing about heard in camera? If it was, did you check with the judge or magistrate what you can use?

Stage three

- ☐ Before doing your accuracy check, have you been able to answer the questions above?
- ☐ How did the report originate?
- ☐ Prime source and telephone number/address?
- ☐ Other people contacted and telephone numbers/addresses?

Checklist

- ☐ Are all names correct and spelt correctly?
- ☐ Are all figures and percentages correct?
- ☐ Are all dates and ages correct?
- ☐ Are the facts correct? (Are there three sources?)
- ☐ Are quotations correct? (Check against notebook.)

Content

- ☐ Are you satisfied that the story is accurate?
- ☐ Are you satisfied that it is angled correctly?
- ☐ Are you satisfied that it is fair to all parties?
- ☐ Did you contact all parties involved? If not, what steps did you take to contact them?
- ☐ Have you put the subject's comments/denial high up in the report, or have you simply added it at the bottom of the report?
- ☐ Are we being fair to the subject?

Legals

- ☐ What legal problems do you foresee?
- ☐ Were you threatened with legal action?
- ☐ Does this report need to be checked by lawyers?
- ☐ Is this a pending case?
- ☐ Is this report based on documents merely filed in court, or based on documents referred to in open court?
- ☐ Do you have all the necessary documents to back up your report?
- ☐ Are they authentic?

Journalists should:

- ☐ be honest, fair and courageous in gathering, reporting and interpreting information;
- ☐ test the accuracy of information from all sources and exercise care to avoid inadvertent error;
- ☐ diligently seek out subjects of news stories to give them the opportunity to respond to allegations of wrongdoing;
- ☐ identify sources whenever feasible;
- ☐ always question sources' motives before promising anonymity;
- ☐ avoid stereotyping by race, gender, age, religion, ethnicity, geography, sexual orientation, disability, physical appearance or social status;
- ☐ support the open exchange of views, even views they find repugnant;
- ☐ balance a criminal suspect's fair trial rights with the public's right to be informed;
- ☐ refuse gifts, favours, fees, free travel and special treatment, and shun secondary employment, political involvement, public office and service in community organisations if they compromise journalistic integrity; and
- ☐ admit mistakes and correct them promptly.

BIBLIOGRAPHY

BOOKS AND ARTICLES

Adey, David; Margaret Orr and Derek Swemmer. 2002. *The new word power*. Jeppestown, Johannesburg: AD Donker.

Allan, Stuart. 2001. *News culture*. Buckingham: Open University Press.

Ansell, Gwen. 2002. *Basic journalism*. Milpark, Johannesburg: M&G Books.

Behr, Edward. 1985. *Anyone here been raped and speaks English?* London: New English Library.

Belsey, Andrew and Ruth Chadwick (eds.). 1992. *Ethical issues in journalism and the media*. London: Routledge.

Berger, Guy. 1999. 'Grave new world: Democratic journalism enters in the global 21st century', Grahamstown. Posted at http://journ.ru. ac.za/staff/guy/, accessed on 4 April 2003.

Berger, Guy. 2000a. 'Submission for HRC investigation into racism and the media', Grahamstown. Posted at http://journ.ru.ac.za/staff/guy/, accessed on 24 April 2003.

Berger, Guy. 2000b. 'Deracialisation, democracy and development: transformation of the South African media 1994–2000', Grahamstown. Posted at http://journ.ru.ac.za/staff/guy/index.html, accessed on 23 April 2003.

Berger, Guy. 2002c. 'More media for Southern Africa? the place of politics, economics and convergence in developing media density', Grahamstown. Posted at http://journ.ru.ac.za/staff/guy/, accessed on 23 April 2003.

Black, Jay; Bob Steele and Ralph Barney. 1995. *Doing ethics in journalism: a handbook with case studies*. Needham Heights, MA: Allyn & Bacon.

Carvajal, Doreen. 1991. 'The great quote question', *FineLine: The Newsletter on Journalism Ethics* 3,1, January.

Cooper, Thomas. 1992. 'The ethics behind the effects: a comparison of national media codes of ethics' in Felipe Korzenny and Stella Ting-Toomey (eds.), *Mass media effects across cultures*. Newbury Park: Sage.

Christians, Clifford and Michael Traber (eds.). 1997. *Communication ethics and universal values*. Thousand Oaks: Sage.

Croteau, David and William Hoynes. 1997. *Media/Society: industries, images and audiences*. London: Pine Forge.

Curran, James and Jean Seaton. 1985. *Power without responsibility: the press and broadcasting in Britain*. London and New York: Methuen.

Curran, James and Michael Gurevitch (eds.). 2000. *Mass media and society*. London: Arnold.

Dahlgren, Peter and Colin Sparks (eds.). 1991. *Communication and citizenship: journalism and the public sphere*. London: Routledge.

Danso, Mansford and David McDonald. 2000. 'Writing xenophobia: immigration and the press in post-apartheid South Africa'. Cape Town: Institute for Democracy in South Africa (Idasa).

Day, Louis A. 2000. *Ethics in media communications: cases and controversies*. Belmont, CA: Wadsworth.

Du Plessis, Deon. 1994. 'Confidentiality and public interest', *Ecquid Novi* 15,1.

Froneman, Johannes and Arris S de Beer. 1998. 'Media ethics: thorny questions with diverse answers' in Arrie S de Beer (ed.), *Mass media towards the millennium: the South African handbook of mass communication*. Pretoria: JL van Schaik.

Gandy Jr, Oscar H. 1998. *Communication and race: a structural perspective*. London: Arnold.

Haffajee, Ferial. 2001. 'Revisiting the ethical codes'. Paper prepared for the Freedom of Expression and Ethics in the Media conference, Sandton, 30–31 October.

Haiman, Robert J. Undated. 'Best practices for newspaper journalists', Freedom Forum, Washington. Posted at http://www.freedomforum. org/publications/diversity/bestpractices/bestpractices.pdf, accessed on 19 March 2004.

Health-e and Soul City. Undated. 'HIV/Aids: a resource for journalists'. Johannesburg: Soul City.

Heins, Marjorie. 2001. 'Violence and the media: an exploration of cause, effect and the First Amendment', First Amendment Center, Nashville. Posted at http://wwwfirstamendmentcenter.org/PDF/ violenceandthemedia.PDF, accessed on 22 March 2004.

Jacobs, Sean. 1999. 'Tensions of a free press: South Africa after apartheid'. Research paper R-22, Joan Schorenstein Center on the Press, Politics and Public Policy, Harvard University. Cambridge, MA: Joan Schorenstein Center.

Karikari, Kwame (ed.). 1996. *Ethics in journalism: case studies of practice in West Africa*. Accra: Institut Panos.

Kasoma, Francis (ed.). 1994. *Journalism ethics in Africa*. Nairobi: Acce.

Kasoma, Francis. 1994. 'Media ethics or media law: the enforcement of responsible journalism in Africa' in *Ecquid Novi* 15,1.

Keene, John. 1991. *The media and democracy*. Cambridge: Polity Press.

Kieran, Matthew. 1999. *Media ethics: a philosophical approach*. Westport, Conn: Praeger.

Krüger, Franz. 1989. 'Word wars: South African media under the emergency'. Unpublished masters thesis, City University, London.

Laurence, Patrick. 2002. 'Patrick Laurence interviews Peter Mokaba: a dissonant view on Aids' in the Helen Suzman Foundation publication *Focus* 26, June. Posted at http://www.hsf.org.za/focus26/focus26interviewaids.html, accessed on 28 January 2004.

Lowe-Morna, Colleen (ed.). 2001. *Whose news? Whose views? Southern Africa: gender in media handbook*. Johannesburg: Gender Links.

Lowe-Morna, Colleen (ed.). 2002. *Gender in media training: a Southern African tool kit*. Johannesburg: Gender Links and the Institute for the Advancement of Journalism.

MacGregor, Brent. *Live, direct and biased? making television news in the satellite age*. London: Arnold.

Madden, Kate. 1992. 'Video and cultural identity: the Inuit Broadcasting Corporation experience' in Felips Korzenny and Stella Ting-Toomey (eds.), *Mass media effects across cultures*. Newbury Park: Sage.

Malcolm, Janet. 1998. *The journalist and the murderer*. London: Papermac.

Manning, Paul. 2001. *News and news sources: a critical introduction*. London: Sage.

Marinovich, Greg and Joao Silva. 2001. *The bang-bang club*. London: Arrow.

Media Monitoring Project (MMP): 1999. 'The news in black and white: an investigation into racial stereotyping in the media'. Johannesburg: MMP.

Mukela, John (ed.). 2001. *Essays and conversations on media and democracy*. Maputo: NSJ Trust.

Nel, François. 1999. *Writing for the media in South Africa*. Cape Town: OUP.

Netshitenzhe, Joel. 2002. Speech delivered on Media Freedom Day, 25 October, at Wits University.

O'Dowd, Catherine. 1995. 'Truth or taste: the depiction of the Hani murder', *Rhodes Journalism Review* 11, December.

Oosthuizen, Lucas M. 2002. *Media ethics in the South African context: an introduction and overview.* Lansdowne, Cape Town: Juta.

Pahad, Essop. 2001. 'Communication in a changing society: a news agenda for development'. Paper delivered at the Sanef/government indaba at Sun City, June.

Pauw, Jacques. 1997. *Into the heart of darkness.* Johannesburg: Jonathan Ball.

Retief, Johan. 2002. *Media ethics: an introduction to responsible journalism.* Cape Town: OUP.

Rønning, Helge. 2002. *Media ethics: an introduction and overview.* Lansdowne, Cape Town: Juta.

Seleoane, Mandla. 2001. 'Towards an African theory of freedom of expression'. Paper delivered at the Freedom of Expression and Ethics in the Media conference, Sandton, 30–31 October.

Shoemaker, Pamela J and Stephen D Reese. 1996. *Mediating the message: theories of influence on mass media content.* New York: Longman.

Stavitsky, Alan G. 1995. *Independence and integrity: a guidebook for public radio journalism.* Washington: National Public Radio.

Steele, Bob. 1996. 'The Bummer beat'. Posted at http://www.poynter. org/content/content_view.asp?id=5540 on 1 May, accessed on 28 January 2004.

Steele, Bob and Jay Black. 2001. 'Media ethics codes and beyond', *Global Issues* 6,1, April.

Steinberg, Jonny. 2002. *Midlands.* Johannesburg: Jonathan Ball.

Switzer, Les and Mohamed Adhikari (eds.). 2000. *South Africa's resistance press: alternative voices in the last generation under apartheid.* Athens, Ohio: Ohio Center for International Relations.

Tomaselli, Keyan and P Eric Louw (eds.). 1991. *The alternative press in South Africa.* Bellville: Anthropos.

Tomaselli, Keyan; Ruth Tomaselli and Johan Muller (eds.). 1987. *Narrating the crisis: hegemony and the South African press.* Johannesburg: Richard Lyons.

Tyson, Harvey. 1993. *Editors under fire.* Sandton: Random.

Ukpabi, Chudi (ed.). 2001. *Handbook on journalism ethics: African case studies.* Windhoek: Misa (Media Institute of Southern Africa).

Uys, Pieter-Dirk. 2002. *Elections and erections: a memoir of fear and fun.* Cape Town: Zebra.

Van Dijk, Teun A. 1991. *Racism and the press.* London and New York: Routledge.

Wakeham, Lord. 1998. 'Can self regulation achieve more than law?' Wynne Baxter Godfree Law Lecture delivered at the University of Sussex on 15 May.

Wallraff, Günter. 1982. '13 unerwünschte reportagen'. Hamburg: Rowohlt Taschenbuch Verlag.

CODES AND DOCUMENTS

Commonwealth Broadcasting Association. 1997. 'Africa Charter on Children's Broadcasting'. Posted at http://www.nordicom.gu.se/ unesco/declarations-resulutions/africacharter7.html, accessed on 23 July 2003.

African Commission on Human and People's Rights. 2002. 'Declaration of principles on freedom of expression in Africa', adopted in 2002 in Banjul, The Gambia. Posted at http://www1.umn.edu/humanrts/ achpr/expressionfreedomdec.html, accessed on 1 April 2003.

BBC. 1996. *Producers' guidelines.* London: BBC.

Broadcasting Complaints Commission of South Africa (BCCSA). 2001. *Review 1999–2001.* Craighall, Johannesburg: BCCSA.

Canadian Broadcasting Corporation. 2002. 'Journalistic standards and practices'. Posted at http://cbc.radio-canada.ca/htmen/policies/ journalistic/index.htm, accessed on 6 December 2003.

Canadian Broadcast Standards Council. 1990. 'Sex role portrayal code for television and radio programming'. Posted at http://www.cbsc.ca /english/codes/sexrole/sexrole.htm, accessed on 20 March 2004.

Council of Europe. 1993. 'Resolution 1003 (1993) on the ethics of journalism'. Posted at http://assembly.coe.int/Documents/Adopted Text/ta93/ERES1003.HTM, accessed on 20 March 2004.

Media Institute of Southern Africa (Misa) and Gender Links. 'Gender and media baseline study'. Johannesburg: Misa and Gender Links.

Independent Communications Authority of South Africa (Icasa). Undated. 'Code of conduct for broadcasters'. Posted at http://www. icasa.org.za/default.aspx?page=1349, accessed on 20 March 2004.

International Federation of Journalists (IFJ). Undated. 'Declaration of principles on the conduct of journalists'. Posted at http://www.ifj. org/default.asp?index=111&Language=EN, accessed on 20 March 2004.

Journ-Aids.org. Undated. 'Reporting on HIV/Aids: ethical guidelines for South African media'. Posted at http://www.journ-aids.org/ Guidelines%20Change.htm, accessed on 28 January 2004.

Media Development and Diversity Agency. 2000. *A draft position paper*. Pretoria: Government Communication and Information System (GCIS).

Media Institute of Southern Africa (Misa). October 2001. 'Misa gender policy and action plan'. Posted at http://www.genderlinks.org.za/ docs/2001/misa-draftpolicy-actionplan.pdf, accessed on 20 March 2004.

New York Times, The. 2003. 'Ethical journalism: code of conduct for the news and editorial departments'. New York: *New York Times*.

Press Ombudsman of South Africa. 2001. 'Press code of professional practice'. Johannesburg: Press Ombudsman of South Africa.

SABC. 'Editorial policies'. Draft (2003) and final (2004) versions. Johannesburg: SABC.

South African Human Rights Commission (SAHRC). 1999. *Interim report of the inquiry into racism in the media*. Johannesburg: SAHRC.

South African Human Rights Commission (SAHRC). 2000. *Faultlines: inquiry into racism in the media*. Johannesburg: SAHRC.

South African National Editors' Forum (Sanef). 2002. Back to basics: the Stellenbosch Commitment. Johannesburg: Sanef.

Truth and Reconciliation Commission of South Africa (TRC). 1998. *Report* Vol 4. Cape Town: TRC.

INTERVIEWS

Unless otherwise indicated, these interviews were conducted by the author. They took place between mid-2002 and early 2003.

Andrew Bolton, news editor of *Cape Talk*.

Peter Bruce, editor of *Business Day*.

George Claassen, deputy editor of *Die Burger*.

Robin Comley, pictures editor of *The Star* (conducted by Rosemary Ramsay).

Johan de Villiers, executive editor of *The Star* (conducted by Rosemary Ramsay).

John Dludlu, former editor of *Sowetan*.

Tim du Plessis, editor of *Rapport*.

Ivan Fynn, editor of the *Cape Argus*.

Pippa Green, head of SABC radio news and current affairs; Solly Phetoe, current affairs editor; and Vusi Sithole, bulletins editor (jointly conducted with Ferial Haffajee).

Zubeida Jaffer, former parliamentary editor of Independent Newspapers.

Ed Linington, press ombudsman of South Africa.

Hope Mahlangu, news editor of Yfm (conducted by Mandla Radebe).

Mondli Makhanya, editor of the *Sunday Times*.

Jimi Matthews, head of SABC TV news.

George Mazarakis, executive producer of *Carte Blanche*.

Barney Mthombothi, editor of the *Sunday Tribune*.

Denis Pather, editor of the *Daily News* (conducted by Ferial Haffajee).

Motalane Phalane, editor of the *Daily Sun* (conducted by Mandla Radebe).

Dumi Shange, executive producer of current affairs on Ukhozi FM (conducted by Ferial Haffajee).

Joe Thloloe, head of news at e.tv.

Mathatha Tsedu, editor of *City Press*.

Kobus van Rooyen, chairperson of the Broadcasting Complaints Commission of South Africa.

Martin Welz, editor of *Noseweek*.

Moegsien Williams, editor of *The Star*.

ONLINE RESOURCES

The journalism programme at the University of the Witwatersrand runs a website, www.journalism.co.za, with news and debate on ethical and other issues confronting Southern African journalists.

The South African National Editors' Forum is building up a collection of South African ethics codes on their website, www.sanef.org.za.

A large collection of ethics codes from around the world (from Albania to Zambia) is posted on the site of the International Journalists' Network, at www.ijnet.org.

The Broadcasting Complaints Commission of South Africa posts its judgments on its website, www.bccsa.co.za.

The *Rhodes Journalism Review* is a forum for debate on issues affecting South African journalists. It is available online at www.rjr.ru.ac.za.

The *British Journalism Review* is a forum for discussion of issues confronting the media. Its site is at www.bjr.org.uk.

The *Columbia Journalism Review* is a forum for discussion of issues in the US media. It is at www.cjr.org.

For a discussion on issues in the Indian media, visit the Indian media review at www.indianmediareview.com/

The website of the Poynter Institute in Florida contains a huge collection of materials, links and columns dealing with ethics. The site is at www.poynter.org.

Note particularly the Ethics Tool of the American Society of Newspaper Editors and the Poynter Institute, which is available to registered users at https://www.poynter.org/ethics/Default.asp.